Love
&
Duty

CIVIL WAR AMERICA

Peter S. Carmichael, Caroline E. Janney,
and Aaron Sheehan-Dean, editors

This landmark series interprets broadly the history and culture
of the Civil War era through the long nineteenth century and
beyond. Drawing on diverse approaches and methods, the
series publishes historical works that explore all aspects of
the war, biographies of leading commanders, and tactical and
campaign studies, along with select editions of primary sources.
Together, these books shed new light on an era that remains
central to our understanding of American and world history.

ANGELA ESCO ELDER

Love & Duty

Confederate Widows *and the* Emotional Politics of Loss

THE UNIVERSITY OF NORTH CAROLINA PRESS

Chapel Hill

*This book was published with the assistance of the Authors
Fund of the University of North Carolina Press.*

Design by Jamison Cockerham
Set in Arno, Scala Sans, Dear Sarah, Jenson
by codeMantra

Cover illustration courtesy of the Library of Congress.

Manufactured in the United States of America

The University of North Carolina Press has been a member
of the Green Press Initiative since 2003.

Material in chapter 5 previously appeared as "Dead Husband, Dead Son: Widows,
Mothers-in-Law, and Mourning in the Confederacy" in *Household War: How
Americans Lived and Fought the Civil War*, edited by Lisa Tendrich Frank and LeeAnn
Whites (Athens: University of Georgia Press, 2020), 248–67. Reprinted by permission.

Material in chapter 6 previously appeared as "Emilie Todd Helm and Mary
Todd Lincoln: We Weep over Our Dead Together" in *Kentucky Women: Their
Lives and Times*, edited by Melissa A. McEuen and Thomas H. Appleton Jr.
(Athens: University of Georgia Press, 2015), 81–98. Reprinted by permission.

LIBRARY OF CONGRESS CATALOGING-IN-PUBLICATION DATA
Names : Elder, Angela Esco, author.
Title: Love and duty : Confederate widows and the
emotional politics of loss / Angela Esco Elder.
Other titles : Civil War America (Series)
Description: Chapel Hill : The University of North Carolina Press, [2022] |
Series: Civil War America | Includes bibliographical references and index.
Identifiers: LCCN 2021046313 | ISBN 9781469667737 (cloth) |
ISBN 9781469667744 (paperback) | ISBN 9781469667751 (ebook)
Subjects: LCSH: Widows—Confederate States of America—History. |
United States—History—Civil War, 1861–1865—Women.
Classification: LCC E628 .E44 2022 | DDC 973.7082—dc23
LC record available at https://lccn.loc.gov/2021046313

FOR

Nathan

HEART VICTORIES

by a Soldier's Wife

There's not a stately hall,
There's not a cottage fair,
That proudly stands on Southern soil,
Or softly nestles there,
But in its peaceful walls
With wealth or comfort blessed,
A stormy battle fierce hath raged
In gentle woman's breast.

There Love, the true, the brave,
The beautiful, the strong,
Wrestles with Duty, gaunt and stern,
Wrestles and struggles long.
He falls, no more again
His giant foe to meet;
Bleeding at every opening vein,
Love falls at Duty's feet.

O Daughter of the South!
No victor's crown be thine,
Not thine upon the tented field
In martial pomp to shine;
But with unfaltering trust
In Him who rules on high,
To deck thy loved ones for the fray,
And send them forth to die.

With wildly throbbing heart,
With faint and trembling breath,
The maiden speeds her lover on
To victory or death;
Forth from caressing arms
The mother sends her son,
And bids him nobly battle on
Till the last field is won.

While she, the tried, the true,
The loving wife of years,
Chokes down the rising agony,
Drives back the starting tears;
"I yield thee up," she cries,
"In the country's cause to fight;
Strike for our own, our children's home
And God defend the right."

O Daughter of the South!
When our fair land is free,
When peace her lovely mantle throws
Softly o'er land and sea,
History shall tell how thou
Hast nobly borne thy part,
And won the proudest triumph yet
The victory of the heart.

From *The Southern Poems of the War*,
created and arranged by Miss Emily V. Mason
(Baltimore: John Murphy, 1867).

Contents

Illustrations

Love
&
Duty

Introduction

> With malice toward none, with charity for all, with firmness
> in the right as God gives us to see the right, let us strive on to
> finish the work we are in, to bind up the nation's wounds, to
> care for him who shall have borne the battle and for his widow
> and his orphan, to do all which may achieve and cherish a just
> and lasting peace among ourselves and with all nations.
>
> *Abraham Lincoln, second inaugural address*

When Jefferson Davis completed his book *The Rise and Fall of the Confederate Government* in 1881, he did not dedicate it to "officers and soldiers," as Confederate lieutenant general James Longstreet would later do. Nor did Davis dedicate his writings to "the memory of the dead," as Confederate brigadier general Edward Porter Alexander would. Instead, when the former president of the Confederacy completed his first book, he dedicated it to "The Women of the Confederacy." In this choice, he honored women before his friends who died in battle. He honored women before the veterans who survived it. In his prolonged tribute, Davis argued that while soldiers "died far from the objects of their tenderest love," it was women who supplied, soothed, and sustained with a "zealous faith in our cause."[1] Certainly, Davis recognized that many wives, mothers, and daughters sacrificed to further the Confederate cause, but perhaps there is something more. If Jefferson Davis turned Americans' eyes to the women, the ones who "shone a guiding star undimmed by the darkest clouds of war," then the nation might not dwell on Confederate states' recent rebellious and bloody behavior. By focusing on the women "whose annual tribute expresses their enduring grief, love, and reverence for our sacred dead," the attention shifts from Confederate soldiers who killed to mourners who loved. Here, the South was not a lynch mob, slaver, or threat that almost destroyed America but a woman who offered "pious ministrations to our wounded soldiers" and "soothed the last hours" of dying men. Rather than a defiant, threatening, and abusive region, this feminized South was a place of grief and healing.[2]

Between 1861 and 1865, approximately 3 million men left for war; as many as 750,000 died. In the process, some 200,000 women became widows. *Love and Duty: Confederate Widows and the Emotional Politics of Loss* examines the complicated emotional and political relationships between Confederate widows and the Confederate state. Throughout the conflict, Confederate newspapers and government officials championed a particular version of white widowhood—the young wife who selflessly transferred her monogamous love from dead husband to the deathless cause for which he fought. Widows were to "preserve green by grateful tears the dearest and most brilliant memories" of their hearts. Only then would their husbands live forever—as would their cause.[3]

But a closer look at letters and diaries of widows reveals that these women spent their new cultural capital with great practicality and shrewdness. Indeed, even as their culture created an entire industry in their name, widows played the role on their own terms to forward their own ends. Prescriptive literature, as abundant and prevalent as it may be, is an incomplete lens without considering the lived experience. Precisely because society invested widowhood with so much significance, it inadvertently created the stage upon which an unforeseen and unprecedented number of young Confederate women could be seen and heard. Death forced all Confederate widows to reconstruct their lives. But only some would choose to play a role in reconstructing the nation. *Love and Duty* argues that the emotional expressions of widows carried new political meaning amid the crisis of war and the battle to establish the Confederacy's legitimacy.

This book is not the first to explore the relationship between women and the Confederate state. Stephanie McCurry has argued that, during the Civil War, the Confederacy became for the first time actually answerable to its fictive family, including women and enslaved people. Similarly, Drew Gilpin Faust noted that "sacrifice and the state became inextricably intertwined" during the Civil War. Or as Thavolia Glymph put it, there were many wartime sacrifices men called upon women to make but "rarely acknowledge as polit-ical." Laura Edwards and Amy Dru Stanley have also explored what might be called the bleed-through between the new legal categories required by cap-italism and the modern state and the more organic and accepted categories of nineteenth-century family and community life. Victoria Ott argued that Confederate women had political power during the war, which they used to uphold the Confederacy in an attempt to preserve ideals of the antebellum era for their own futures. These opportunities for political engagement were particularly available to the Confederacy's widows.[4]

As soldiers' widows, Confederate women could leverage the label, and their particular relationship with the Confederate administration, in attempts to receive support, recognition, or political influence. Likewise, government officials had the opportunity to use Confederate widows to further their own political agendas. This relationship between widows and politics remains relevant even today. Take Carryn Owens, a recently widowed woman who received one minute and thirty-six seconds of applause, the longest ovation of the night, in President Donald Trump's 2017 address to Congress. Her hus-band was the first military service member killed in combat under Trump's administration. Carryn's father-in-law, who had refused to meet with Trump and criticized the raid publicly, was not in attendance. But Carryn's presence, and seat beside Ivanka Trump, sent a powerful political message of support. Or consider Cindy Sheehan, the mother of a U.S. soldier killed in Iraq, who protested the Iraq War by camping outside President George W. Bush's ranch in Crawford, Texas. Sheehan gained media attention where thousands of other protestors didn't because she had what we might call cultural *standing*. She had given a son to the state, and now she had some say in what the state should do and be. Confederate war widows, though they might be as young as seventeen, had, if anything, *more* cultural standing. Mothers who lost sons in the Civil War still had husbands and, thereby, as the culture understood it, protectors. Many also had additional children, even additional adult sons. Death left Confederate widows without husbands but with a tremendous opportunity to engage as key participants in the new emotional regime of the Confederacy.

The Confederacy desired legitimacy and aspired to become a stable polit-ical government. As William Reddy defined it, an emotional regime is "the set of normative emotions and the official rituals, practices, and emotives that express and inculcate them; a necessary underpinning of any stable political regime." In other words, if a widow recommitted herself to the Confeder-acy and poured her emotional resources into the war, that was a powerful endorsement. If she withdrew her emotional resources or, worse, used her new standing to criticize the war, that was a powerful indictment. Emotional expression served as a conduit for political expression. The concept of emotional regimes is a useful construct to help us better understand the political power of grief, especially in the mourning processes of Confederate widows. The Civil War marked a shift in emotional regimes from one that supported the white patriarchy to one that supported both the patriarchy and the Confederacy. In the antebellum South, official rituals of mourning supported the structure that placed men in political and social positions of power. For example, wives mourned their husbands for over two years, as custom directed, while husbands formally mourned only three months for late wives. With war, the experience of Southern white widowhood gained heightened political significance, transformed by the necessity of proving Confederate validity. The cause needed ardent advocates.[5]

Confederate widows had a new and powerful political identity, more so than soldiers' wives, because they sacrificed their husbands to the war effort not temporarily but permanently. Every time the political and military leadership of the Confederacy described a deceased soldier as "gallant" and "brave," it highlighted that this was a man who should be missed. And each time the leadership described a widow as "poor" and "helpless," there lay the implication that she should be shattered by this loss. This language was everywhere, from speeches and newspapers to condolence letters. As Reddy emphasized, "In these regimes, a limited number of emotives are modeled through ceremony or official art forms." Widows should cry, widows should find solace in religion, and widows should continue to support the Confederate cause. And in turn, white Southern society had a duty not to let these women's sacrifices be in vain. They, too, must invest everything into the Confederacy. But in order for this construct to work, Confederate widows must appropriately play their role. Those that did would be praised by their friends, their family, and their communities. They would be publicly applauded and rewarded.[6]

Take this example from Jefferson Davis's speech on December 26, 1862. For Confederate widows, Davis promised government support. From Jackson, Mississippi, he argued that widows must receive financial backing from the state. "Let this provision be made for the objects of his [a soldier's] affection and his solicitude," Davis began. "Let him know that his mother Mississippi has spread her protecting mantle over those he loves, and he will be ready to fight your battles, to protect your honor, and, in your cause, to die." In other words, if a soldier believed that the state, Mississippi, would take care of his loved ones, particularly his wife, then Davis believed that soldier would be ready to die for the Confederate cause. Davis then spoke of the "glorious dead of the battle fields of the Confederacy" and the "desolate widows and orphans, whom the martyrs of war have left behind." In this speech, these widows had sacrificed to the cause and loved their glorious husbands so much that they were desolate without them. Therefore, as Davis had outlined at the start of his speech, the Confederacy should care for them. Widows had a special relationship to the Confederate state. Further, as a message to the rest of the crowd, if wives could give up their husbands to be martyrs, what else might others be able to give? Davis called for the House Chamber, and the larger audience, to "not delay a moment, but rush forward and place your services at the disposal of the state." This speech, like many of Davis's speeches, was published by newspapers across the Confederacy, speaking not just to the state of Mississippi but to the Confederacy as a whole. Here, themes of government support for widows, the sacrifice of widows, and the call for others to sacrifice to the Confederacy as these widows did are intertwined. The emotional expressions of widowhood carried important political meaning, particularly in the struggle to establish the Confederacy's legitimacy.[7]

This book offers three major takeaways. First, analyzing the expressions of white Confederate widows, across regions, changes the way we think about the Civil War household. Though they shared a gender, women did not wound the same, work the same, or share the same strengths and weaknesses, and these differences emerged particularly when their relationships were put under stress. Second, emotions mattered; for Confederate widows, the political was personal, and the personal political, a fact that left a lasting impression on both Confederate officials and widows' communities. As historian William Blair put it, "Political mobilization depended on outdoor rituals, processions, torchlight parades, and other activities characteristic of nineteenth-century America." Or as historian Elizabeth R. Varon has argued, "If we define politics broadly, to include not only electoral contests but a variety of battles for social authority, we bring into focus not only the stunning range of women's public activism, but also their private agonies and triumphs." In the Confederacy, political mobilization rested, in part, on the public mourning of its widows. War widows had a tremendous amount of influence, and Confederate leaders were anxious to oversee how they used it. And third, widows existed. It is worth exploring why, and how, tens of thousands of women faded in much of our academic narrative, only to reappear in popular culture as Scarlett O'Hara.[8]

Let us take each point in turn. First, examining the emotional expressions of white Confederate widows changes the way we think about the Civil War household, shedding important light on the emotional costs of war. Union widows, Black and white, lost husbands but won the American Civil War. Their investment had tangible results and tangible rewards for the nation, celebrated with fireworks. Confederate widows lost husbands, but then they also lost the war. For some widows, that emotional trial was too much. Not all widows marched in step to support the emotional regime of the Confederacy. Martha Harbin, a twenty-two-year-old mother with two children, attempted to burn herself after becoming a Confederate widow, leading to her institutionalization in a South Carolina asylum in 1864. Frances Campbell, also with two children, also in her early twenties, also entered an asylum in 1864, after losing her husband at the battle in Chancellorsville. She experienced delusions, depression, and restlessness and had a family history of suicide. Unlike Union widows, the sacrifice of Confederate widows had no national value in 1865; their late husbands were Southern traitors. Or as one New York captain put it, "A rebel against the *best Government* the world ever saw is worthy of one of two things to wit a *bullet* or a *halter*. . . . If I hated a rebel before I left home I hate him double now." And in addition to bearing the double burden of lost war and lost husband, Confederate widows faced financial losses; the majority of the fighting had occurred on Southern soil. As historian Diane Miller Sommerville argued, "Ex-Confederates, steeped in the shared experiences of pervasive material and emotional misery that sometimes culminated in suicide, refashioned their identity on the basis of that suffering." For many Confederate widows, this refashioning, and the experience of suffering, seemed inescapable.[9]

We have long appreciated that mourning was woman's work, but we have not yet lifted the veil to reveal the complex internal female politics that lay behind the patriotic rhetoric that invoked sacrifice. As the *Savannah Republican* printed in 1863, "Women of the South! Do your spirits faint, or your hands falter? You, who so nobly urged this work, will you sustain it still? Are you not ready, if need be, to fill every possible post at home, and send the last man to the field?" Many papers printed sentiments like this, lumping sisters, mothers, and wives into a singular gendered category. Similarly, the *Arkansas True Democrat* lauded, in 1861, "Thus it is with the glorious women of the South. . . . The laughing maiden, the busy mother and the mourning widow have vied in their efforts to advance our cause. Day by day and night by night, they have toiled at the work until an army of heroes, clothed by beauty, grace, and worth, stand forth, as did Achilles on the Trojan plain, invincible." In the narrative of the time, and the historical narrative to follow, Confederate "women" sent men to war and Confederate "women" put men back on their feet afterward. This attempt to put women back into the historical narrative produced the essential foundation on which women's history of the war must be built. But perhaps because a solidarity among women was necessary to produce this feminist wave of scholarship in the first place, we have inadvertently stitched an assumption of solidarity into the treatment of our subjects, in effect reproducing an essentialization of women that, while not as problematic as leaving them out of the narrative in the first place, is still an oversimplification of their lives and expressions.[10]

The way scholars understand the Civil War household, and even women's history more broadly, changes when we cast a critical eye on the myriad experiences of Confederate widows. Much research has been published on the vast economic, political, and cultural work that women performed during and after the war, from their roles as nurses to their dominating presence in the Ladies Memorial Associations and, ultimately, the United Daughters of the Confederacy. But less attention has been paid to the degree to which, in all of these roles, these women often differed from and fought *with one another*. No cultural work gets done without friction; all human beings have their own (sometimes prickly) sense of the way things ought to be. This was no less true of the work of mourning. The American Civil War was a war grounded in the household with all of its systems of support and all of its interpersonal tensions. In our appreciation of women's common grievances under patriarchy, we have sometimes massaged away the very natural, very human process by which disputes arose and were settled as women went about their common work.

These stories that follow reveal that widows mourned in a variety of ways. By delving in and allowing these women their individualities, we broaden and deepen our understanding of the white female world. Additionally, investigating the conflicts that emerged *between* women, and the means they used to try to address and resolve them, takes us at once away from and deeper inside the "sisterhoods" and "female world of love and ritual" that have dominated feminist readings of social history since the 1970s. Elite white women may not have dueled or engaged in drunken fistfights (often), but they will not appear fully whole or human until they are allowed their own competitive codes of honor that governed the social slights, punishments, and penances they doled out on one another. If we grant, as we now do, that women did critical cultural work in prosecuting the war and interpreting its meaning, we must pay greater attention to the way they went about their work. Indeed, historians must consider the way the war continued on as a conflict between generations of women, such as mothers and their widowed daughters-in-law, and how the tensions of war played out within households that were sometimes fractured, cracked, or destroyed by the burdens they placed upon women to hold them together.[11]

A second major takeaway of this project is that the mourning and grieving of widows had real potential political consequences for the Confederacy. Emotional expression could be manipulated, as it had been for centuries in fictional and nonfictional worlds. Even mythology, centuries old, contains links to the political and emotional roles of Confederate widowhood. For instance, when her husband died, Deianeira plunged a sword into her side. Hylonome fell upon a spear. Alcyone drowned herself in the sea. Evadne and Oenone threw themselves on their husbands' burning funeral pyres, while Cleite and Polymede hanged themselves. Laodamia, Marpessa, and Polydora are also among the ranks of widows in classical mythology who committed suicide after their husbands died. When they became widows, it was their duty to mourn, and they carried this task out to the ultimate expression—death by their own hands, a preferable alternative to life without their husbands. Language reflected this idea of the empty life of a widow. In Greek, *cheroo* means to make desolate. *Chereuo* is to lack. In Homer, a widowed wife is called a *chera*. The masculine form, *cheros*, did not appear until Aristotle applied it to birds. The Old English *widewe* has an Indo-European root, *widh*, meaning to be empty or separated, while the Sanskrit *vidh* also means to lack or be destitute. Neither Greek vocabulary nor mythology affixed similar meanings or implications to widowers.[12]

This ancient notion, that a woman is filled by a marriage and emptied at her husband's death, persisted through time and across space. Nineteenth-century America called children who lost their fathers "orphans," even though their mothers still lived. As one condolence letter read to a recently widowed woman, "Can you not come, my afflicted young friend, with your orphan babes and remain with me until you can return to Kentucky?" Southern etiquette suggested a mourning period of two and a half years for widows and glorified those who mourned longer. Widowers mourned three months with an unassuming black armband affixed to their everyday attire. Like Queen Victoria, who mourned Prince Albert for decades beginning in December 1861, some elite American widows donned black and dedicated themselves to the part for the rest of their lives. Their communities served as an audience, applauding those who played the role well and ostracizing those who did not.[13]

And all of this was particularly fraught in an age when the American state had relatively little power and relied to a heavy degree on emotional resonances to glue the country together. In his first inaugural address, Abraham Lincoln compared secession to divorce. Confederate diarist Mary Boykin Chesnut did the same: "We are divorced, North from South, because we hated each other so." Familial metaphor dominated nineteenth-century politics because, in a still young country, almost without history, patriotism had been planted in the sturdier soil of family love. As journalist Henry Adams said of America in 1860, "The Union was a sentiment, but not much more." Familial language was not mere rhetoric, then; it was a wellspring of state legitimacy and was deeply political. *Uncle Tom's Cabin* was effective because it attacked slavery on *familied* grounds. Politicians spoke endlessly of "founding fathers" and "sister states." In cartoons, the nation was still as likely to be embodied by the character of "Brother" Jonathan as it was by the more distant "Uncle" Sam. "The state" as we know it—invasive, protective—did not exist. Government was a union and nationalism a romantic sentiment, both rooted and understood in the language of marriage and family.[14]

Relations between war widows and their communities, then, could not simply remain personal; they had political implications. Confederate armies fought to bring legitimacy to the Confederate States of America. The relationship of a soldier to the government was political and definite. The death of a soldier did not dissolve this household connection to the Confederate government. But the Confederacy also needed soldiers' widows' emotional endorsement for the cause. Recommitment to the Confederacy sent a powerful message to local communities, particularly to other households with men not yet in the armies, that there was more they could give. Women who had sustained such losses, then, had a staggering amount of social capital, something Jefferson Davis implicitly recognized, decades later, when he dedicated his book. By using the term *social capital*, this study refers to a mixture of respect and influence earned by widows, from fellow white Southerners. Particularly toward the end of the war and during Reconstruction, many widows used this newfound status in society for personal provision. By reminding their communities of their sacrifice to the Confederacy, in petitions, newspapers, and personal letters, these women requested (or, in some cases, demanded) support.[15]

This book builds on the powerful new work on emotions, love, and trauma in the American Civil War. In recent decades, historians have no longer left the study of human emotion to psychologists, philosophers, and biologists. As Peter N. Stearns argued, "We short-change our power to explain if we leave out the impact of emotional culture." He further maintained that "the potential for examining the wider consequences of emotional change—for taking emotions seriously as a source of social behaviors, within families to be sure but also in a variety of other, more public settings—has not been tapped." Similarly, William Reddy's theoretical defense of emotions history, that there is "a core concept of emotions, universally applicable, that allows one to say what suffering is," allows for cultural variation. Historian Diane Miller Sommerville's work on suicide is a powerful example of emotions history in action. She argued that stories of broken Confederate soldiers "get us closer to a full accounting of the personal cost of the Civil War." Physicians, chaplains, and soldiers described people's emotional distress when a spouse died, such as Captain Thyssent, who shot himself through the head when he learned that his wife had passed away. Emotional distress was not limited to men; the death of a husband was also a traumatic experience for most wives. War distributed widowhood unevenly across the South. Some towns lost entire companies, and gained entire companies of widows, while other widows found themselves isolated and alone in their positions. Moments of breakdown provide a clearer understanding of the depth and expression of widows' emotional wounds and the process by which women struggled to recover from them.[16]

Like historian Nicole Eustace's work, this book analyzes "not the internal experience of emotion, but rather the external expression of emotion through language."[17] It is impossible to fully recapture the emotional experience of nineteenth-century Americans, but we can interpret their emotional expressions, charting the broader experience. Feelings may be human, even universal, but how they are expressed and how people describe them depends greatly on time, place, and culture. For example, when Civil War–era women described love, they often described it as almost overwhelming. For young relationships this might be expressed, as Susan McCampbell wrote to her fiancé, as feeling "so delighted as to grow dizzy." For those with a few more years of marriage, letters like Rosa Delony's were typical; she wrote her husband, "I must send you a little love message to night and tell you over again how constantly you are in my thoughts." To describe grief, women turned to adjectives such as *crushing* and *broken*. Widows who used these types of adjectives affirmed the Confederate death culture, supporting a political narrative that placed great value on soldiers. Anger, alternatively, served as a social signal that threatened the emotional regime. Anger at God, at a widow's community, or at her situation all undermined the narrative that this sacrifice was worth it for the greater good of the Confederacy. With regard to change over time, no significant shifts occurred in the ways men and women described emotions such as love, sadness, or anger over the course of the Civil War. While the quantity of loss increased tremendously, the loss remained personal to each individual, each wife. Many died, but this was the first time her husband had died, and the words used to describe that experience in 1865 did not differ dramatically from the words used to describe it in 1861.[18]

Even though Confederate popular and political culture championed the selfless widow, the defiant widow trope won out in twentieth-century popular culture through Scarlett O'Hara. But in the nineteenth century, the Confederacy was largely successful in the maintenance of normative mourning rituals. Most widows wore black, even if it meant dyeing their only dresses. Most widows cried, publicly and privately. Most widows followed etiquette. Exceptions existed, but during the war, the deviant widow did not shift the national discourse. The patriarchal white South emerged from the war in place, but notably, most widows did not lead the charge to uphold it, or the Lost Cause, after the war.

And finally, this book offers a third contribution to the historical field by returning widows to the narrative of the American Civil War. The war created widows, by the tens of thousands, then hundreds of thousands. *Love and Duty* focuses on widows whose husbands died between 1861 and 1865 while soldiering for the Confederacy and on widows who were politically aligned with the Confederacy, not widows who lived in the South but sympathized with the Union cause. Drew Gilpin Faust and Mark Schantz have documented how dying and killing prompted significant cultural shifts. In doing so, their work reclaimed the human experience, the important ways the individualized experience should not be lost in the grand scale of casualty rates. Faust's discussion of the Good Death, condolence letters, and grief rituals all contribute to an understanding of widowhood as a lived experience. *Love and Duty* joins this conversation, building upon this strong foundation, yet is unique with a focus on Confederate widows and widowhood in the white South.[19]

This book offers some discussion on widowhood in border states and conflicted counties, but the bulk of the sources consulted are from the eleven states that seceded from the Union. Richmond appears in several chapters to include the urban experience of some widows and as an important stage for performative politics as the Confederacy's capital, but the majority of this project's source base is small-town and rural in its focus. To the extent source material allows, working-class widows are included in this discussion, though the majority of written records are from those with the time and financial security to produce them. Unfortunately, one book cannot encompass all aspects of widowhood with the depth and breadth this topic craves, and yet, this project challenges historians to explore nineteenth-century womanhood and how the nascent emotionalization, even feminization, of patriarchal politics is proving relevant today.

Love and Duty is ultimately a story of love, loss, readjustments, and in some cases, a lack of readjustments. By blending cultural and emotional history, this book provides perspective not only on the emotions of Confederate widowhood but also on the struggles of families, communities, and white Confederate society as a whole to cope with both the loss of men and the high number of young widows. As war widows, these Confederate women had a moral platform and an opportunity to make a statement. They had social capital, and they could withdraw that capital from the bank of Confederate nationalism or continue to champion the Confederate cause that put their husbands in early graves. With an analysis of emotional expression, emotional power, and the political significance of mourning for a Confederate nation struggling to establish itself, this book gives us a much-needed chapter in the history of widows in the American Civil War.

1

Be My Wife

Love and Loss in the Antebellum South

Tivie if you cant be my wife we must be strangers.

Winston Stephens to Octavia Bryant, February 20, 1859

"I do not think I will ever forget that ride and frolic out to the Plantation," sighed Octavia "Tivie" Bryant to her suitor in October 1856. Her choice, Winston Stephens, was a twenty-six-year-old plantation owner of almost 360 acres.[1] "The question you asked me about where the house should stand is rather difficult to answer. . . . I will live wherever you wish," she replied. Tivie simply wanted to remain his, and the feeling was mutual. With her pale complexion, brunette hair, and expressive black eyes, Tivie had captured Winston's heart so completely that he would later write, "You had as well bid the Sun cease to wander the earth with its heat, giving life to vegitation and thereby producing plenty for all Gods creation as to bid the heart of Winston not to commune with the object of its adoration." He loved her, and lucky for him, she wished to marry him.[2]

They met in Welaka, a town founded by Tivie's father in 1852, about seventy miles south of Jacksonville, Florida. The town's warm winters, easy river access, and reputation as a hunters' paradise attracted tourists and settlers alike. By 1860, just eight years after its founding, the town boasted 317 white residents, 66 homes and stores, and 137 enslaved people. Winston was a slave owner, holding ten of that number, and combined with the acreage he owned and his reputation, he was quite the eligible bachelor. But when he asked Tivie's parents for their blessing, her parents vehemently refused. Their daughter, after all, was just fourteen.[3]

This chapter examines love and loss in the antebellum South, 1820–1860, to reveal the power of emotional expression and to provide a baseline to allow us to more fully understand how the Civil War affected courtship, engagement, marriage, and widowhood. Even as women increasingly sought the love match of a companionate marriage, the South remained a patriarchal world dominated by men, defined by relationships and customs. Relational labels such as daughter, fiancée, wife, mother, and widow came with a set of behavioral prescriptions. In this social contract, a white woman who behaved appropriately could expect certain comportment from those with whom she interacted, based on her age, stage, and financial situation. The wealthiest must comply or risk social ostracization, while the poorest might choose which elements applied best to their situations. But even as custom influenced experiences such as courtship, emotional expression played a major role in guiding (and sometimes misguiding) actions. To be sure, sermons, literature, and gossip affected those searching for love, but so did sentiment. For all the formal and informal rules of the world Tivie and Winston lived in, emotions often took over. The pages to come highlight the hopes and expectations of many women, as well as the etiquette of the antebellum era. They also emphasize the social benefits that white, married women in a white, enslaving, patriarchal society cultivated. This was a social standing they expected to bring with them into the new Confederacy.

For most Southern white families, a successful marriage was the ultimate goal for their young daughters. Definitions of *successful*, of course, varied family to family. Southern women generally married younger than their Northern counterparts, in their late teens and early twenties, pushed toward the altar by families but also by strong economic, social, and cultural forces. Though the objective seemed clear, sometimes, as in Tivie's case, a young woman had a difficult time balancing her desires, her family's desires, and her suitor's desires. The more money a family had, the higher the stakes in this balance. On her fifteenth birthday, Tivie could hardly believe how her life had changed. "A year ago to night I was dressed in a pink muslin dress low necked and short sleeved. . . . To night high necked and long sleeved black dress," an outfit less to her taste but more befitting of a sensible young woman. Sent away by her parents to her uncle's Massachusetts boarding school in hopes that she would move on from Winston, she did not need to reflect long before concluding, "Oh how I would like to be home." Tivie's family intended for her to marry, of course, but not yet. With a little time and distance between them, they hoped a more successful and appropriate match might be made.[4]

The entry into boarding school served as a defining phase for elite girls of the antebellum South and offered the opportunity to practice courtship rituals. At female academies, schoolgirls, often about fourteen years of age, experienced a new degree of freedom. Intimate friendships, sometimes highly romantic, offered the opportunity to exchange physical affection, pen lengthy letters of love, and engage in other rituals of courtship, from gifting flowers to exchanging rings. "Linda I am almost crazy to see you dearest," wrote one schoolgirl preparing to return to Wesleyan Female College in Virginia. "I suppose you will not fail to choose our desk and remember we are partners for everything next session." A Georgia schoolgirl similarly missed her friend, sighing into her diary about desires to feel her "breath on my cheek," "her hand, (my hand), clasped in mine," and "her sweet ruby lips pressed to mine." A third expressed the sorrows of heartbreak, explaining, "I have had many crys about you my darling, last night I sat by my window and the tears trickled down my cheeks, and I do not think my heart ever ached worse and it was all for you Lou." Through the acts and practices of finding close friends, young ladies experienced the emotional turmoil of lust and love, jealousy and loneliness—emotional expressions not unlike those of formalized courtship. Graduation marked both an end and a beginning, which most women realized all too well. "Today is my last school day! Time is ever rolling onward. . . . The childish heart must be exchanged for a garb of dignity, the hallowed books must be thrown lightly away, and I am to be ushered a mass of whalebone & starch into the fashionable world," reflected one graduating schoolgirl in 1857. Through these schoolgirl relationships, young women gained confidence and experience for courtships to come.[5]

Surprisingly, upon their return home many young women felt uncertain about, and some openly opposed to, the idea of marriage. "Monotony kills me as dead as a door nail," pronounced one twenty-three-year-old in 1826. "It will never do for me to be married." "Two people coming together in holy wedlock always remind me of two Birds in a cage. Unless they sing in concert, what discord ensues," agreed the opinionated and wealthy Mary Telfair. Likewise, Ann Reid informed a friend "that I was enjoying the independence of my Spinstership . . . and I should be very sorry to think, that only those who were to be launched on the sea of Matrimony, were happy." Others did not object to marriage outright but simply worried about their own abilities to fall in love, such as Mary Francis, who felt "my heart seems made of granite as far as men are concerned." Young women worried over marriage, and for good reason.[6]

These uncertainties surrounding matrimony came from a variety of places, from a love of independence to a fear of making a poor choice. "Marriages are said to be made in Heaven," reflected Martha Richardson, "but surely they are so jumbled together they get terribly mismatched by the time they reach us." Drunkards, gold diggers, gamblers, adulterers, and the aloof were all to be avoided. Many young women confessed something along the lines of "I see so many unhappy matches it almost discourages me." In their diaries and letters, young ladies often poked fun at their suitors, deeming them "great bores" and "loafers," giving them unflattering nicknames such as "Doctor Kill-pill" or "the fat proffessor." These nicknames and descriptors hinted at a darker truth in the importance of making the right choice. For all the fun they had in their flirtations and collection of suitors, most realized marriage was serious business. "So Sally is all but on the scaffold," reflected one friend. "I hope sincerely she may not find this being noosed, decidedly inconvenient, to say nothing more." Because husbands held so much power over a woman's private and public life, anxiety remained.[7]

Young women had the opportunity to take a greater role in selecting a husband with the rise of the companionate marriage ideal. In this type of marriage, instead of parents selecting a marriage partner, women might marry for love and hope for a partnership characterized by shared decision-making. But as Suzanne Lebsock's research discovered, even as the ideals of companionate marriage spread, marriage remained "fundamentally asymmetrical. Men retained the upper hand in almost every aspect of marriage; mixed with the new ideal of mutual affection and respect were substantial elements of male dominance and coercion." As Lebsock went on to explain, "Consensus and mutual respect did not come easily when the law, the economy, custom, and nature still conspired to make husbands vastly more powerful than their wives." Some women may have achieved a companionate marriage, characterized by mutual respect, affection, and increased power, but most fell short. The disappointment of these wives was palpable and an important caution to those selecting a partner.[8]

For example, the marital choice had serious legal implications, because when a woman married, she surrendered her legal identity to become a "covered woman," a feme covert. As the English judge Sir William Blackstone stated, "By marriage, the husband and wife are one person in law: that is, the very being or legal existence of the woman is suspended during the marriage, or at least is incorporated and consolidated into that of the husband; under whose wing, protection, and cover, she performs everything." A husband controlled his wife's property, represented her in court, retained custody of her children, and even had the legal responsibility to govern her behavior with physical force if he thought necessary. When married, an antebellum wife fell under the protections of her husband, without a legal or economic identity of her own. And so her choice was of paramount importance, not simply for her happiness, but for her survival.[9]

While Mary Telfair believed "stupid men are often the best matches," most young white women preferred a well-educated, financially stable suitor, if possible. "I will not give away my heart, and am afraid to exchange it, lest I should not get one in return equally valuable," explained one young South Carolinian. Southern society expected white women to marry, and even though some may have expressed hesitation, most young ladies focused on the positives. "I have long sought for one on whose confidence to rely, to whom I can without restraint, pour out my inmost secrets," hoped Elizabeth Ann Cooley in November 1845. She would marry but ultimately died at age twenty-two of fever. Many women sought what John N. Shealy sought in a marriage: two people who "openly acknowledge their preference for each other, voluntarily enter into a league of perpetual friendship, and call heaven and earth to witness the sincerity of the solemn vows." John was in love, but his intended, Jennie Burson in Georgia, worried ceaselessly about a marriage to him. He promised her a heart that would "always reflect and beat in union and unerring fidelity with yours." But Jennie felt anxious. "I am left now without Father or Mother to keep me from difficulties," she wrote, reflecting on the death of her parents, and worried, "I may innocently get into with scheming young men, I know I am very young and with but little or no experience." John persisted, and in the end Jennie yielded, honored "to think I have won such a heart as I believe yours to be." They married in 1859. She, like many women, overcame her fears and accepted the match she deemed best.[10]

For the upper class, the process of introduction, courtship, and engagement was fairly ritualized. A young lady's days and nights were filled with social activities—teas, parties, weddings, balls, concerts, lectures, and picnics. While arranged marriages were few in the antebellum era, parents kept a close eye on their children, ensuring the social events they attended contained a guest list of suitable partners. As superficial flirtations turned serious, young couples sought semiprivate and private moments for more personal and serious conversation. In the carefully monitored courtship process, these moments were rare, so couples often turned to letters as an opportunity for intimacy. Judiciously written and analyzed, letters were of tremendous importance for courting couples, as explained in the 1858 *Dictionary of Love*. "Love letters, billets-doux, are among the sweetest things which the whole career of love allows," begins the author, under a pseudonym. "By letters a lover can say a thousand extravagant things which he would blush to utter in the presence of his fair charmer. He heaps up mountains of epithets and hyperboles, expressing the inexpressible heights, and depths, and lengths, and breadths of his affection." It is in these letters that the lover "dissolves into sighs, and spreads himself out, on a sheet of gilt-edged note paper, into transparent thinness." Kissed, carried around, and cherished, love letters became quite sacred to a person in love and played an important role in the courtship process. In this emotional experience, the ritual of letter writing offered evidence to a couple in love to see if a successful partnership might be made.[11]

Even with the rituals and structure of courtship, emotions could, of course, sail a courtship into dangerous waters. Returning to the story of Tivie and Winston highlights how even the most beautifully written and ardent letters were not enough. In 1858, Tivie returned home from boarding school, scarcely 100 pounds and just over five feet tall. Perhaps a more dutiful daughter, or perhaps having learned her lesson from her last broken engagement, she promised her parents not to entertain any more suitors until she was at least eighteen years old. When Winston returned from fighting in the Third Seminole War, she informed him, "I was too young, and am now too young to judge for my happiness in my future life. . . . We all esteem you as a friend, and wish you to visit the house as gentlemen do, but not in any other position as regards myself." This reflected a proper course as defined by her society's standards. She would obey her parents and entertain a marriage, yes, but at the proper age.[12]

In the following months, Tivie and Winston saw each other often at parties and dinners. Spring blossomed and then another hot Florida summer began, harkening back to the summer they fell in love just two years earlier. Despite Tivie's repeated insistence that they were simply friends, she took great pleasure in Winston's continued attention. "While I played [piano] he watched me the whole time and when the melon came he began throwing seeds at me and I at him and we became quite friendly," she wrote in her diary. His letters put "roses to my cheeks," she added. Despite all the beautiful and eligible ladies in Welaka, Winston "talked to me most of the evening" at parties and always "danced the first dance with me and the last." It was not long before Winston, or the "Dear Crabid old Bachelor," as he called himself, began openly expressing his devotion to Tivie once more.[13]

When he proposed again in September, Tivie hesitated. "Forgive my keeping you in such suspense but you know Yes or No are the hardest words in the world to say," Tivie tried to explain to Winston. After much thought, she attempted to satisfy her heart and remain a dutiful daughter, deciding, "I will agree to be engaged to you secretly until I am 18, then I will ask my parents again and I hope gain their consent." Winston would continue to press for an earlier wedding date, but Tivie remained resolute. "Dear Old Man I do indeed pity you in your loneliness," she replied, "but oh I cannot yet give up my single life, you know I did not wish to marry for years yet."[14]

By February 1859, Winston had grown impatient. He requested a secret meeting with Tivie among the stones of a graveyard. There was "no other safe way" to have the discussion he planned. Between graves he attempted to convince her to marry him without parental approval, but his efforts backfired miserably and Tivie broke off their engagement. "I never cried so much in my life," Tivie wept into her diary. Winston sent her angry letters, claiming, "I have ben led astray by your smiles and sweet words of promises." He accused Tivie of "an irreparable wrong you have done an innocent and unoffending heart." He wrote, "Go to your parents for forgiveness as it seems they are the only ones you care for." Unable to stomach her presence, Winston concluded, "Tivie if you cant be my wife we must be strangers." This disagreement reflected a break in the standard courtship procedure, and for many, that would be that.[15]

But Tivie's eighteenth birthday approached. Though he would rather forget her, Winston continued to believe their marriage would be a superior choice to "matches that are formed by parents and friends to suit their wish." Putting his pride aside, Winston combined logic and compliments in an attempt to win her over, again. By July 1859, she was back to being his "angel purity of love and Goodness!" Resigned to the fact that she would not budge on her parents' demands, Winston began signing letters with a countdown to her eighteenth birthday in October. "Two months and twenty one days," he would write. Tivie began planning the wedding yet again, but this time gained the confidence of her mother. She wrote a letter to her father, who was traveling, requesting his permission. "I would dislike to marry without [your consent]," she explained, "but if you do not, I will be obliged to for my own happiness." This time, Winston would come first. Tired of fighting his daughter and perhaps realizing the futility of doing so, Tivie's father granted his blessing. Happy to have the tumultuous four years of courtship behind them, Tivie and Winston finally wed on November 1, 1859. Winston was thirty years old, Tivie twelve years his junior. This courtship of Tivie and Winston reveals that though society had particular procedures for engagements, and rules (such as obeying parental wishes), emotional expression played a significant role in guiding young couples through the process.[16]

While most women had less eventful journeys to the aisle than Tivie, the majority of women in the antebellum South, across social class, would marry. Most would also be excited by it once they found a suitable match. "Were you ever so delighted as to grow dizzy, I have been so often, and to you I am indebted oftenest for that exstatic pleasure," wrote one engaged Tennessee woman to her fiancé. The wedding day marked an important shift in a woman's life, no matter her class. For one nineteen-year-old bride, the ceremony brought "the pain of adieus and separation from my home and kindred" and "the happiness of loving and being loved." With marriage, a woman joined a new family, took on a new set of responsibilities, and moved to a new household. Wedding ceremonies in the antebellum South were typically small, attended by close family and friends to celebrate the transition to full womanhood. Young ladies met this transition with various degrees of excitement, but either way, most young women would have a moment such as this young bride, who wrote in her diary, "The wedding is over, and I am MARRIED."[17]

The ideals defining marriage roles came from many places, including prescriptive literature and, particularly, etiquette books. Although primarily read by elite white women, these books spread ideals to much of white Southern society. Antebellum America did not lack for advice manuals, for "aside from frequent revisions and new editions, twenty-eight different manuals appeared in the 1830s, thirty-six in the 1840s and thirty-eight more in the 1850s—an average of over three new ones annually in the pre–Civil War decades." In addition to the pricier, bound editions, publishers also released shorter, less expensive manuals, such as the 1859 *Beadle's Dime Book of Practical Etiquette*, at seventy-two pages, and the competing 1860 *Etiquette, and the Usages of Society*, at sixty-four pages. Each cost ten cents. In addition to the many American-published volumes, conduct books had a transatlantic air about them. In 1820, British writers authored roughly 70 percent of the etiquette books published in the United States. By 1850, that number dropped to 30 percent, as American-born authors began writing their own codes for behavior. Even so, much of the advice mirrored that of the British originals. These advice manuals mattered because they guided women's actions and set expectations for their gender.[18]

Lydia Maria Child penned one such popular etiquette book, *The American Frugal Housewife*, in 1828. By 1833, it was in its twelfth edition, sharing admonitions against waste and frivolity. According to Child, a young woman should not enjoy herself "while she is single" but rather see the "domestic life as the gathering place of the deepest and purest affections; as the sphere of woman's enjoyments as well as her duties." Catharine Beecher, sister of the famous author of *Uncle Tom's Cabin*, similarly believed that of all female experiences, a woman's domestic life was most important, and she devoted her life to writing advice, including the annually reprinted *Treatise on Domestic Economy*. The manual contained advice on everything from early rising to childcare and mental health. She believed women from New England to Virginia "would encounter many deprivations and trials" and attempted to prevent women from these trials through her advice. Dancing, for instance, was a recreation to be avoided. Beecher described a room where conversation ceased, "where the young collect, in their tightest dresses," and begin to dance, causing blood "to circulate more swiftly than ordinary," pores of the skin to become "excited," and stomachs to be "loaded with indigestible articles." She concluded that in fifteen years, she had never seen a situation in which dancing had not had "a bad effect, either on the habits, the intellect, the feelings, or the health" of young ladies. Because Beecher expected most women would become wives and mothers, she cautioned against this unhealthy activity. The pervasiveness of these publications and the consistency of the advice offered clear social expectations to nineteenth-century white women.[19]

Literary journals and magazines proved similarly influential in the antebellum North and South, particularly *Godey's Lady's Book*. In 1822, Sarah Josepha Hale began writing and editing to support her family when she found herself widowed with five children. Her career brought her to the editorship of *Godey's*, a magazine whose circulation reached 150,000 monthly subscribers by 1860. From 1837 to 1877, Hale compiled issues that included essays, poems, engravings, and music to interest and educate her female readers. Often, the advice came through a story, such as "The Constant; or, The Anniversary Present" in January 1851. This tale shared the story of a young and beautiful wife, Catherine, and her husband, Willis. Each night, Willis left his wife and baby for a club, remaining unaware of the "injustice of his conduct" until he overheard a friend of his wife's urge her to attend a party. "Why, every one's talking about it, my child, how you are cooped up here, and Willis at the clubhouse night after night. . . . If he went to the club, I'd flirt, that's all, and we'd see who would hold out the longer." Catherine reminded her friend that two wrongs "never make a right" and shared she would "try to make his home as pleasant as possible, and when he is weary of his gay companions he will return to me with more interest." "Dear Kate," Willis wrote from a business trip three months later, "I have searched all over Paris, and could not find anything that I thought would please you more than the included, which is my resignation of club membership." Upon his return home, he informed the friend, "Kate's way was the best"; supposedly the friend could not help telling the story, and thus it was a secret no longer. The advisory message could not be clearer to young wives, for as the patient young Catherine reflected, "Nor would it be wise to annoy my husband with complaints. Nothing provokes a man like an expostulation." And so ideals also spread in this way, through published stories such as this, celebrating the dutiful wife.[20]

Religion, and religious figures, also influenced feminine ideals laid before women. Often, the advice of conduct books and Christian ministers overlapped, reinforcing each other and reappearing in sermons and theological study. "Let me say to both, seek, by all proper means, to promote each other's happiness; and especially remember that the great object of your union is to help each other to heaven," urged James Andrew, a bishop of the Methodist Episcopal Church, South, in 1847. This proper means came with a slew of expectations for a young bride that mimicked the advice found in etiquette books. She should "keep a pure heart, a bright eye, a kind look, loving words, a clean house, a well-managed pantry and kitchen: be neat and tidy in dress and person; love your Bible and your prayers" in order to "be certain to deserve your husband's love." Rev. E. P. Rogers of the First Presbyterian Church of Augusta, Georgia, also offered advice to unmarried young women, urging them to not "wear the bright apparel of the butterfly," for there "is no beauty like the beauty of goodness." In his view, a young girl "prostituting" herself "on the altar of vanity" and "running a giddy round of gaiety, frivolity, and dissipation" was a "sad, heart-breaking sight on earth." Ministers believed a godly wife met the preferred ideals by avoiding such activities.[21]

A powerful message of the superiority of husbands, and men more generally, came through ministers' admonishments. "The apostle says, 'Wives submit yourselves to your own husbands,'" chided Bishop James Andrew in 1847, continuing, "There are some wives who seem to me to act very unwisely in this matter." The Bible was commonly used as a common defense of male superiority; as one plantation mistress put to her diary, "Our mother Eve when she trangress'd was told her husband should rule over her—then how dare any of her daughters to dispute that point." Methodist minister John Bayley likewise believed a true wife cultivated attitudes of "mildness, softness, sweetness of temper" and regarded her husband with "reverence" above all else. James Andrew agreed: "Let your husband see, let him feel, that next to God, he is enthroned in your heart." That proof would come "in your looks, your words, the neatness of your person, and the arrangement of your household matters. . . . Study his peculiar tastes and temperament, and accommodate yourself to them." A proper wife would not chide, guide, or disagree, for "doubtless many husbands, once kind, have been ruined by such management." And a proper husband would "remember that your wife is a fallen and imperfect creature. . . . You will therefore have need to understand well and practise on the maxim bear and forbear." In order for women to perform in their societal roles, men also had to play their part.[22]

Episcopal bishop James Madison, in Virginia, agreed that feminine obedience was key, advising his daughter to "never to attempt to controul your husband by opposition of any kind." He believed "a difference with your husband ought to be considered as the greatest calamity" and urged her "to believe that his prudence is his best guide." This letter, though written in 1811, would be published and republished continually—in the *Richmond Enquirer* in 1818, the *Southern Literary Messenger* in 1834, and the *Watchman of the South* in 1839. Through obedience, women met society's expectations.[23]

In addition to ministers, families offered formal guidance to women, especially young brides. "You will have to study housekeeping. You are too young to have learnt much of it; but you have been an apt scholar in other branches and I hope so in this," directed one father to his recently married daughter. Another father advised his eighteen-year-old daughter, "You are now in the most interesting and critical period of life—a young married lady—your own welfare and happiness and that of your husband depend much upon yourself and your early adoption of those rules of conduct that are suited to your situation." To love a woman who complained, cried, or scolded, in his opinion, "is more than a mortal man can do," so she should instead seek "kindness and gentleness" as the "natural and proper means of the wife." Mothers agreed with the advice, hoping their daughters "may be one of those wives whose price is far above rubies," with a calculated amiability "to increase the esteem and affections of your companion." Surprisingly, one mother admitted, "A single life has fewer troubles; but then it is not one for which our maker designed us." Agreeing with the messages of etiquette books, literature, and sermons, families also encouraged their daughters to behave by obeying their husbands. As pro-slavery intellectual George Fitzhugh put it more bluntly, "A husband, a lord and master, whom she should love, honor and obey, nature designed for every woman, for the number of males and females is the same. If she be obedient, she is in little danger of mal-treatment." Families echoed the guides of ministers and etiquette books in their letters, reinforcing the role that wives must play.[24]

Just as ideals circulated widely in print, influencing expectations and actions of girls such as Tivie, so too did cautionary tales. Some women, such as Anna Cooke in Kentucky, chose to take an unconventional path. Her family had money, connections, and a plantation, yet she chose not to wed and in 1820, at age thirty-five, delivered a stillborn baby. The father, she claimed, was a wealthy Kentucky politician, and the baby was conceived while his wife was at church. A reader of romantic literature and a poet herself, Anna transformed her story into a tragic seduction straight from the pages of her well-worn novels. Antebellum women commonly read sentimental books featuring fallen female characters, such as Susanna Rowson's *Charlotte Temple*, which warned young ladies against the dangers of making sinful choices during courtship. According to his confession, eighteen-year-old Jereboam Orville Beauchamp heard about the politician's dishonorable behavior and visited Anna, after which the woman nearly twice his age "began to haunt my thoughts and my dreams." Unable to resist her, he proposed, and she informed him that "she would kiss the hand and adore the person who would avenge her," desiring that her former lover "die through her instrumentality." She married Jereboam, and in return Jereboam approached the politician "and muttered in his face, 'Die you villain!' And as I said that I plunged the dagger to his heart."[25]

Anna stayed with her husband in prison. They attempted a double suicide via laudanum but botched it. The morning of his execution, she tried again, but could not keep the laudanum down. The third time being the charm, they turned to a knife, smuggled in by Anna, to fatally stab themselves. Anna's suicide proved successful, and a bleeding Jereboam was taken to the gallows to be quickly hanged. Their corpses were arranged in an embrace, placed in a single coffin, and buried together, as they requested. One of Anna's poems graced the tombstone, which included the stanza "Daughter of virtue! Moist thy tear, This tomb of love and honor claim; For thy defense the husband here, Laid down in youth his life and fame." Their story, and their unique take on honor in the South, became infamous overnight, published in newspapers across the nation. It mattered because it highlighted not only the power of emotional expression but also the tragedy of following passion to sex outside of marriage.[26]

While Anna and Jereboam dressed their story in the pervasive moral language of the day, some white women, often of the lowest economic class, did not place a priority on following etiquette strictures at all, as the exceptional case of Edward Isham highlights. As a miner, lumberjack, herdsman, farmer, gambler, drinker, and fighter, Edward's world was awash with foul language, violence, and sex. In 1848, Mary Brown of Alabama abandoned her first husband, married Edward, and moved to Georgia. "I saw her and she and I agreed to run off and we did so. . . . She was 20 yrs old and very pretty," recalled Edward. Through his autobiography, Edward, a poor white laborer who murdered his North Carolina employer in the 1850s, offers insight into the lives of working-class women in one man's life.[27]

What Edward and men like him lacked in social prestige and wealth, they overcompensated for with flashy exhibits of masculinity. Success in drinking, gambling, and brawling bought a hardened reputation that demanded respect. The poorest of white women, who lacked formal power and legal rights in the antebellum South, often relied on these men for protection. A dark side to this world of brazen action, of course, was the effect it had on those whom men loved most—themselves and their women. Edward's mother, three wives, and many lovers provided him with moments of refuge, comfort, and adventure throughout his short thirty-two years of existence. In this masculine world, women often served as prizes to be won from fathers, lovers, or even other husbands. Women manipulated these situations, pitting men against one another, choosing the best situation as it became available, and abandoning that situation when a better one appeared. Edward's reckless and relentless thirst for violence would bring about not only his eventual execution but the loss of Mary to another man. After a stint of carousing, Edward returned from Chattanooga and seemed surprised to find "something wrong with Mary, she did not treat me kindly and I became jealous." He followed her and at dusk discovered another man "sitting on a bed with her and his arms around her." Not surprisingly, Edward tried to shoot him and, when that failed, "jumped off and pursued him with my bowie knife." Rather than endure Edward's abusive behavior, when he left for Tennessee, yet again, Mary decided to shape her own circumstances, revealing the mutable nature of antebellum relationships among some poor white couples.[28]

Prescriptive literature and elite society prized the female practice of patience, politeness, meekness, chastity, self-sacrifice, and loyalty. For women such as Mary with a husband such as Edward, however, this moral code promised a life of frustration and destitution. Instead, Mary chose a new path, a new partner, and a new marriage as it suited her. In Edward's world, marriage appeared informal and fleeting, suggesting that these unions lacked legal sanction and are perhaps more accurately viewed as common-law liaisons. Even so, they reveal a world of relationships quite unlike the ideals of the upper class.

While the experience of courtship and marriage for elite women such as Tivie Stephens fell on one side of the spectrum and for poor wives such as Mary Brown on the other, the majority of wives did have one eventual commonality: the experience of motherhood. On average, the antebellum Southern wife had at least five children, and up to fourteen, numbers which do not account for miscarriages, stillbirths, and infant deaths. Put another way, most women experienced a pregnancy about every two years until menopause. Husbands often announced the happy news of a new baby's arrival via letters. Some felt overwhelmed with gratitude, such as R. M. Price, who described the birth of a son as "an event which caused my heart to overflow with tears of gratitude to our great Preserver." Others chose to boast: "He of course is the finest boy that ever was born, given already strong indications of both eminence and usefulness." Another bragged of a new baby daughter "fat and lusty" who was "destined doubtless to be the smasher of many hearts." Some mothers wanted daughters, for "how much less trouble they give than boys," while others hoped for a house of "bustling sons" over the "prospect of having old maids in the family." Motherhood was a central experience for the majority of antebellum wives.[29]

But at minimum, most young women simply hoped to survive the whole experience, for all knew that pregnancy and childbirth in the antebellum South were risky business. Each time a wife became pregnant, she faced the possibility of death. It was not uncommon for pregnant women to be found as physician Charles Hentz discovered one of his patients, "lying on the floor—cold—almost pulseless and flighty—foetus hanging by the cord." He saved her life with his linen handkerchief, checking the hemorrhaging. Newspapers ran a constant stream of obituaries with stories such as that of Mary Dale, age nineteen, who died "and left her first child of about two hours and an affectionate husband to lament their loss." Simple slate tombstones also shared the sad tales of laboring gone wrong, such as that of "Mary Adaline Patterson who departed this life on the 9th of May 1825 aged 20 years 6 months 10 days also her infant who lies by her side." In 1850, the South had twice the maternal mortality rate of New England and the Middle Atlantic states. Bloodletting, opiates, disease, lack of sanitation, and lack of general knowledge about pregnancy and childbirth contributed to the high mortality rates.[30]

Rearing a child required a great deal of energy and dedication, which was met with mixed responses by those who undertook it. Elizabeth Fischer told her sister, "I feel with you that my responsibilities are doubled; and sometimes am almost in despair about ever being able to do my duty." Another sympathized with a friend, "I received your letter of the 21st a few hours ago and read it pretty much as you say it was written, amid the bustle of half dozen children and in the intervals of attending to their wants." After a pause, she continued, "I do everything now and my mode of locomotion is no longer a *walk* but rather a half run." But others, such as Rebecca Turner, embraced motherhood so fully that she could not even imagine ceasing to breastfeed her eighteen-month-old son. "It will be a trial for me to wean him," she wrote in her diary. "How am I to relinquish so sweet an office—that of giving nourishment to my darling? Are these foolish tears that dim my eyes when I think of the times, when he will no longer nestle in my bosom through the silent watches of the night?" As the years passed, many women felt tremendous satisfaction in their roles as wives and mothers. "All my anticipations have been more than fully realized," rejoiced one wife. She assured her friend she was "as much in love as ever and am perfectly happy." Another found married life to be "far preferable [to single life] & wonder much that we should have been so long a time making up our minds concerning it." For some, wifehood and motherhood suited them well, inspiring the next generation of daughters to seek a similar situation.[31]

Of course, not all marriages were of love, or even a physical presence, in the antebellum South. A repetitive loop of desire and disappointment exhausted the emotions of many antebellum plantation mistresses, such as Anna Page King. Born in 1798, Anna grew up on St. Simons, an island off the coast of Georgia, on the Retreat, a plantation with a raised cottage and more than 100 varieties of roses. Her world was one of fragrant flowers, education, and parental devotion but also a world of persistent heat, mosquitoes, and a long row of slave houses facing the beach. Anna's siblings all died before they reached adulthood. Her father, a wealthy and successful planter, personally invested in her education, training her to be an unusually capable manager of plantation affairs.[32]

This combination of wealth and education made Anna an especially desirable candidate for marriage. In 1824, at twenty-six years of age, she wed Thomas Butler King, a handsome man two years her younger, with piercing gray eyes, a light complexion, and lips that met in a stern line. This was her second fiancé, after a failed dowry negotiation with an Englishman left Anna with a broken engagement and a broken heart. But in Thomas, she found an initial happiness. Early in her marriage, she reflected to a friend, "My dear Husband ever kind and attentive to me is well. Have I not many instances of his divine goodness? Have I not still more blessings than I deserve?" Thomas, too, was pleased with his improved reputation as a planter of extensive land holdings and more than 350 enslaved people.[33]

But by 1843, Thomas's world had crumbled. "My husband has probably been one of the greatest sufferers from these successive disasters," Anna
explained to a friend of her now-deceased father, who was also a trustee of
the property left to her in her father's will. The collapse of cotton prices, the
Panic of 1837, and a variety of elaborate financial schemes had left Thomas
penniless. Local papers ran notices of the family's misfortune and attempts
to satisfy the debts against Thomas, including the sale of 247 enslaved people
and 20,000 acres across three counties. It wasn't enough, and Anna worried
creditors would come after her. "I do not impute any blame, or mismanage-
ment to my husband, nor has his misfortunes, in the slightest degree impaired
my confidence in his integrity, or his ability to manage property," she emphasized, but she asked permission to call on the trustee "to protect my property,
as my husband cannot act." In the end, the family kept only the Retreat, the
home of Anna's childhood, and the fifty enslaved people (and their children)
left to Anna in her father's will. Thomas would spend the rest of his life on
the move—Washington, D.C., California, Texas, England—chasing a political and business career, continually grasping at opportunities to restore his
fortune and reputation and hounded by creditors for nearly twenty years.[34]

This left Anna lonely, unhappy, and at home, a fact she reminded her husband of constantly. Despite being surrounded by the noise and activity of nine
children and more than 100 enslaved people, she felt alone. More prison than
"retreat" to Anna, the management of the plantation demanded her constant
attention, with "hands full and in the midst of this house full." Of course, the
workload helped distract from her sorrows, in some ways. "I have more to
do than I can attend to—but perhaps it is well that it is so as I am thereby
prevented from brooding over the absence of my dear husband," wrote Anna
typically to a friend in 1839. She was not alone in her feelings. Many plantation
women, like Anna, did not have a community such as those offered to women
who lived in cities and towns. Large land and slave holdings served as a hedge
of protection against poverty but simultaneously were a barrier to community
and an institution dependent on violence. In this isolated realm, the physical
presence of a husband offered necessary companionship. Letters, too, helped,
as Anna, like many plantation mistresses, turned to correspondence to create
intimacy. Her daughters provided emotional support, while her eldest son,
who preferred plantation life to that of a traveling occupation, took over the
management of the plantation when Anna grew older.[35]

And yet no matter how disappointing, how remote, or how unsuccessful
her husband may have been, Anna invested and reinvested her faith in him.
Certainly she chided, begged, and even belittled him at times with barbs such

as "Hard—hard have you laboured for a reputation to leave your children but that will not give them bread." But even as the decades passed, her pleas for his permanent return never ceased until her death in 1859. This marriage, with all its financial difficulties and emotional distance, and the accompanying motherhood, remained a central component of Anna's life.[36]

Anna's difficulties paled in comparison to those of white women caught in verbally, physically, or mentally abusive marriages. In 1849, one wife petitioned the North Carolina courts for a divorce after her husband continuously drank heavily, beat her, locked her out of the house overnight, slept with an enslaved woman, and in one instance, forced his wife to watch them have sex. The chief justice did not grant the absolute dissolution of the marriage, believing there was reasonable hope for the couple's reconciliation. Another wife, in Virginia, would flee to the swamps when her husband drank. If he caught her in the kitchen seeking protection from the weather, he attacked "with his fists and with sticks." A third husband "stamped" on his wife, after knocking her to the ground with fireplace tongs, until her ribs broke. A fourth "beat her head against the bed post and wall till her sense had nearly left her." Another forced his wife "to ride a wild and dangerous horse in a violent storm" to cause a miscarriage. Another woman witnessed a William Ball drag his wife "around the house by the hair of her head" while "cursing and threatening to kill" her. Divorce, while a possibility, remained a difficult and lengthy process, discouraged by social and religious beliefs. And within the patriarchy, men maintained the right to correct their wives.[37]

Some husbands did kill their wives. One slit his wife's throat "and pulled out the sinews." Newman Roane assaulted his wife with an ax. A third husband, with a fondness for alcohol, Alvin Preslar, beat his wife so brutally that she fled with two of her children toward her father's house, dying before she reached it. Three hundred people petitioned against Preslar's sentence to hang, arguing his actions were not intentional but rather "the result of a drunken frolic." Alcohol seemed to bring out the worst in men with unkind inclinations. "Like a dog returning to his vomit, and the Sow Wallowing in the Mire, he again became more and more intemperate and more and more Morose in disposition, and harsh and unkind," shared one wife with the court. Her husband was known for giving her "severe and violent blows with his fist." He confessed to nothing more than having "played Roughly with her" because "liquor set me crazy." These extreme cases, of brutality, adultery, and murder, reveal the dark side of patriarchy in the antebellum South. As the ideals of companionate marriage grew, there remained a strong undercurrent that a woman must make a match she could not only enjoy but survive.[38]

Another form of infidelity, common in the antebellum South, involved the sexual relationships between married planters and enslaved women. Certainly, some white women did have sex with African American men. Dorothea Bourne of Virginia, for example, engaged in an extended sexual relationship with a man enslaved on a neighboring plantation. Her husband stated there was "no room to doubt that an illicit intercourse" was "regularly kept up between them," while neighbors testified to her children "by a slave." In 1831, a different husband, Thomas Culpeper, also in Virginia, attempted to divorce his wife, claiming she "sacrificed her virtue on the altar of prostitution" and had "carnal intercourse with black men or negroes." Elizabeth Walters's husband alleged that she had "lived in illicit carnal cohabitation with a negro slave, become pregnant by him, and had a negro child." Married wives turned to enslaved men for sex for a variety of reasons, including lust, love, passion, and power.[39]

While these relationships are notable, far more common were the relationships, usually of the coercive sort, between white men and African American women. As Mary Boykin Chesnut famously wrote, "Every lady tells you who is the father of all the mulatto children in everybody's household, but those in her own she seems to think drop from the clouds, or pretends so to think." The extent to which slave owners sexually assaulted enslaved women will never be known, but it was common enough that even travelers noted the relationship. For example, James Davidson wrote of New Orleans in 1836, "Married men in this City are frequently in the habit of keeping quadroons," whom he described as prostitutes for exclusive use. The fancy trade, or sale of young, attractive enslaved girls at high prices, became more than just a sex trade but a platform for planters to display dominance, power, and wealth to other slave owners. Flirting with the edges of respectability, married men purchased young girls far above market prices, described with phrases such as "13 year old Girl, Bright Color, nearly a fancy for $1135." More common, though, were slave owners who used enslaved women they already owned for their sexual desires, owners such as James Norcom, who repeatedly whispered sexual propositions into a girl's ear when she turned fifteen. "If God has bestowed beauty upon her [a female slave] it will prove her greatest curse. That which commands admiration in the white woman only hastens the degradation of the female slave," reflected formerly enslaved Harriet Jacobs. For African American women, beauty brought male attention, from Black and white men alike, and increased likelihood of sexual assault. White married women would rarely be ignorant of it.[40]

Whether false or faithful, cruel or kind, all men met the same end: they died. In this antebellum society, a widowed wife met an entirely new list of challenges as a single woman once again. Immediately, there were practical considerations. One of her first tests included the management of her dower thirds, an automatic inheritance of approximately one-third of a husband's assets, to provide for her in his death. Sometimes, widows also inherited the management of entire estates until children came of age. For many, there were also emotional considerations, such as grief. But like in courtship and marriage, there were also ideals, a combination of ritual and etiquette, guiding mourning practices.[41]

Ideally, a person's death was a communal ritual, taking place at home, witnessed by close family and friends, and with strong religious themes. When John C. Calhoun, political defender of slavery as "a positive good," died in March 1850, his widow encouraged their daughter, "Begin from this hour, to give your children religious instruction. Tell them how calmly and resigned their Grandfather died." Of utmost importance to the white antebellum South was a Good Death, *ars moriendi*, a ritualistic passing-away experience in the home, surrounded by loved ones, culminating in the peaceful acceptance of God's will after a long-lived life. Death did not happen in a hospital or doctor's office but at home, in the bed one slept in every night. Women, as central components in the rituals of death and mourning, expected this type of death for their loved ones. When Charlotte Verstille's brother died with strangers, she was furious and wrote her sister, "I feel as if I dont care whether I live or die when I give up my contemplation of the subject. I know it is wicked—but my heart almost murmurs against the decrees of Being, of whome we are told that mercy is his darling attribute." Just as important as being surrounded by family was the utterance of last words, often reaffirming a faith in God, offering a resignation to death, and providing last words of wisdom for the family. It was at this moment, observers believed, that the true and honest status of a soul could be assessed. When dying of cholera in Kentucky, Methodist bishop Henry B. Bascom was able to reply, "Yes! Yes! Yes!" when asked if his faith in God remained firm, but he was unable to speak once more of Jesus or the resurrection, much to the disappointment of his wife. Nonetheless, his faith was reaffirmed, so his family felt relieved. He had an *ars moriendi*.[42]

After a death, certain mourning prescriptions fell upon the family and especially the widow. Antebellum custom suggested that husbands mourn the death of a wife three months, with a simple black armband. Siblings

Example of mourning attire, from "Women in Mourning, Cemetery in New Orleans," *Frank Leslie's Illustrated Newspaper*, April 25, 1863. *Image courtesy of author.*

should mourn the loss of a sibling for six months, and mothers should mourn the death of a child for one year. But for a widow, the mourning period for the death of a husband should last two and a half years. During this time, male relatives filled the void her late husband left behind by managing property and legal obligations, so a widow's attention could turn to her private grief and the management of its public portrayal. Clothing, as an outward expression of inner turmoil, was an important aspect of mourning widows' lives. As the 1856 etiquette book *How to Behave* explained, "Dress has its language, which is, or may be, read and understood by all." The authors believed "there should be a harmony between your dress and your circumstances." The color black aimed to remind the widow, her friends, and strangers alike of her grief.

Thus, in the first year of heavy mourning, "the bereaved wore solid black wool garments," a "simple crape bonnet—never a hat—and a long, thick, black crape veil." Her jewelry, too, would be black and frequently contain a piece of the deceased's hair, often braided. In the second year, a widow could progress to wearing "a silk fabric trimmed with crape and use black lace for her collars and cuffs" and "shorten her veil and make it of tulle or net." Eventually, she "might vary her wardrobe with garments or trim of gray, violet, or white." The subtle shifts in wardrobe reflected a slow transformation of grief and signaled to the community how they should approach and behave around a widow, particularly an elite widow. Mourning etiquette offered structure when emotions threatened to overwhelm her.[43]

Some antebellum etiquette books described the mourning costume to an almost comical extreme. Emily Thornwell's *Lady's Guide to Perfect Gentility* devoted an entire paragraph to mourning bonnets. Initial descriptions of the hat appear rather benign. Thornwell informed the reader that mourning bonnets ought to be made of black silk and "covered in crape." Thornwell became more particular when describing the hems of the bonnets, that the bow and strings should be "broad-hemmed, the double hem being from half an inch to one inch broad." Then, she proceeded into descriptions of the bonnet for deep mourning. The front of the bonnet should have "a fall or veiling of crape" measuring "half a yard deep, and a yard and a half long." The ideal and respectable widow, according to this description, walked about with a foot and a half of dark, heavy fabric in front of her face. For short women, the veil, over four feet in length, could nearly drag on the floor before them. In this mourning bonnet, a community could easily identify, watch, and speak to a widow but not with. The mourning attire placed her in the world but not quite interacting with it.[44]

Etiquette books offered directives for widows' behavior as well. The idea that "the true wife, when widowed, remains a widow, till death re-unites her to the being—complementary to herself . . . [and] perpetual widowhood is alone consistent with our Ideal of woman" met mixed reactions. Many antebellum widows did remarry. A greater portion of society readily accepted the other directives, such as a renewed devotion to religion and children. Lizzie Torrey's *The Ideal of Womanhood* offered the example of a touching letter between a widow and son, with "sentiments we cannot but approve." The widow looked forward to reuniting with her husband in heaven, "and confiding in the grace of God, I am resolved to suffer all the troubles of widowhood, and brave alone the storms and tempests of life." The widow promised her son "to devote the remaining years of my life to your education, and contemplation of the virtues of your beloved father." This widow agreed with the notion that she should not remarry, concluding, "Preserving the memory of my husband, whom I shall never cease to love, I shall refuse all offers to contract a second marriage." These commitments, to her God, her son, and her husband's memory, set a high standard for mourning widows.[45]

Family and friends did not expect recent widows to rely solely on etiquette books, of course, and also attempted to guide recently widowed women. Frances Douglass, for example, struggled when her husband, a minister in North Carolina, died speechless. This was not a Good Death. "I look a round I see many things which he begun that are incomplete," she reflected, wondering why her Lord "called him home in the midst of his labours," leaving her with his heavy financial debts. Her family and friends had much advice for her. One friend of her late husband reminded her "how great his gain. Everlasting rest. Joy unspeakable, a crown of glory" in heaven. Another minister reminded her that she would meet her husband in heaven, for "the separation is but for a season; our dear friend is not lost." As a widowed pastor's wife, she should show the world "that the religion you profess is a glorious reality, not an empty name," by using it to "console and strengthen" herself. Receiving all these messages, Frances concluded to her son, "I was too happy for earth, & now I am made to know that this is not my rest." The notes and advice from family continued emphasizing themes of religion and peace.[46]

Like it did for good wives and mothers, antebellum society held up properly behaving widows as an example in a variety of printed forms. Take a sermon that described "the fond and devoted wife, [who] has just received the dying benediction of the faithful and affectionate husband, and exclaims, with heart-breaking anguish, Oh! what will now become of us? My husband was my all—was my everything—friend, counsellor, nay, was next to God himself." This level of devotion and grief reflected the ideal relationship between husband and wife. He was the most important thing in her life, next to her religion. As such, it was appropriate sermon material. Antebellum visual imagery, too, shared messages about the ideal female mourner. Beginning in the 1820s, printed images lifted off carvings made in stone, called lithographs, began to spread across states in large quantities. Printers frequently created and copied various depictions of a neatly dressed woman, with her head in her hands, leaning against a large, well-kept graveyard monument with the description "In Memory Of." In these images, women mourned; it was their task to weep and remember, and they leaned bent, but not broken, over the grave.[47]

After conducting an extensive analysis of prescriptive literature for widows in the colonial period, historian Vivian Conger concluded that "within those texts, ministers and others variously labeled widows as sober, grave, temperate, just, honest, faithful, charitable, peaceable, modest, chaste, kind, virtuous, and pious but also as deceptive, wanton, angry, scheming, haughty, sorrowful, pitiful, discontented, odious, and sinful." These descriptors are significant because they hold true in the language of the antebellum era as well. While etiquette books championed the well-behaved widow, they also warned of the sexual attraction of widows. Take an advice book published in 1846, which conceded that "there is a peculiar fascination about widows . . . whether it by sympathy for the weeds of mourning, the interest excited by a lady in distress, or a certain air acquired by experience in matrimony, widows are very commonly the objects of a tender passion." Their allure stemmed from the fact that "they have more experience than maidens have." Recognizing this desire, this book included instructions, and a model letter, advising interested men on the proper way to introduce the idea of a second marriage. The formulaic letter reveals that even though remarriage was an option, the idea was still surrounded by a specific set of expectations, including an address as "dear madam" and an expression of sympathy for her misfortunes. Not all widows would be content with the status of widowhood forever or financially able to survive it.[48]

In addition to etiquette books, historical precedent and popular culture also warned of the sexually experienced, and often badly behaved, widow. Sarah Stickney, living in the colonies and widowed before the American Revolution even began, reportedly called to a passing man, "A you roge, yonder is yor Child under the tree, goe take it up and see it." Sarah had multiple illegitimate children and, in a different instance, successfully sued for child support from a married man. The stereotype of the hypersexualized American widow sprung from stories such as these. Widows appeared without a proper male chaperone. Take Aphra Behn's popular play *The Widow Ranter, or The History of Bacon in Virginia*. The central character came to Virginia as an indentured servant, married her rich master, outlived him, inherited his entire plantation, and performed lines such as "We rich widows are the best commodity this country affords, I'll tell you that." As a widow, she drank, smoked, argued, donned male clothing, fought, and lived her life unfiltered and unchecked, with a healthy sexual appetite. Audiences with traditional leanings likely found comfort in the fact that by the end of this tragicomedy, the Widow Ranter was married once more. Under the control of a husband, she better fit into societal structures.[49]

Marrying a widow wasn't always such a challenge, as the character Porgy believed in the 1852 novel *The Sword and the Distaff; or, "Fair, Fat, and Forty,"* set in the South. Porgy, in need of a wife, must decide between two widows. "Widows are, after all, the best materials out of which to make good wives; always assuming that they have been fortunate in the possession of husbands like myself, who have been able to show them the proper paths to follow," he explained to a friend. Widow Griffin was a deferential, domestic, humble, and virtuous middle-class widow. Widow Eveleigh, on the other hand, was a bold, charming, beautiful, intelligent, and upper-class widow. After lengthy speeches weighing the pros and cons of each choice, he ultimately chose Widow Griffin. Even though she "is not wise, nor learned; is really very ignorant; has no manner, no eloquence; is simple, humble and adhesive" in comparison to Widow Eveleigh, Widow Eveleigh ultimately "appeared to him to be quite too masculine," for one "does not want an equal, but an ally in marriage." This play highlighted the tension of widows in a patriarchal society and the delicate balance of surviving as a feme sole, a woman alone, while negotiating gender norms.[50]

Like their literary counterparts, some antebellum widows did seek remarriage after the mourning period had passed. Generally, widows of older ages, with grown children, found life as a single widow to be preferable. Moving into an adult daughter or son's household provided companionship as well as economic and social security. But single life in the antebellum South brought a great deal of stress some younger widows did not desire, especially those of a lower economic status or those with young children. As one widow struggling for economic stability wrote, frustrated, "My only recourse will be a lawsuit. I have authorized him [the lawyer] to act according to his own judgement and I have left everything for him to do and make the best of. Alas! two lawsuits already! What is to become of me! and I with only one quarter of a dollar in my purse!" In 1831, another plantation widow similarly lamented, "I have so much to perplex me at times that I scarcely know how to bear all things as it comes. . . . If I had no children, I would gladly leave this world." Often, finding other people to live for, such as children, eased the difficulties of widowhood, even as they increased the workload. Even so, remarriage had the potential to ease the burden of navigating a patriarchal society alone.[51]

Dolly Lewis, who buried three children in addition to her husband, found an empty house to be a tremendous trial. Thirty-two years old, lonely, heartbroken, and working as a teacher in 1849, she accepted a marriage proposal only to quickly regret it. "What have I done? Am I not dreaming? What means it all. Why these heavy forebodings?" she poured into her diary. "I have often joked & laughed about marrying & though I have when asked always refused yet I am caught this time. Is my heart truly interested?" She broke the engagement, mended it, and married "with trembling & fear." A year after the wedding, she reflected, "O it has been a year of happiness a year of *heartrest* for after striving & toiling alone for years in this cold hearted world thus to find a heart that truly loves & a home full of every comfort—O How my heart expands with love to him that has thus taken me to himself." After nine years, she found herself widowed once more, when her husband had a cough and died. She recorded his last night in her diary for her baby daughter, sharing that "after preparing himself for the night he solemnly clasped his hands & said, 'I commit & conjure myself with all that I have & am into the Hands of my Heavenly Father for this night & for all Eternity.'" With his final good-bye, and affairs in order, he died in his sleep, leaving a widow who felt "it was my privillage to wait upon him until the very last moment of his life." Dolly had found comfort and support in her second marriage, something antebellum widows often hoped for.[52]

But not all widows found such happiness in a second marriage. In 1839, Martha Trice, in North Carolina, widowed and remarried, petitioned the court for a divorce from her second husband. Not only did he beat her, deny her basic necessities, and commit adultery, but he squandered the money she brought into the marriage. Unfortunately for her, he was also justice of the peace at the time of the case. She lost the suit, was left penniless, and returned to her father's home.[53]

Lucy Harris Price, a widow aged thirty-six, made a similarly poor choice in a subsequent husband. She was anxious for "a life of contentment and happiness" after the death of her wealthy husband. In November 1842, she rushed to the altar and married a not-yet-twenty-one-year-old James Norman. He proved to be a poor choice indeed. Within a year of the nuptials, James informed his wife that he desired she leave. She refused; he responded with verbal and physical abuse. She refused again. He began an affair with an enslaved woman named Maria. He brought her into Lucy's bedroom, slept with Maria on a nearby cot, and when Lucy protested, he suggested that "if she not like it she might look out for other quarters." To make matters worse, he flaunted his relationship with the woman "not of his own color" before Lucy's family and friends. "He often embraced and kissed her in my presence," one guest testified in court. Another described how James insisted Maria join them at dinner and threatened Lucy with punishment if she touched the woman. Lucy "burst into tears and asked me if it was not too much for her to stand," to which James responded, "It was nothing to what he intended to inflict upon her." The state of Virginia did grant Lucy her divorce in 1849, not because of the racial dynamics of the case but rather because of the concrete proof of infidelity. In a grave understatement, Lucy later described this second marriage as "an unfortunate connection."[54]

It is not a surprise, then, that many older and wealthier widows chose not to remarry. To be a wealthy widow in the antebellum South brought its share of concerns but also its share of power. "I cannot allow you to dictate from which friends I shall or shall not receive advice and assistance. As your views and mine of the duties and position of a gardener differ so widely, I shall have no occasion for your services an other year," Martha Rutledge Kinloch Singleton informed her overseer. When Martha's husband died in August 1854, he left her with debts owed to fifty-two creditors across multiple states, 281 enslaved people, 5,000 acres, and three children under the age of ten. Well educated and named sole executrix of her husband's will, Martha inherited this entire South Carolina estate in addition to her late husband's problems. Martha could have done what many other wealthy widows did: ask a close male relative, perhaps a father, brother, or cousin, to manage the estate on her behalf while she focused on her grief and children. But she was not alone in the ranks of widows who decided to manage things herself. She began by selling off enslaved people, furniture, and land to satisfy the debts. From there, she appeared in person to settle business affairs, sign receipts, and shop in the same cities as her husband had done. She continued to receive her late husband's numerous subscriptions to agricultural publications such as *American Farmer* and the *Horticulturalist*. For decades, Martha had watched her father, then her husband, manage plantations. Now it was her turn, and she thrived. The 1860 census, taken six years after her husband's death, revealed that Martha had increased the plantation's cash value by over $70,000, added 1,600 acres to her holdings, increased the number of work animals, and diversified the crops to include more wheat, peas, beans, sweet potatoes, hay, and corn. She also switched her mill from water to steam power in 1860, increasing its value, and added nearly 200 enslaved people to the plantation holdings. While she dealt with many aspects of daily life and management on her own, she did rely on male relatives and friends for legal assistance, particularly her brother-in-law, in a land dispute with a neighbor. In the end, as Mary Boykin Chesnut put it, "she is the delight of her friends, the terror of her foes." Martha is an example of a strong, independent, business-minded widow who handed life's twist and turns well.[55]

And she wasn't the only one. "Mama has paid off the heavy land debt which has been due for several years. She has been decreasing the amount ever since Papa's death—this year she paid off every cent—and is now intirely out of debt—she makes fine crops," bragged one daughter from North Carolina in 1835, continuing, "Every year has something of all most everything to sell such as corn fodder, bacon, wheat, oats, etc., etc. She is now building an excellent house will have it completed this fall." She thrived as a widow in a patriarchal society not built for her. When another North Carolina woman, Frances Bumpass, had a husband pass away and leave his editorship of a newspaper behind, she decided to carry on her husband's legacy, and provide for herself financially, by continuing its publication herself. At first, she lost money and experienced pushback as a female editor. But Frances clung to her belief that "I should fear I might do wrong to give up. I believe [God] will succeed my efforts." Her tenacity won in the end. Frances remained editor of the paper, and a widow, for twenty years. Keziah Brevard was a third woman who had no desire to remarry. Physicians found her late husband to be "deranged," as he imagined "that every one about him as tried to poison him" and felt "jealous of his wife & deems himself in honour bound to find out her delinquency & challenge her paramour." He spent most of their marriage in an asylum, and after his death, his widow did well for herself. According to the 1850 census, she managed 2,600 acres of farmland in South Carolina, 180 enslaved people, 185 swine, 90 cattle, 42 sheep, 20 mules, and 6 horses and produced 7,073 bushels of corn, 1,700 bushels of sweet potatoes, 700 bushels of peas and beans, 525 bushels of oats, 200 pounds of butter, 190 bales of cotton, 45 pounds of wool, and 43 tons of hay. By 1860, she raised her holdings to 6,000 acres and 209 enslaved people and added 1,200 pounds of rice to her annual harvest. As all of these stories reveal, not all widows sought remarriage, and many did well without it.[56]

As important as the ideals and realities of widowhood were, the fact remained that wives greatly outnumbered widows in the antebellum South. Young widows existed more as an exception, not a rule. In a world defined by relationships, custom mattered, even as emotion influenced women's lives. White women across economic classes most typically lived as wives with husbands and babies. This was the life they knew. This was the life they expected. Their days were busy as they semiconsciously managed societal expectations and more intentionally managed husbands, homes, and children. And as they tucked in those children, blew out their candles, and climbed into their beds on April 11, 1861, most wives did not realize that what they knew, what they expected, and what they depended on was all about to change.

2

Prepare for It

Weddings, War, and Uncertain Futures

Now prepare for it. I am in earnest. Every day I feel more reluctant
to go into an uncertain life without having the consciousness of
being yours entirely. I could fight better & I would do everything
better. Should I fall, you could have at least the satisfaction to be a
soldiers widow who I trust will only die in honor. Besides, though
I know you do not want me to tell you this, some pension would
insure to you the prospect of a humble but honorable existence.

Frank Schaller to his sweetheart

"He came in this afternoon & gave me the news from Charleston—Said Ft.
Sumpter had been taken," wrote Keziah Brevard, a wealthy widow in her
fifties, in her diary on April 13, 1861. She lived about ten miles east of Columbia, South Carolina. "I am thankful it [Fort Sumter] is no longer a terror,
but Oh my God we may still tremble for we have enemies in our midst," she
continued. "A few months ago & 'twas said man could not take Ft. Sumpter
unless walking over five or ten thousand dead—it has been taken—& not

one life lost of those who aided in taking it—My God the work is thine." She described her desires for a peaceful resolution of the situation, hoping the Union would leave the Confederacy alone or make new laws for their protection. She then turned to what the shots on Fort Sumter could mean for the women and children of the Confederacy. "My God be with all thy dear Children—Oh how desolate many are now—Husbands & sons gone to the scenes of war—to save their [country]." Husbands gone, like hers, potentially forever.[1]

The war had officially begun, and husbands enlisted by the thousands. While some men left behind wives that they had married decades ago, other soldiers left spouses of mere weeks. The first shots of war carried with them a slew of hurried courtships, engagements, and weddings, as many couples made certain of their relationship status, particularly as they marched into an uncertain future. Meanwhile, Confederate wives weighed exactly what this war was worth. On their wedding day, most women (particularly those who married before 1861) expected the marriage experience of their antebellum mothers. But the war changed their daily experiences and the power dynamics of the South. In order to understand widowhood, we must first reckon with the realities of wartime marriages. Exploring these marriages, the good and the bad, the deep and the superficial, uncovers exactly what wives lost when their husbands died at war. The letters between spouses also reveal the pervasive power of emotional expressions. During the war, many soldiering husbands and wives expressed themselves as never before, with ink and paper. Their letters discussed a range of topics, including love, sex, duty, power, slavery, children, flirtations, and finances, and offer a rare look into the emotional expressions of a range of couples, spanning age, education, and geography. As the war grew long and battles grew bloodier, another topic joined the list, as soldiers increasingly reflected on death and their own mortality. With each letter, a wife had the opportunity to express hope or despair, to cheer or to chastise, to support the Confederate war effort or say no, come home. Their words carried power.

"Onward! Onward!" urged Nettie Fondren, of Thomasville, Georgia, to her fiancé, "until the vile invader is driven from our sunny South!" When the war began, a flurry of marriages swept up young couples across the region. In a changing world, some white Southern women increased their dedication to seemingly unchanging institutions such as marriage. As a result of these wartime weddings, newlyweds who lost their husbands in war found themselves in a situation where they were expected to mourn longer than they had even been married. Georgia Page King would be married fifteen months when her husband died. Laura Cornelia McGimsey had been married seventeen months at the time she received word of her husband's death. And Ellen "Nellie" Richmond Ramseur lost her husband to a Yankee bullet just eight days shy of their first wedding anniversary.[2]

One of the most striking examples of short marriages, and long widowhoods, was that of Hetty Cary. When Hetty Cary kissed her husband goodbye in February 1865, she did not expect him to die. She had just kissed him, after all, before her entire community, of friends, family, and officials, at the altar. Hetty Cary was pretty, so pretty that one soldier believed her to be "the most beautiful woman of her day and generation . . . altogether the most beautiful woman I ever saw in any land." On Thursday, January 19, 1865, the war was almost over, though she did not know it. Richmond's belle walked down the aisle and married a Confederate colonel, John Pegram. In spite of the raging Civil War, "all was bright and beautiful" at their wedding, which took place in St. Paul's Episcopal Church. John soon returned to duty, and on February 5, he received a gunshot wound above a lower rib and died almost instantly in the snow. Exactly three weeks from the date of her wedding, Hetty found herself in the same church, with the same people, the same minister, walking down the same aisle, for the funeral. One female diarist wrote, "Again has St. Paul's, his own beloved church receive[d] the soldier and his bride—the one coffined for a hero's grave, the other, pale and trembling, though still by his side, in widow's garb." Twenty-nine-year-old Hetty "was like a flower broken in the stalk," so heartbroken that earlier she had to be torn from the body "almost by force." Three weeks a wife, Hetty would remain a widow for more than fifteen years. The story of Hetty Cary is a story of Confederate widowhood that is quite like, and quite unlike, thousands of others.[3]

During the war, most young women were less worried about widowhood and more worried about finding a husband to marry, period. In 1863, Ardella Brown would lament, "If I Can get any Body to have me you Shall get to a weding But there is nobody a Bout here only Some old widiwers for all the young men has gone to the army." From Virginia, Judith McGuire believed there to be "a perfect mania on the subject of matrimony," explaining that "some of the churches may be seen open and lighted almost every night for bridals, and wherever I turn I hear of marriages in prospect." "It looks like the girls will marry anybody these days," agreed another mother, warning her daughter, "Keep a strict watch over your affections and don't be deceived, men are very deceiving," particularly soldiers. Esther Alden in South Carolina reflected, "One looks at a man so differently when you think he may be killed to-morrow. Men whom up to this time I had thought dull and commonplace

... seemed charming." While some women would use the war as an excuse to delay marriage, the shortage of eligible men did worry others who intended to become wives and mothers. As historian Drew Gilpin Faust elegantly put it, "A married woman feared the loss of a particular husband; a single woman worried about forfeiting the more abstract possibility of any husband at all." Not only was marriage a key component in the ideal of nineteenth-century womanhood, but for most Southern white women, it also provided a clear societal position in this time of uncertainty. While single white women of the Civil War era feared their chances for marriage would lessen, it turned out to be a false fear; "the vast majority (approximately 92 percent) of southern white women who came of marriage age during the war married at some point in their lives." But they didn't know this, and so wedding bells rang.[4]

Many young men also sought wartime weddings, wanting the reassurance of wives awaiting their return as they marched toward an undecided future. On July 2, 1861, Frank Schaller of the Twenty-Second Mississippi Infantry sent a letter to his "dearest Sophy" in South Carolina. He had recently had a conversation with a minister and felt it necessary to share. "I do not know how it happened, but we talked about marriage and I told him I would like to marry before going into battle. He strongly advised me and I told him that as soon as I got my commission, I would make a strong effort to get a wife." Frank would rise to colonel in the war. "Every day I feel more reluctant to go into an uncertain life without having the consciousness of being yours entirely," he reflected. "Now prepare for it. I am in earnest." Not only did he believe that he "could fight better & do everything better," but he also was thinking about her future. "Should I fall, you could have at least the satisfaction to be a soldiers widow who I trust will only die in honor. Besides, though I know you do not want me to tell you this, some pension would insure you the prospect of a humble but honorable existence." Frank would be shot but ultimately survive the war. For Frank, a wartime marriage was not just about emotional stability but also about economic stability for Sophy.[5]

Frank was not alone in his urgency to secure the label of marriage—take Georgia Page King and William Duncan Smith's story in St. Simons Island, Georgia. On January 19, 1861, the state of Georgia seceded from the Union. "Oh! How I wish, from my heart, it could have been otherwise—As I tear it all from my heart, I am not ashamed to say, I weep," William wrote from Milledgeville, the state capital, in 1861. "It was very hard to sever the silver tie which had bound me, willingly, for some many years to my noble commands and to well tried friends," he lamented to Georgia. When he handed in his resignation from the U.S. Army, "my heart yearned—my brothers, once;

"Jeff Davis Reaping the Harvest," *Harper's Weekly*, October 26, 1861.
Image courtesy Library of Congress, Washington, D.C.

now perhaps, my foes." But within these wrenching emotions, his heart also yearned for something, or rather, someone, else. "And now, My dear Miss Georgia, I must beg you to listen to me calmly," he began. "Immediately after my arrival here, I sought your Father—found him—told him what I wished to win—and asked permission to write you," he explained. Upon listening to William's wishes, Georgia's "kind and courteous father (as he always is) . . . granted the privilege which I desired." And so, their courtship began.[6]

Scarcely three months passed before William was in love. "You cannot imagine, my dear Miss Georgia, how sad, how—very sad I felt at our parting" nor "how profoundly I love you," he explained. "But you do love me, do you not?" William sought reassurance. Though they had been courting only three months, William wanted to be married. "A war is fast approaching. Oh Let me claim you as my own! Let me have the right to protect you, and shield you by my earnest love," he begged. Realizing Georgia would object to a rushed wedding, he urged, "Do not let, oh! do not let, any slight obstacles, or conventionalities, prevent you from being mine as soon as you can. We know not what may happen!" William wanted Georgia as a wife to write home to, to protect, to think about. And as a wife, she could champion his wartime successes and send him letters of encouragement and love. "How will I be able to manifest my affection, if you are not my wife," he asked.[7]

But Georgia was a dutiful daughter, one who would not make this decision hastily or without family approval. "Do listen to me!" begged William, struggling to undo decades of her upbringing. When Georgia was a child, her mother, Anna Page King, had praised her as "an old fashioned little thing," raised to be practical and dutiful. Anna's own antebellum marriage had been plagued by a distant (and indebted) husband. When she died in 1859, Georgia became the family's matriarch, managing the Retreat, their extensive island plantation off the coast of Georgia. But perhaps William did not have so hard a task as he assumed, for even as he begged, she was already explaining to her father that she was "so sick of living in this lonely place with so many cares & so few pleasures." She did not want her mother's life; she wanted an adventure. On April 19, William wrote again, declaring, "I will not be so formal, when my heart contradicts all formality." He again pressed her to marry him immediately. Playing on her notions of duty, he asked, "If anything mortal should happen to me who you love, would it not be doubly trying to grieve over him, for whom you would not have a right to grieve except in the studied retirement of your own feeling heart?" As a widow, she would have the right to publicly grieve him for years, beyond that of an unmarried sweetheart. Even so, Georgia hesitated to rush down the aisle.[8]

"I tremble," Georgia wrote to demonstrate the strength of her conflicting emotions over the courtship's hurried timeline. Though her father and older brothers were absent, in the tenor of the times she decided to seize her own independence and marry William. In July, she anxiously wrote her brother Henry Lord "Lordy" Page King that "the hour has come—the man who . . . I have consented to marry . . . is about to leave for war." She explained that "I have at length after weight of prayer—after tears and with earnest faith in God's direction—determined to marry him before he goes to Virginia—and follow him there in a few weeks." She knew that their short courtship would concern her brother and preemptively replied, "I am perfectly satisfied that I love him dearly sufficient to sacrifice a great deal for his sake." Together, William and Georgia wrote a letter to her brother Floyd. "My deep regret at the absence of our beloved Father—dear Lordy—and yourself—cast a shadow over my happiness," she assured him. "I feared that you all might not approve—but my heart relented." William added an addendum to the note thanking him "for your kind consideration and for your unselfish and appreciative consent to the dearest wish of my reason and of my heart." Not waiting for a response, on July 9, 1861, Georgia married William. In a time when everything seemed changeable and everyone seemed to be declaring independence, Georgia claimed her own in choosing to marry William.[9]

Family members quickly dashed off letters in return. "It is impossible to describe my feelings when I read your letter of the 7th," Lordy began. "The tumult was so great that I will not attempt to unravel the maze of emotions which oppressed me." He seemed in shock, surprised his sister would take such radical action without her father's or brothers' consent. "That you, Georgia, should be married and I not present is what I never conceived before to be possible!" he explained. Despite the surprising news, Lordy realized that "whatever I might have thought of the wisdom of the vital step you have taken matter nothing now, for I will stand by you to the last and my hard heart melt in prayers." He wished her happiness and hoped to love her new husband as a brother.[10]

Lordy's letter to William took a more boisterous tone. "I am half jealous for you taking my dear sister away from me, but you are such a fascinating fellow that I suppose she could not help herself," he wrote. He proceeded to give "a regular benediction on you both—May you ever be healthy, wealthy, & wise in peace and happiness." "You will doubly need the rest of my good wishes," he warned, unless William showed "more wisdom than you do in spending your honeymoon in a camp." Lordy worried about his younger sister and hoped "dear Georgia has not had so rough a time in camp as I fear

46   *Prepare for It*

she had." Still struggling to realize that his dutiful sister was now married, he attempted to assure himself that William would make a good husband. But no matter the brothers' opinions, the couple was wed, and William was thrilled. "Beloved, you are my beautiful fascinating bewitching little wife. I am yours—Altogether yours, in soul, mind, and body, my heaven-given wife." Marriage gave William what he wanted: a supportive wife. For Georgia, this union provided an escape from the place she longed to leave.[11]

Young white women who rushed to the altar, defying expectations, drew strength from a culture of female resistance. In the antebellum era, some young women "exerted female agency throughout the process of coming-of-age" by prolonging each life stage, taking their time to transition from girl to wife and mother. As highlighted in the first chapter, though most women did marry, some young women did express hesitations. Historian Anya Jabour argued that this "female youth culture of resistance" would shift into a "politics of rebellion" in the coming war. Young women who married quickly at the start of the war, ignoring custom, were not altogether unlike young women who hesitated to marry in the antebellum era. In this time of transition, women seized the opportunity that made the most sense to them, given the circumstances. At the start of the war, much was out of their control, but the decision to marry, and marry at that moment, remained theirs.[12]

When husbands departed for war, some wives joined them, traveling with the regiments. This was a difficult experience, though, typically limited to those of the upper class. Laetitia Lafon Ashmore Nutt, of Louisiana, was one wife who joined her husband. She crisscrossed the Deep South with three daughters in tow, following her husband and his company of partisan rangers. By the end of it, she wished she had "left the children with my Mother and devoted all my time and energies to our sick and wounded." She had seen much and found it trying, in both physical and emotional ways. The shortages and movement made for many challenges. As such, most wives did not join their husbands in war.[13]

Letters, the primary method of communication between spouses in wartime, reveal an authenticity of expression and highlight the changing nature of correspondence. During the war, correspondence departed from prevailing etiquette. Letters closed the distance at a time when there were no other options. "Writing what I know your eye will rest on," explained one wife in 1862, "cements me with you more closely than anything else." Many aspects of marriage, shrouded by Victorian sensibilities and closed doors, appear with a greater intimacy in letters and from a wider variety of people. Farmers who rarely traveled, and therefore rarely wrote, and husbands who only whispered sweet nothings behind closed doors appear in full force in archival collections. Those who had not expressed frothy romantic sentiments since courtships returned to them in this time of war. "Old lady, I want to see you mighty bad.... I would give lots just to have one pouting smack, and I would give any thing I've got to have you serve me as you did you know when," penned Winston Stephens, who left Tivie to fight with a Florida regiment. He was not the only husband to express this sort of sentiment. "Honey, I feel in a loving mood and if you were here I would hold you in my lap and kiss and kiss you to your hearts content," wrote another husband, William Pender, to his wife in 1863, adding, "Darling, did you think about yesterday being the anniversary of our marriage? Four years how short they seem.... We are more violently in love by far than the sweethearts." Unable to speak into their wives' ears, husbands penned their whispers on paper. The moment demanded authenticity of expression.[14]

Wives also seized this opportunity to express themselves more freely, the emergency of the experience bringing with it a longing for genuine connection. "I miss you sleeping with me as much or more than anything else," Mary Bell wrote her husband, lamenting the loss of their physical connection. Another wife, Malinda Waller Averett, was pregnant when her husband, Harris, joined the Fifty-Fifth Alabama Infantry in 1863, and she likewise missed her husband's physical presence. "I wish you could come home for I am as fat asa pig in a pen.... I wold write som which wold make you laugh but I am afread som man wod see it," she wrote shortly after he left. Three weeks later, she informed her husband that "I have staded so long as I can." She planned to "make my new dress an I am a coming." The separation was hard on the young couple for "it seames lik you has bin gon a year," Malinda wrote. Her pregnancy was progressing rapidly, leading her to explain that "I want to com befor I get to big so you can hug me good. I am geten pretty bigh around. I am afread you cant get your arms around me." Once again worried that her letters might be discovered, she asked, "My dear Harris do birn up this letter when you read it. I am afroad somebody mite get holt of it." Harris did not follow his wife's directions, so this letter survives as an example of a candid dialogue between spouses. "How I wist I was with you now," Malinda informed her husband, adding, "I wold eat a peace of you." Wartime conditions prompted new forms of correspondence, a surprising number of which include directives to burn or destroy. Because letters offered the only opportunity to communicate, some sentiments that never would, or should, be written, according to etiquette, would be. Broadly, correspondence changed to express more physical and emotional desires. The letters met the needs of the moment, a moment in which temporary separation could become permanent loss in an instant.[15]

Holidays, such as Valentine's Day, offered opportunities for special moments of expression and retrospection. On February 14, many soldiers wrote poetry and mailed special letters to their wives. One particularly special valentine came from Confederate soldier Robert H. King, who created a paper heart with a penknife for his wife, Louiza. When opened, the seemingly random holes in the paper reveal two people separated from each other, crying. On November 8, 1861, Robert had written to his wife, "It panes my hart to think of leaven you all," and signed his letter as many soldiers did, with "yours til death." Ultimately, this would be true, and all Louiza would be left with was this paper heart. Robert died of typhoid fever near Petersburg, Virginia, in April 1863. She kept this valentine until her own death decades later.[16]

Letters not only allowed couples to express desires, emotional and physical, but also offered an opportunity for a soldier to remember a world left behind. "I can imagine your loneliness and measure it by my own. I never was so homesick, restless, and down hearted in my life. Here I am away from all I love, sleeping on the wet ground, my horse poor, nothing to do, nobody to see, nothing to eat and an oven & a pot to cook it in," reflected William Gaston Delony in March 1862. "I shall miss you all now more than ever & I hardly know what will become of me without the prattle of my precious little children, all alone in my tent, with my poor little wife too all alone at home. ... Dont give up, it will all turn out right I hope and believe." This letter offers another example of how the logistics of separation expanded the opportunities for William to communicate romantic feelings of love and loneliness.[17]

Like William, Stephen Dodson Ramseur, a Confederate general from North Carolina, professed his love abundantly in letters. "My Heart's Most Precious Darling! You are the light and delight of my life. I live for you. And Oh! your love makes life so delightful for me," he wrote in a characteristically beautiful letter. And yet Stephen felt words were insufficient, for while he wished "I could give expression in this letter to the intensity, the deep devotion, of my love to you," he simply believed, "Dearest little wife, this is impossible." The separation was tough on the couple, who had married in 1862. And yet letters were the only way in which he could express his sentiments, so he wrote, "My Sweetest Darling, My Heart's Queen, my Best beloved, My beautiful little wife, how earnestly, increasingly I long to be with you." Similarly, Ebenezer B. Coggin, a farmer with only $100 in personal estate in 1860, wrote a steady stream of letters to his wife, Ann, until his death. They were from Alabama. "My deare wife," he would write, "my heart is fild with greef and my eyes with tears to think that we ar so far apart that I cannot See you and my Sweet little Children." He died in 1863. The letters were the only ways she would hear his voice again.[18]

For Georgia and William Smith, who rushed to the altar without the blessing of Georgia's father or brothers, letters also served as a tool to reconnect emotionally. For his beloved wife, William wrote a lengthy poem to celebrate their first wedding anniversary. He began with their courtship, when "a nation's wrong had waked a nation's ire," and then likened her to a heavenly angel:

> She spoke, and from her pearly mouth did gush
> Sweet liquid words, which to my heart did rush
> Her lovely eyes, beamed as from Angel's face
> My soul, unsandaled, stood in Holy place.

He continued following their courtship and then described their wedding day:

> Happy the husband who can truly say,
> "Hail sweet return of Heav'n-blessed Wedding Day!"
> I hail this day! Hea'vn's blessing o'er us throw
> Profusely, as were giv'n one year ago!

William concluded his poem with this stanza:

> If virtue e'er can bless a husband's heart,
> And Purity can e'er its charm impart,
> My soul will make to purer, better life,
> By the sweet teachings of my modest wife.[19]

Poetry provided William an outlet for emotional expression. On July 9, 1862, he and Georgia celebrated their anniversary unaware that they would not celebrate another. William would be sick by the end of the month and dead by the end of the year.

For those who did not rush to the altar at the start of the war, letters were a place not simply to express love but to fall in love. Elodie Breck Todd, little sister of Mary Todd Lincoln, met Nathaniel Dawson at the inaugural ball of Jefferson Davis. "I fell in love with you in Montgomery," he later confessed to Elodie, "and tried to restrain my feelings, but they were too powerful." By the night's end, he had "made up my mind to endeavor to make the star mine in whose beams I had wandered." After this meeting, Nathaniel began sending her little presents, while drilling his new company in Selma, Alabama, where she lived. A few days before he and his men were scheduled to depart, to be mustered in as Company C of the Fourth Alabama, Nathaniel asked Elodie for her hand in marriage. She was shocked; Nathaniel was an unlikely suitor. He had been married twice, both wives dying in childbirth, and was twelve years her senior. "Ever since I can remember," Elodie wrote, "I have been looked upon and called the 'old maid' of the family and Mother seemed to think I was to be depended on to take care of her when all the rest of her handsomer daughters had left her." And even if her mother could be brought around, what about her older sisters? What about Mary Lincoln? Even with all this, Elodie said yes. "My family may think I am committing a sin to give a thought to any other than the arrangements they have made for me," she said, but "as this is the age when Secession, Freedom, and Rights are asserted, I am claiming mine." Some combination of the man and the times made her willing to take a chance. She wanted to be in charge of her own life.[20]

Over the following year, Nathaniel and Elodie fell in love by mail. Words were all they had, as they flirted, fought, and fumbled toward each other. Nathaniel was almost ludicrously ardent in his early letters, carried into raptures by the strength of his own affection. "My whole soul seems to swell with love for you," he wrote Elodie typically, "and if I could die at this moment, all my thoughts would be of you." Nathaniel was inclined to see Elodie as a glorious abstraction, a vessel for all his hopes and dreams of outliving the war. Elodie tended to correct such rosy excesses, poking holes in his ego and his lavish language. "I am a troublesome somebody at all times," she assured him. "I am a Todd, and some of these days you may be unfortunate enough to find out what they are." Nathaniel seemed gradually to understand that these were not warnings but invitations—to know and love Elodie whole. With each letter, they had an opportunity to bare a bit more of themselves, to fall a bit more in love. The war would break Elodie's family into smaller and bloodier pieces, damage Nathaniel's reputation, and delay their wedding month after month. Their letters would be their lifeline.[21]

Nathaniel equated wife and country. "My loved Elodie," Nathaniel reflected to her, in a letter, "*She is my country*, and without her, I would have no country, to live for, and to die for. I would make a better soldier, if you were now my wife, as you could take publicly an interest in my welfare, and not be subjected to many annoyances that must now disturb you." He was not alone in these feelings. In March 1861, the war not even truly begun, another newly enlisted officer explained to his wife, "I cannot feel contented, quiet, or happy away from you. You have become necessary to make me feel all was right. I feel exactly as if some part of me was absent." And yet this closeness is why he fought. A farmer from Alabama put it more clearly. He was grieving the unexpected news of the death of their daughter but could not return home. "If it were not for the love of my country and my family and the patriotism that bury in my bosom for them I would bee glad to come home and stay there," he began, continuing, "but I no I have as much to fite for as any body else but if I were there I no I could not stay." These loves, to him, were one and the same. His wife responded, "I trouble all most to death about you and our little cricket death it all most breaks my hart to think that you are gone so farr from me and the children." He would remain at war until May 1865, fighting to defend his wife and his country.[22]

When husbands marched off to battle, most did not view their actions as shirking husbandly duty but rather as fulfilling it. "A man who will not offer up his life for his family when necessary takes a very low view of his Christian duty and does dishonor to his wife and children," explained one father to his daughter. The question of where a man's duty belonged, wife or country, was rarely asked at the outset of the war. In a letter written just one week before he received a mortal wound in the Battle of Seven Pines, Sydenham Moore wrote, "I feel that our lives are at the disposal of an over ruling Providence and that if it is his will that I should fall . . . I feel that I am doing my duty to my wife and children, expelling a foe." While patriotic ideologies certainly bolstered their resolve, "it was for her that he was fighting; it was for her that he would suffer and die"; she was his reality amid the mass of abstractions.[23]

Some wives, however, had trouble accepting this argument and believed their husbands happier, or at least happy, away at war. "You appear to think that I am more easily weaned off than you thought I would be, from my dear family," acknowledged one husband. "I really thought that you knew my disposition better than to think that I ever could be weaned off, when my whole thoughts and affections are with you." Another husband assured, "Catherine, don't think that I run off on purpose to keep from staying with you. I want to see you mighty bad." But sometimes, the needs of the two entities, wife and country, conflicted directly. When forced to choose between his wedding and his country's orders, Stephen Ramseur missed his wedding. He immediately wrote a letter to his beloved fiancée, revealing "my disappointment has almost unmanned me. But no, I will perform my duty here & there. I'll come & claim your love." Though they would marry just over a month later, on October 28, 1863, the missed wedding highlights which duty Ramseur placed precedence upon. As the war grew long, food grew scarce, enslaved people became increasingly rebellious, U.S. troops marched closer to hometowns, and desertion rates escalated. While duty to country and to family did not necessarily conflict in men's minds, as the war continued, these kinds of tensions rose.[24]

For some men, such as Theophilus Perry of Texas, absence truly did make the heart grow fonder. Theophilus took his father's enslaved man, joined Company F of the Twenty-Eighth Texas Cavalry, and rode off to fight for the Confederacy in the summer of 1862, before realizing how important his marriage was to his happiness. Not two months into his life as a soldier, he wrote to his wife, Harriet, "I never knew how much my life is wrapped up in you and daughter, as I now know. . . . All the world is blank and sadness unless your face shines upon it." His wife was similarly dejected: "You are my life," she told her husband. "It is all I can do to live separated from you." She attempted to remain encouraging in her letters to Theophilus, but to her sister she shared the secrets of her heart. "I am here so lonely and uneasy," she wrote. "It seems to me that Mr. Perry's being in the army will kill me. I am no better reconciled than I was at first." She claimed she could not "sleep nor take pleasure or interest in any thing in the world" while he was away. Harriet felt "so low spirited I dont know what to do. . . . I dont know what is to become of us—we are sorely scourged if any people ever were . . . for I have no idea he will ever return to stay—war makes its widows by the thousand." And in 1864, war made a widow of her. Stories like this expose the depth of felt love, of emotional expressions, in some marriages.[25]

Because of this absence of husbands, the war required most married couples, whether celebrating their first or fifteenth wedding anniversary, to negotiate a new balance of power and responsibility. "We have a part to perform as well," reflected a recently engaged woman to her diary. "We must make our men comfortable, we must encourage them by brave words and keeping stout hearts, we must try to turn their hearts to the guider of all destinies, and we must cry mightily unto Him day and night, and must trust in Him to deliver us." Women must support soldiers, physically and psychologically. But because of the gender roles in the South, many wives also desired direction. Even with prayer, many wives, accustomed to leaning on husbands for a variety of daily tasks, found themselves lacking direction. "If you would only tell me to do something, I would like it so much—I should feel like I was your wife, and that you claimed your property," wrote Emma Crutcher to her husband in 1862, feeling "wearied of acting for myself and deciding for myself" after six months of separation. In this way, the South remained patriarchal throughout the war. Certainly, patriarchy was built "on a male assumption of power and privilege, justified in the physics of bone and muscle and biology, policed by courts, churches, fists," as George Fitzhugh wrote in 1854, but it was also upheld by women who championed and polished this image of manhood. "Your little wife is tired, and wants to give up the reins, and lay her head on your shoulder and rest," Emma concluded. Whether she was tired or not, the reins remained in her hands.[26]

And many husbands provided direction. "I want the rye sowed in the barn lot as soon as the hogs have eat out if there is any seed left let it be sowed down to the woods field," advised James Nixon to his wife. When another husband, James Rains, heard of his wife's recent illness, he wrote for her to come to him, believing "you would be so interested in keeping house for me that you would not get sick again." "You must not be troubled at the news," instructed a third husband, William Pender, to his anxious wife, "but like a brave woman as you are bear up, reflect that you are not the only wife whose husband will likely be in the trouble." He also offered advice on his new baby son. "You must love Dorsey as I said before, for Turner is mine. I raised him and must love him without rival. The Mother always takes to the younger and the father the oldest," he wrote. Even though he had not met the new baby, he knew "none can ever be so dear to me as that incomparable boy, Turner; the greatest boy in the world." From farming to children, patriarchal direction came steadily from soldiers.[27]

John W. Cotton, an Alabama farmer, was another husband ready to direct. When he marched to war as a private in 1862, he left behind his wife, Mariah, their seven children, his land, and a couple of enslaved people. Like many husbands, he constantly requested more letters, writing lines such as "rite I havent got nary letter from you yet." It seemed to him that he always wrote more letters than he received. In addition to worrying about his wife not writing enough, he worried about the farm. "I am very sorry that I cant get to come home I no you are at a loss to no what to do with your farm," he wrote in December 1862. "You must try to get somebody to tend your land for I dont no what you will do if you don't get somebody to make some corn for you." She did find someone to hire, but John still expressed frustration: "I think you have lost smartly by selling your corn when you did." The next month, he felt unhappy again, for "I was not very well pleased when I herd what you had to give for salt." More typically, he tried to direct his wife as clearly as he could in her additional duties. "If your hogs ant all dead you had better have them fed about once a day with green corn give them about one stalk a piece a day I think that meat will bee of more value than corn and you should make your hogs do as well as you can," he wrote. And Mariah sought this counsel, as reflected in his responses. "You said you wanted to no whether you must kill

Prepare for It

that steer or sell him," John wrote in one letter, while also directing, "I want you to hire him," regarding an enslaved man; "I want you to tell me how much tax you have to pay" on the brandy; "I reckon you have not forgot where I told you to have wheat soad"; and "I would bee better satisfied if I new what ailded you." Mariah was pregnant, a condition that no doubt added to her struggles. These letters reveal the strong influence of many husbands, even from afar.[28]

Even as Southern society remained tied to its patriarchal structure, the mechanics of war encouraged some soldiers to relinquish power to their wives. C. D. Epps felt quite confident in his wife's wisdom and ignored her constant pleas for instructions. When he finally addressed her requests, he replied, "You wrote to me to write to you about managing. You know best now. Do the best you can to make something to eat." Likewise, E. P. Petty told his wife, "I approve anything you do. . . . I am not now the head of the family and dont pretend to dictate," while Morgan Callaway reflected, "Dear me, why should I advise an experienced farmer like yourself?" One war widow, who did not embrace these additional responsibilities during the war, struggled to manage after her husband's death. She recalled in a letter to her brother that her husband "told me that I ought not be so dependent on him, but to learn how to manage." A little management know-how would have gone a long way in his permanent absence.[29]

Certainly, slavery was something else to be managed by the Confederate South. Some wives struggled to keep the system intact at home, as their husbands fought to maintain it elsewhere. In a region where power came from violence, and violence fell outside the acceptable range of feminine behaviors, management had the potential to become tricky for some women. "Is it possible that Congress thinks . . . our women can control the slaves and oversee the farms? Do they suppose that our patriotic mothers, sisters and daughters can assume and discharge the active duties and drudgery of an overseer? Certainly not. They know better," concluded one Georgia newspaper in 1862. The image of white women whipping slaves, as male masters did, clashed with gender norms. Some women had no issues claiming this social and economic power, while others found themselves struggling to manage enslaved people while maintaining their image as a docile and vulnerable example of her sex. Some elite women penned their frustrations to their husbands, such as Mary Bell, who complained she often felt "ready to give up and think surely my lot is harder than anyone else." In 1862, she wrote, "I wish I could be man and woman both until this war ends," after she discovered that their hired enslaved man Tom both stole meat and poisoned her brother-in-law's dog, while Liza, an enslaved woman, disappeared for days at a time. James J. Nixon, who enslaved ten people in 1860, informed his wife, Louisa, that "sometimes it appears to me like that it would be better for me to hire out our darkies than to undertake to make another crop under the circumstances." Lizzie Neblett wrote her husband that, when it came time to pick cotton in 1863, their enslaved people "are not doing that job. . . . Some of them are getting so high in anticipation of their glorious freedom by the Yankees I suppose, that they resist a whipping." A South Carolina congressman's wife echoed Lizzie's sentiments with "I tell you all this attention to farming is uphill work with me. I can give orders first-rate, but when I am not obeyed, I can't keep my temper." The change in household command, along with the rumors of occupying armies coming near, offered enslaved people even greater opportunities to push against the system, much to the frustration of their female masters.[30]

Despite some wives' failures in slave control, most Confederate wives could and would not imagine a life without the institution. In the midst of all her annoyances and difficulties, Lizzie simply wanted "one good negro to wait upon me." Similarly, Mary Bell, though frustrated with Tom and Liza, desired a "woman that can get up and get breakfast. I am getting tired of having to rise these cold mornings." Though many women agreed with Mary Boykin Chesnut's opinion of African Americans as "dirty—slatternly—idle—ill smelling by nature," white women realized enslaved people offered valuable labor not just to plantation crops but to the lifestyles many Confederate wives epitomized. This was what the war was about; the Confederate constitution that their men fought for had made the issue clear. Infamously, in March 1861, Confederate vice-president Alexander Stephens explained to all that the cornerstone of the new nation "rests upon the great truth that the negro is not equal to the white man; that slavery—subordination to the superior race—is his natural and normal condition." As such, many white women desperately wanted to hold the South's racial hierarchy together via methods of violence or persuasion until their men could come marching home.[31]

Slaveholding was not the only source of tension; like marriages before the war, marriages during the conflict also had their share of challenges. After graduating from West Point, William Dorsey Pender met Fanny Howard, the fourteen-year-old little sister of a friend and classmate. They married four years later, on March 3, 1859, and had a son by the end of the year. William enjoyed a professional military career, with a commission in the U.S. Army, often fighting in the West against Native Americans. "Darling do not trouble yourself about the Indians," he wrote in 1860. "Fighting is supposed to be my profession, and my wife must get used to the idea."[32]

Fighting may have been William's profession, but it also entered his personal life when his fondness for flirtation brought him to verbal blows with his wife during the Civil War. At twenty-seven years old, he resigned his commission with the United States and joined the Confederacy in March 1861. His steady stream of letters to his wife contained missives of love, notes of encouragement, and compliments amid the news of war. They also revealed his weakness for pretty girls. "Tell Pamela that her good opinion of me is ten fold returned. I think her the prettiest woman I have yet seen, and the most loveable one," he wrote of Fanny's younger, unmarried seventeen-year-old sister. "There are lots of beautiful girls here, and good many fine horses," he wrote from Virginia, "so when I have nothing else to do, I can look at something beautiful or fine." A couple days later he "dined today with the most beautiful girl in Suffolk—and it was [a] great many very pretty ones." The next week, he let his wife know that "the ladies keep my table covered with flowers and smile on me in the most bewitching manner." In the same letter, he expressed concern for his wife, who had just given birth. "Honey I hope they have not let your figure be spoilt by not keeping your bandage sufficiently tight. . . . Do not lose your figure." Later that month, he described a woman who "has intimated once or twice that she has fallen in love with me." Then in his next, he had had "a very nice time dancing and flirting with a very nice girl" who told him she would "do anything for me." In case the message was somehow muddled, the next letter contained evidence. "To show you what a favorite I am with some of the ladies," he bragged, "yesterday one of them had two peaches—all the way up from Georgia—given her, she ate the small one and kept the large one for me with the request that I should eat it all. . . . David says everything I do is complimented. They certainly treat me very politely."[33]

Fanny had had enough. With her infant not yet two months in this world, her husband flirting his way through Virginia, and her health leaving her "weak as a baby," she decided it was her turn to write a frank letter. She first addressed his scolding about her letter writing. "Remember, Mr. Pender, that I am not quite as strong as I might be, and I have a good many duties to attend to that distract my attention from the sheet before me. I never sit to write a letter that I do not have to get up half a dozen times to perform some little service for the baby or someone else. And often, I attempt to write with both children screaming in my ears." She then turned to her concerns, beginning by establishing her own actions as a wife. "I have never in the whole course of my married [life] done anything deliberately that I knew would pain you— your will has always been my law—and I have ever tried to *obey* to the very letter the commands of my Lord and master," she began. She then quoted back to him one of his stories of flirtation. "Now, I ask you candidly, in your sober sense, why you wrote me such a thing as that? Was it to gratify your vanity by making me jealous, or to make me appreciate your love still more? You are very much mistaken," she informed him. "I feel indignant that any woman should have dared to make such loose speeches to my husband and that he should have encouraged it by his attentions, for you must have gone pretty far for a woman to attempt such a liberty." She could not believe he would "stoop to listen to such improper language" nor "admit that you had been *flirting*." She then turned the tables. "What would you think to hear me use such an expression?" she asked. "And would it be more immoral in me than in you?" This apparently, was a milder response than that which she first imagined, for "I have forgotten all the anger I felt at first—but I can never forget that letter—nothing you have ever said—nothing you have ever done, nothing you have ever written in this whole of our married life—ever pained me so acutely or grieved me so deeply." And off the letter went.[34]

William returned the letter to her two days later, adding a notation. "You have torn my heart . . . brought tears, bitter tears [to] the eyes of one who has loved you and tried to honor you," he wrote. "Oh! Fanny, my letter was cruel," he admitted, "but you have surpassed me." He found the charges hard to bear, nor could he bear "that anyone should know that I had ever received such a letter from my wife." "I have loved life dearly, but tonight I feel this war has no terrors for me," he confessed darkly, adding, "I feel the want of support under this greatest blow I have ever received." This blow, he believed, was that his wife believed him "not only a tyrant, but a vain unprincipled wretch."[35]

A few days later William wrote again. "To my great surprise I received a letter from you today. . . . I should not have been surprised if I had not received any more letters from you. I had about made up my mind that we were henceforth to be as strangers," he began, before again revisiting the pain of Fanny's accusations and expression of her feelings. "If you knew what I have suffered," he explained, "that letter was in my mind awake and sleeping, again and again would my grief have to be relieved by tears." "If you had simply said I do not love you I could have stood for it," he confessed, "but to accuse me of dishonorable acts." That was too much. Reflecting on the incident a few letters later, he added, "I did not love you the less at any time but felt miserable at the insane notion that I might be losing you. Honey say nothing more about [it]."[36]

From there, they set the argument aside, and William no longer wrote of his flirtations. "There are no ladies to trouble you this time," he wrote in

December 1862. "I had a pressing invitation yesterday to dine where there were several pretty ladies but did not go." In February 1863, "Mrs. Walker is considered a great beauty, but I was comparing you last night while there and I came to the conclusion that you were the prettiest, and by far more intelligent than any lady I met," he assured her. Even as he tried to ease her worries, he also constantly asked for her prayers, expressing sentiments such as "I know you pray for me and darling I need it for with all my efforts I am a great sinner" and "help me my wife for you know how hard it is to do right and how many temptations surround me."[37]

William also struggled with the physical side of their marriage, fearing a pregnancy each time they visited each other. After Fanny became ill (likely of urological issues) in the late summer of 1861 after a visit, he blamed himself, writing, "Oh! Darling, and I have to reproach myself for it. Honey, the same that causes you so much trouble is my stumbling block in this world. When I think I am getting better it rises up and stares me in the face to my great mortification, for I do feel humbled and mortified that the most dangerous of all our passions and the most sinful when indulged, should be the one that I cannot conquer." After he saw her again the following spring, he worried once more that she had become pregnant. The following month he received news. "I must say I am heartily glad you had a miscarriage," he wrote. "My mind was very much relieved to hear that you were not as I had imagined, very ill. . . . Surely if you do not want children you will have to remain away from me, and hereafter when you come to me I shall know that you want another baby." She visited again in late February, so when he was mortally wounded at Gettysburg in 1863, she was just twenty-three years old and pregnant again. Upon hearing the news of his death, she locked herself in her room, emerging three days later, reportedly with her hair turned white. She never remarried and in 1922 finally lay beside her husband once more, buried after a long eighty-two years of life. This extended example reveals a marriage, and subsequent widowhood, complex and human. The politics of mourning were complicated—though the Confederacy may showcase a soldier such as this as a hero, his widow would remember him as a man, fully human, with faults. Ultimately, it would be Fanny's choice to champion his name or tuck it away, remarry quickly or mourn evermore, attend veterans' reunions or quietly fall out of contact with the men her husband fought alongside. She shaped his memory, and she would choose which stories to share, or not share, with the world.[38]

Fanny and William were not the only ones who argued via the mail during the war before a soldier's death. "I received your unkind letter of the 30th," wrote James Edward Rains to his young wife. Married in 1858, Ida Yeatman was at home in Tennessee with their infant daughter while James fought for the fledgling Confederacy. At the outset of the war, James reluctantly supported the concept of secession, but he quickly rose through the Confederate ranks to the position of brigadier general in the Eleventh Tennessee Infantry. "You scold me very severely when I am with you," James wrote his wife, but "I did not think that you would write me such a letter at a time when I may be called away from you, perhaps forever." Ida accused her husband of spending their money selfishly, to which he replied, "The single article of caps is the only thing about which I have been extravagant. On this point I plead guilty to the charge." As an officer, James argued, "I am obliged to support my rank." Questioning his wife, he asked, "Are you unwilling for me to make myself comfortable and support the position I occupy?" James went on to describe the hunger he was currently experiencing, informing Ida that "under all these circumstances I do think your scolding exceedingly unkind and undeserved." "I will endeavor to live on salt pork and stale bread and you will have all you want," he concluded sharply. Tension, disagreements, misunderstandings, and arguments did not always cease when husbands left for war and could make for complicated mourning.[39]

James was shot in the heart and died instantly on December 31, 1862, at a battle in Murfreesboro. "What must have been the feelings of the . . . young wife . . . environed by Yankees . . . in Nashville, unable to come to him," wondered a funeral attendee, who recalled that "it seems but yesterday since we laid our hands on the cold, dead face of General Rains." Indeed, what were the feelings of the young widow? Was she perhaps a touch relieved that she could now manage the family's financial situation herself? With James's death, hat purchases would no longer come before her daughter's needs. It is impossible to know, but the letters do reveal that no two marriages were the same, and certainly no marriage was perfect.[40]

As the months turned to seasons, and seasons to years, the length of the war brought on a weary heaviness for many women. Their newspapers reminded them daily of their losses, as the *Semi-Weekly Standard* in Raleigh, North Carolina, did, acknowledging, "Whilst we write, the warm blood from the heart of many a strong man and bright eyed boy no doubt reddens the soil. The whole nation is a vast house of mourning. Christmas, once so merry and joyous, now finds the widow and her little ones clustered together in grief." This was a region where "carnage, blood, fiendish malignity, devilish hate, all the horrors of hell, seem to rise uppermost and turn the land into a vast slaughter-pen!" Many women agreed with this newspaper's sentiment.

"Thus we bury, one by one, the dearest, the brightest. . . . O God! help us, for the wail is in the whole land!" reflected Judith McGuire on January 1, 1864. "Oh how I wish the war never had started," sighed another wife characteristically to her husband in 1863. "I think we had better give up, and have our husbands with us." Life, she went on, "will be much harder when we are subdued after our husbands have been killed." Patriotism and sacrifice no longer held weight to her. Mariah Cotton, who wrote in the same style as her husband, similarly rambled:

> I hope that happy day will soon com when you can com to see
> me and you little children I hope the war will com to a close and
> you can com home to me to stay it wood bee a day of joy to see
> you a com home saft again I think if peace was made it wood be
> the joyfullest times that ever has ben in wood bee to me if you
> was to com saft. . . . If I cood see and talk with you won time
> more I wood bee so glad I cant beegen to tell you any thing about
> how bad I want to see you I hope that happy day will soon com
> when I can see you lovely face noth mor I re main you true loving
> wife till death Mariah Cotton to her dear beloved husband in the
> war good by my dear husband.[41]

Not surprisingly, many wives worried, and mourning began even before husbands died. Couples not only grieved physical separations but feared deadly outcomes. Minerva McClatchey believed she worried ceaselessly because "we hear thousands of rumors—but nothing reliable." Another future widow, Rosa Delony, told her husband, "Faith and hope and every thing else nearly dies out of my fearful heart in view of the monstrous fact of our indefinite separation." She felt "as restive and impatient as a young unbroken colt," aching for news of her husband and for the day he could finally return home. Like for many women, for Rosa constant anxiety seemed to be tearing out her very spirit. "I wonder if the time will ever come when you will come home to remain. God grant that it may," she wistfully penned. Tivie Stephens was blunter. "Give up now while you have life," she begged her husband. Even wives who bore the separations well in the day could find themselves haunted by night. While dreaming, Emma Crutcher's "powers of self control" were "somewhat benumbed" by sleep, as she imagined her husband returning to her at night. "I never should have allowed [it] had I been fully roused," she assured him. Fears about death led to emotional days, and nights, for many wives.[42]

William Pender scolded his wife for her fears. "Honey, you say you get perfectly desperate. I too get low in spirits and want to see my precious wife worse than ever," he sympathized, "but we must fight against it. We are only in the same condition as others, and my wife to talk so unpatriotically, I am astonished, after your talking so bravely sometime since. Cheer up." James J. Nixon, a soldier of the Eighth Florida Regiment who would die of wounds he received at the Battle of Brandy Station, told his wife to "enjoy yourself as much as you can" for "it is just as well to live while we are living." Even so, husbands reflected on the possibilities of death. "I have often thought if I have to die on the battlefield, if some kind friend would just lay my Bible under my head and your likeness on my breast with the golden curls of hair in it, that it would be enough," wrote one soldier to his wife in Georgia. Death tolls rose, and along with them anxiety, particularly in letters.[43]

Bloody battles, anticipated or experienced, forced husbands to recognize their own mortality. Anticipating a heavy fight in October 1862, C. D. Epps, a private in the Sixth Georgia Regiment, informed his wife that "I will write you the straight of it if I come through. I don't know whether I will or not, but I am in hopes I will. . . . Don't be uneasy about me." As with all letters, he signed his name with the phrase "I remain yours truly 'till death." Likewise, in January 1863, William Delony reflected on the future with "sink or swim live or die, survive or perish if I know my own heart, I am willing to fight on until the end is accomplished." His admissions that "my fear is that the worst hasn't come yet" and "I can see nothing bright in the future" did not bring comfort to his worried wife. Ebenezer B. Coggin preferred to express his thoughts on death in poetry. On July 14, 1862, he wrote:

> Remember me tho many miles apart we Be
> I shall Remember thee if you on Earth no more I see
> If on Earth we meat Nevermore
> I hope that we may meat on Heavens happy shore.[44]

As the death toll rose, and soldiers watched friends, male relatives, commanders, and strangers die in rapid succession, a hardened, almost callous acceptance seemed to overcome soldiers, Union and Confederate alike. When a soldier fell dying in the path of Col. Charles Wainwright, the colonel reported, "I had no more feeling for him, than if he had tripped over a stump and fallen; nor do I think it would have been different had he been my brother." Similarly, William Delony believed "the loss of a man makes but little impression upon the Army," while his wife urged him to take "vengeance for our murdered thousands." Insurance companies also took advantage of this situation, bluntly advertising, "Think of your wife and family if you die." The Confederate Insurance Company, which sold life insurance, was unable to understand why

"The Rebel Lady's Boudoir," with caption "Lady (reads)—'My dearest wife, I hope you have received all the little relics I have sent you from time to time. I am about to add something to your collection which I feel sure will please you—a baby-rattle for our little pet, made out of the ribs of a Yankee drummer-boy,'" *Frank Leslie's Illustrated Newspaper*, May 17, 1862. *Image courtesy Indiana State Library Digital Collections.*

every soldier did not purchase a policy. And yet, even as callousness grew, the experience of a particularly bloody battle could break down all the carefully constructed walls in an instant. Emotions interceded. Though John McCorkle had seen countless men die in battle, he wrote his wife in 1864 that he still "felt awful as the misels of death was filing in every direction." He witnessed men dying around him and told her, "I feel thankful that the good lorde has sparde my life." John was captured five months later and died of pneumonia in Chicago's Camp Douglas prison. The heavy emotional toll required heavy emotional labor from everyone, including soldiers. In the face of battle, death, and life insurance policies, men developed new coping strategies to try to process it all, including putting up walls, in order to emotionally survive.[45]

As they witnessed, heard about, and thought about death, many soldiers processed this experience through their letter writing, directing their wives to prepare. "Dear Linda," penned one husband a month before his untimely death, "let nothing change you from the path of faithfulness to me and the children." He did not want to be forgotten. Similarly, John F. Davenport wrote his wife that "I feal like I will return home to the sweat imbrace of you and our sweat Little Children," but he added that "if I should fall remember I am fighting for the rites of Liberty for you and our Little ones." Not only did he want Mary Jane to remember that he was fighting for liberty, but the fear that she would not remember him also haunted his letters. "Oh my dearest earthlay Jewel . . . if we should never live to see each other again in this life oh let us live so we will be sure to meet in haven thare we will never never parte again," he wrote, describing an everlasting love. At the bottom of the letter, he wrote "forget me never" and circled the sentiment. Death haunted his letters and, finally, caught up to him. A bullet ended John's life on July 9, 1864.[46]

A different John, John Cotton, took a more practical approach to the topic of his possible demise. "Now you need not bee uneasy about me if I get killed," he wrote, anticipating a battle. "Just say I dyed in a good cause ould abe lincon and his cabinet could not daunt me now." A couple of months later, he added, "If I never come back again I want you to do the best you can for your self and the children lern them to love you and obey you and try to lern them to bee good children and if I never return I want you to keep you land and such things as you need and raise your children the best you can I don't want you to bee uneasy." "Pray for me," he wrote, "thew the war til we have moved the yankeys back from our soil and peace is maid and that I may return safe home to you all again." He continued to fight and could not believe he continued to escape death. In late September 1863, John reflected, "The grape shot shells fell around us like hail but we got behind trees and places so none of us did not get hurt they shot off three horses lags clost to us and killed one man. . . . If I could tell you all I have seen it would make your heart ache to think of it." By the end, February 1865, he was longing for peace. "Nothing would do me more good than anything else for them to make peace for I want to come home very bad for I dont want to spend all of the best of my life in this cruel and unholy war but I hope to outlive it." He returned from the war in May 1865 and died in December 1866 at the age of thirty-five. Family tradition recalls that he came home from the war in the rain, with measles, and never recovered. These stories are significant because they highlight the strain of death on marriages, before deaths even occurred.[47]

While upper-class women could pour their doubts onto the crisp pages of their diaries and letters, a lack of resources, time, and education left many working-class women without this option. In her diary, Judith McGuire recorded one unnamed woman's struggle with fears about her husband's life. On February 28, 1864, Judith and a friend encountered a poor woman who lived in "a small and squalid-looking" home in the "streets and lanes of Butcher Flat" in Richmond, Virginia. Most of the people living in this section of town were supplied with food and government work. In this way, urban wives had additional opportunities for economic support, different from those living in rural locales. This particular working-class woman stood at a table cutting out her work when she stopped Judith and her friend, calling, "Ladies, will one of you read my husband's letter to me? For you see I can't read writing."[48]

As the women began to read the "badly written but affectionate letter," the poor woman could not contain her emotion. "The tears now poured down her cheeks," Judith penned. The suffering woman explained to her visitors that her husband "always writes to me every chance, and it has been so long since he wrote that, and they tell me that they have been fighting." She was wrestling with her deepest fear: that "may-be something has happened to him." Judith tried to comfort the woman and "assured her that there had been no fighting—not even a skirmish." The unnamed woman appeared calmer and "turned to the mantelpiece, and with evident pride took from a nail an old felt hat, through the crown of which were two bullet-holes." The tattered hat belonged to her husband. In the Battle of Chancellorsville, a bullet had come "very nigh grazing his head," piercing the hat. Judith "remarked upon its being a proof of his bravery, which gratified her very much." The woman carefully hung the hat up again, near her bed, for all to see. Judith and her friend endeavored to comfort the poor woman, for despite her immense pride in her husband, she still "felt uneasy, because something told her he would never get back." How many situations existed like this one, of illiterate women consumed with worry?[49]

And so, uncertainty weighed heavily on women as they waited for confirmation of their worst fears with the arrival of each letter. War affected marriage, but if affected marriages differently. That categorical label, marriage, masks the variety of experiences within the institution, affected by age, geography, economic class, and personality. The war provided many opportunities for soldiers' wives. They could fall deeper in love with their husbands with each letter, or they could fall out of love with them. They could seize increased political and economic freedoms, or they could falter under the weight of such responsibilities. This was a world of many possibilities, good and bad, and in this uncertain world, one telegram, one letter, one combination of words was all it took to turn them from wives to widows. As they courted, married, gave birth, farmed, managed enslaved people, wrote letters, argued, sewed, cleaned, and cooked, this possibility remained ever present in the back of their minds. And for 200,000 women of the war, this possibility became a reality.

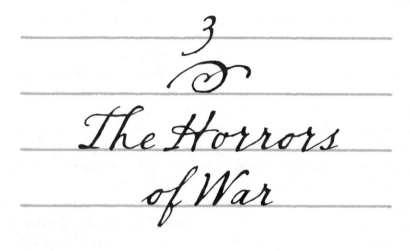

3

The Horrors of War

Outliving a Husband

Redus was kild show Tabithey this and tell hir the very first
chanc he was kild last wensday the 31 day of Desember 1862
he was kild barin the flag for our Ridgment he died like a
tru solger.... He seemed wilen to die he wanted to se his
wife and child before he died.... One cannot emagen the
harows of war unless thay cold see sutch abatle as this.

Norman Fields to his wife, Abigail

In "the dead of the night," her galloping carriage arrived at the heavy gate
and halted. The rider bounded from the coach, cut through the shadows of
the evening, and moved quickly up the steps. She was weary, for when the
telegraph "brought the dreadful news that he was dangerously wounded, she
never waited an instant nor stopped a moment by the way, day or night." The
wounded man was her husband, a Confederate captain who had lost both
legs in a fight below Petersburg. Throwing open the door and rushing into
the hospital hall, she anxiously asked for her husband. She had traveled far to
arrive in Richmond, Virginia, that night. The guard to whom she directed her
query hesitantly replied, "Captain T. is dead, madam, and was buried to-day."

The moment the words reached her ears, the woman "fell to the floor as one dead." The news was like "a thunderbolt at the feet of the poor lady." At length, she found her voice. The new widow "made the immense building ring with her bitter lamentations!" "What *shall* I do?" she cried.[1]

The widow was a day too late. When the chaplain had gone to see her husband that morning, "there was nothing in his room but the chilling signal of the empty hospital bunk." Surgeons moved on to other patients and the chaplain turned to other weary souls in need. All believed that Captain T.'s story had ended, just like thousands of others', with the burial of his body. But his story was not over—not for the widow. After hearing the news and collapsing, she became "wild with grief" and could "hear no voice of sympathy." Ignoring those surrounding her, she launched into "the story of her married life as if she were alone." "I shall never see his face again!" the widow realized abruptly and asked, "Where is he buried?" After learning the location of the grave site, she insisted, "I must go there; he must be taken up; I must see him!" "But madam," the guard responded, "you can't see him; he has been buried some hours." The widow was resolute. She wanted his body, not for its own moldering sake but to take it home, put it in the ground, and have a place to mourn him. They dug him up that morning and she "carried him back to his own house and his children." It was time for her to seek a grave for the man she loved. One day, one sentence even, was all it took to shatter a wife's expectations for her future and change the ways in which the world saw her.[2]

While emotions, actions, and thoughts varied among widows, across age and region, all widows experienced this shift from wife to widow. By definition, she lost a husband. Now, she was a widow and must live as one. This chapter explores the often-emotional transition from wife to widow, in three loose phases. First, how did he die (and how did she know)? Second, what did she feel? And finally, how should she behave? The initial reactions of widows were of particular importance to the young Confederacy and carried even more questions. Families and communities watched to see if a widow reacted with too much feeling, or too little. Did she selflessly accept that her husband died for a deathless cause? Or was the Confederacy unworthy of her great sacrifice? Analyzing the initial reactions of widows, which the widows recorded in diaries and letters, reveals responses that sometimes met expectations. It also reveals reactions that challenged etiquette and gender norms. Unwilling or unable to accept the news that their husbands had died, a surprising number of women frantically dug up graves, collapsed on floors, lamented bitterly, clutched bodies, and demanded proof. This, in part, helps explain why widows attracted so much attention during the war and why, in

The Horrors of War

turn, it is so important to explore Confederate wives' complicated emotional reactions to the initial news of their soldiering spouses' deaths. How he died, what she felt, and how she should behave fell heavily upon a widow during the war, at a time when so many other pressures had already mounted. It is important to remember though, that even as these women were feeling intense emotions and navigating real tragedy, they were also performing their power, even in the earliest days of mourning. Their decisions shaped the Confederacy and how it would be remembered.

By definition, before this work of mourning could begin, death must visit a soldier. For more than 250,000 Confederate soldiers, the fears and dread of dying became a reality. Unlike modern bullets, as historian Frank R. Freemon explained, Civil War minié balls did not pass directly through tissue but rather "tumbled, tearing a terrible swath through muscle and bone. . . . Bones splintered and shattered into hundreds of spicules, sharp, bony sticks that were driven by the force of the bullet through muscle and skin." Getting shot was no small matter. C. D. Epps was wounded in the Battle of Chickamauga. Another officer would recall of that same battle, "Never in any battle I had witnessed was there such a discharge of cannon and musketry." Hurtling through the air, the leaden ball lodged itself into the base of Epps's right knee joint. Before the war, he worked as a farmer in nearby Murray County, Georgia, an occupation that required mobility. "Dear wife," Epps calmly wrote from Polk Hospital in Rome, Georgia, "I take the pleasant opportunity to write you a few lines to let you know that I am getting along well at present." He felt encouraged by his doctor, who "told me he thought I would be able to come home by next Sunday week." From his cot he ordered Catherine to "bring one good straw bed and one good feather bed and two pillows so you can carry me. . . . The doctor won't let me go until you come well prepared to carry me good and easy." Catherine received his note and immediately left to retrieve her husband. "I went to the battlefield and brought him to his home before he died," she wrote on her pension application, decades later. Her attempts to nurse him back to health failed. Epps passed away on December 20, 1863, just before Christmas. They had been married less than five years.[3]

While Catherine witnessed her husband's last breath, most wives did not. In October 1863, Ann Coggin received a letter with unfamiliar handwriting, closed with her husband's name. Like Epps, Ebenezer B. Coggin fought at Chickamauga and fell victim to a Yankee bullet. His bone shattered. The note Ann received was likely transcribed by a sympatric nurse or visitor in Atlanta's Empire Hospital. "I am doing as well as I can be expected for a man with his foot amputated," the note read, though he wished his friends would "come see me as I am here among strangers and their presence would give me comfort and pleasure." Coggin informed his dear wife that over the past days he had "waited anxiously" for a note in her loving hand. Though disappointed, Coggin excused Ann's silence "thinking probably you did not get my letter." Six days later, having still not heard from her, he dictated another letter. "Having written you twice and as yet have not received an answer makes me feel quite uneasy," he told her. "I need someone here. The Doctor told me that he would send me home if any of my people were here to take me." Coggin then cautioned Ann that "I am not doing as well as I was." Underneath Coggin's plea, Lt. F. L. Boathby added his own note to the wife, writing, "Madam, I would advise you to come or send some one here to your husband as he is not doing well." Five days later, still at the Empire Hospital of Atlanta, Coggin died. This story, of death far from home, surrounded by strangers, was more rule than exception.[4]

On July 7, 1861, Solomon P. Solomon called across the house to inform his daughter Clara that "Charley Dreux is dead; he was shot in the head in a skirmish." Charley, a Confederate lieutenant colonel from New Orleans, was the "first of the Louisianan Officers who has paid the penalty of his life." The news shook sixteen-year-old Clara. "I was horrified," she confided to her diary, and "I immediately thought of his young wife and child." Clara imagined herself standing alongside the young widow. "In the agony of her grief will she exclaim, 'Why was he not spared!' Will this be selfishness?" she wrote, before continuing on, "It does seem hard.... Tis said that officers stand the least chance of being killed. But stop, we are quarrelling with Divine Providence." She assured herself that when the soldier was shot, "thoughts of his dear wife and child must have crossed his mind." Above all, Clara did not envy the person who would inform the wife of her widowhood. "How painful will be the duty of the one who will unfold to her a tale, which will blight her young life, crush her dearest hopes, and perhaps, forever cast a gloom over her future—who knows what a day may bring forth," she wrote. The Civil War had just begun, but Clara could not help but wonder "how many heart-rending tales like this, have we yet to hear."[5]

Many men died without the opportunity to get final words home. In his diary, Confederate soldier Joseph Mothershead reflected upon the soldiers who died instantaneous battlefield deaths, crumpling lifelessly on the field. The "noble spirits who dashed bravely forth to meet the foe went not far before they fell ... weltering in blood." These were husbands torn "from the embraces of wife and children and the enjoyments of home." Their voices "had been forever hushed by the fatal minnie." On the battlefield, they lay "quiet in death, stained with gore." As the Missouri man witnessed death and walked among the bodies of his comrades, he did not write about their honorable deeds or lost potential. Instead, Mothershead dwelled upon the "wailing at distant homes when the news goes swiftly back." His thoughts returned often to the "loss of husbands slain," a loss that would cause "many to mourn as widows." Though June 13, 1862, was a day won for the Confederacy, he could not forget the widows produced by the success. Mothershead did not know that in two years he, too, would be dead, and his wife would become one of those widows.[6]

Sometimes, a letter from a loving husband would lift a wife's hopes only for them to be dashed by dark news. "My dear wife," James Nixon began on August 8, 1863, "this is to inform you that my wound is still improving slowly. . . . I am under the best medical and surgical treatment and hope to be able to start home in a few days." James would be dead by Christmas, dying under his wife's care and leaving her with four sons under the age of ten. Likewise, when a different doctor wrote Ann Coggin about her husband's health, he assured her that her husband was "not considered in danger," though he died by the end of the week. In Arkansas, another Confederate widow, just like the widow of Captain T., rode her horse without escort more than 300 miles through contested territory in order to reach her wounded husband. She arrived safely but was "left only the mournful consolation of a visit to his grave." The difference between minor and mortal wounds could be difficult to determine. On average, wounds and sickness affected Confederate soldiers about six times during the war. Minor wounds could quickly turn to mortal ones with the help of dirt and disease. The frequency of sickness and injury would leave many with a false sense of security about odds of recovery.[7]

When a wife sent her husband to war, she expected that should death come, it would come by way of an honorable battle wound. Most quickly learned that even if husbands could survive the actual wounding, the battle was not over. Disease lurked on the next dirty instrument or watery sponge. Lack of food, sleep, and sanitation allowed germs to flourish on wounded soldiers. For example, when William Gaston Delony arrived at a hospital, he had "lost too much blood, and was too weak to rally" for an amputation. Doctors were unable to remove the bullet lodged in his left thigh, and gangrene set in. He died October 2, 1863. A terrible threat, gangrene "was black and exuded the terrible odor of putrefaction, similar to spoiled meat." One surgeon described the infection as a most "fearful and unwelcome guest in any hospital. . . . It claims many victims in its fierce attacks, and often puts to naught all the resources of the most skillful surgeon." This slow, painful, pungent demise was not what wives envisioned for their husbands. This was not a valiant battlefield death while destroying the enemy. This was much worse.[8]

Some men died without any exposure to either battlefields or bullets. When Nancy Gilliam kissed her husband good-bye at the start of the war, she certainly did not expect to receive a letter that read, "Your Beloved husband he Departed this life about 6 o clock this morning after suffering some 3 or 4 Day very horriable with the Brain fever." And yet, letters like this were far more common than wives imagined. Diarrhea, typhoid fever, typhus, malaria, yellow fever, smallpox, measles, and other diseases thrived in the camps, battlefields, and hospitals. Unfortunately, an 1865 fire in Richmond destroyed almost all of the Confederate Medical Department's records. Records did survive from Chimborazo Hospital, the largest hospital of the Confederacy, which served as a model for smaller hospitals throughout the South. While operating, the hospital admitted 77,889 patients; 50,350 of these admissions were for "sickness," while only 14,661 fell under the category of "wounded." These statistics demonstrate the rampant nature of disease in the war, which not only seized the bodies of the wounded but also stalled the hearts of the healthy.[9]

Malinda Waller Averett, an Alabama woman, was one such wife who would lose her husband to disease. She was pregnant when her husband, Harris, joined the Fifty-Fifth Alabama Infantry in 1863. "Dear husband," Malinda penned on October 2, 1863, "I never hird talk of so much sickness in my life, sick an a dying like sheep with chills and feavor. I think it must be dry weather." Her husband would catch this sickness by the end of the month. Malinda received a letter from P. Zimmerman, who felt "it to be the duty of someone to let you know the condition of your husband." Harris had been seized by a severe chill that continued to run its course unabated. "Should you wish to come and see him, you may probably get here before he dies, should that be the result," Zimmerman advised. But by the time Malinda received the letter, her husband had been dead for days. In fact, Harris died on October 27, 1863, just hours after Zimmerman wrote the ominous letter. Harris never saw combat. He also never met his third little girl, Harriet, who was born the following spring.[10]

Likewise, Gertrude Clanton recorded a story in her diary of another wife made widow by disease. Like so many others, the widow arrived at the hospital just after her husband's burial. "She was a plain respectable looking young woman, the mother of three children," explained Gertrude. The youngest was six weeks old. Unlike some other widows, though, "she was giving way to no outburst of sorrow. She could not indulge in the luxury of grief." Feeling for the new widow, Gertrude "seated myself beside her and told her how sorry I was for her—that I too had a husband in the Army. Her lip quivered and shaking her head, she replied, 'You'll lose him I reckon.'" The widow's husband had been a Confederate soldier just five weeks, killed by measles. "Oh the desolation of that house when she returns to it," concluded Gertrude, before moving on to write about the tobacco juice, noise, and lack of privacy in the hospital. The widow would not move on so easily.[11]

Of course, there were other, more unusual ways in which soldiers could lose their lives, beyond bullets and disease. "My dear wife and children," an emotional Asa V. Ladd wrote on October 29, 1864, "I take my pen with trembling hand to inform you that I will be shot between 2 and 4 o'clock this evening." A thirty-four-year-old farmer from Missouri, Asa was married with four children. He joined the Confederate forces in early 1861, served as a private in the Third Missouri Cavalry, and endured capture on October 16, 1864. U.S. military authorities in St. Louis, Missouri, had selected Asa, along with five other Confederate soldiers, for execution. "I am condemned to be shot," he explained to his father, "in retaliation for some men shot by Reeves. I am an innocent man and it is hard to die for an others sins." To his wife, Asa further explained, "There is 6 of us sentenced to die in room of 6 union soldiers." Col. Timothy Reeves, a Confederate guerrilla leader, had shot Union prisoners earlier in the month, on October 3. Federal authorities did not discover the bodies, which lay in shallow graves forty-five miles west of St. Louis, until October 25. Two of the bodies were "so badly eaten by hogs, they could not be identified." Authorities of the Gratiot Street Prison inspected the rolls and chose Asa as one of the six men to suffer retaliatory measures. The decision was final. Asa concluded his last letter with words of love, lamenting that "I must bring my letter to a close, leaving you in the hands of God. I send you my best and respects in the hour of death.... Good-by Amy." Escorted by the Tenth Kansas Infantry, the prisoners rode a short distance south of Lafayette Park. Several hundred spectators surrounded the men. Asa was tied to a post, blindfolded, and shot at 3:00 P.M.[12]

Of course, most prisoners did not suffer death in this manner. Certainly, few men knew the exact hour they would die as Asa had. Many prisoners likely assumed that life in a prison, while miserable, would be less deadly than life on a raging battlefield. Approximately 410,000 men experienced incarceration during the Civil War; 56,000 would not survive their imprisonment. "The horrows of the prison are so grate.... If everybody could Know & feel as I do I think there would be nomore Jales built," wrote William Speer

A couple on Christmas Eve separated by gravestones.
"Christmas Eve," *Harper's Weekly*, January 3, 1863.
Image courtesy Met Museum Digital Collections.

while imprisoned at Johnson's Island in Ohio. From 1861 to 1865, 12 percent of all Confederate prisoners in Union prisons died, mostly from disease. For men such as Isaac Brownlow of Tennessee, death would not come on a battlefield but in a prison. On March 12, 1863, he married, then left with the Fifth Mississippi Cavalry for war. He died at Camp Douglas in Illinois, just two months before the war came to a close, leaving not just a new wife but a new son. Many widows, and society as a whole for that matter, angrily came to believe that "the roll of death is fearful—the cruel monster is insatiable."[13]

Once wives learned of this death, however it came, their lives changed. Most wives reacted with expressions of sadness and grief, but the loud wails of heartsick wives distract from the wives who experienced their husbands' deaths as a release: a release from passionless marriages, abusive marriages, and marriages riddled with deception, greed, laziness, or promiscuity. A widow in a mourning gown might, in all actuality, be a woman quietly celebrating a new morning in her life, free from verbal and physical abuse. The war did not simply cloud sunny marriages; it also quieted stormy ones, washing demons away and ending domestic battles fought for far longer than four years. For some, widowhood was not an obligation but an opportunity for emotional and financial freedom. But while some women quietly celebrated widowhood as a release from unhappy marriage, a larger number found themselves emotionally and physically traumatized by the experience. Drained by food shortages, housework, marching armies, and fears for the future, Confederate wives often learned of their soldiering husbands' deaths at a precarious time in their own lives, in a region torn apart by war and heavy with uncertainty. The news led some wives to act uncharacteristically for a few days, some for a few weeks, and left others permanently damaged, all while a heavy load of cultural expectations fell upon them. Family, community, and society may have provided a script, but the part of mourning was one a widow had to play herself.

Almost immediately, a new widow sought information. Before the war, a wife expected to sit beside a bed, hold her husband's wrinkled hand, and witness his passing, fulfilling the antebellum Good Death. This, in part, explains why many wives so desperately tried to reach their sick and wounded husbands, often risking their own lives. Wives traveled with or without a companion for protection, through enemy lines, with little money, and with little rest, in hopes that they could nurse their husbands to health or, at least, see them one last time. One soldier, like many others, described a poor woman who came "from Alamance County to see her husband who she supposed was in [the] hospital." It was March 1862. "Poor creature, she came to find that he had been buried four or five days," the soldier explained to his wife. "She spent her last cent to get here. She walked out here from town—two miles—through the rain and mud to see his Captain. I sent her back in the ambulance and gave her $5." Seemingly reflecting more to himself than to his wife, he added, "Wasn't her case a hard one. Many is the poor heart that will be broken by this war. May God spare yours is my daily prayer." His own wife's heart would not be spared; he was killed in 1863.[14]

Since most wives would not be beside their husbands at time of death, a well-written letter allowed a widow to place herself next to her husband mentally. For instance, a letter informed Louisa that her husband David was stricken "with yellow fever Monday evening, suddenly, and from the commencement was a very ill man." The writer described David's "most alarming symptoms," the aid he received, the fluctuations of his health, who visited him, who was with him when he died, who held his hand, and the final messages he wished to be repeated to his family members. These details would bring comfort to wives such as Louisa. She now knew that her husband did not die abruptly on a cold battlefield or in a busy hospital surrounded by strangers. As historian Drew Gilpin Faust explained, chaplains, nurses, doctors, and soldiers tried to keep "as many of the elements of the conventional Good Death as possible" alive in their letters, aiming to soothe faraway loved ones. The comfort these letters provided, however, was often fleeting, for no letter could bring a wife's husband back.[15]

A husband's final moments were of particular importance to his widow. Widows wanted to know as many details as possible of their husbands' deaths and would spend years attempting to discover them. On November 28, 1863, Rosa Delony received a letter in response to her "enquiries in regard to the death of your husband." To her first question about the religious state of her husband, Chaplain W. H. Channing responded that "the Chaplain who was with your husband has lately died" but he had heard that Will's close had been peaceful. Rosa had also asked about Will's wound, the location of his body, and where they kept his possessions. It was not until December 3, 1863, two months after Will's death, that Rosa received an official notice from the hospital announcing the death of her husband. "Any further information concerning his death will be most freely given," the clerk assured her. It would take years to get his body transferred back to Georgia.[16]

For many widows, the desire to get the body home was strong. Even before the war, a cemetery was more than a place to store bodies or a formal memorial to the dead; it was an intimate link to those who had passed on. Mary Gray often prayed in and contemplated life after death in cemeteries, reflecting, "I often feel as if it would be a privilege to live near the graves of buried love, 'tis a good & proper place for meditation." Similarly, Frances Bestor grew to appreciate her mother's grave, writing, "'Tis a very sad place to visit—yet it always makes me feel so very near to Mother, I feel when I leave it as tho' I had seen her." If a Confederate widow could manage to determine the location of her husband's body, she should "seek a grave for the dead" at home, "close by those he loved, among kindred and friends in the fair sunny land he died to defend." Both graveyards, which were typically connected to churches, and cemeteries, larger burial grounds often not connected to religious sites, offered a place to reflect on and commune with the dead. The word *cemetery* was derived from a Greek word, *koimētērion*, meaning "sleeping place." At the dedication of one in 1831, the orator shared his belief that cemeteries "may preach lessons to which none may refuse to listen and which all that live must hear. Truths may be there felt and taught, in the silence of our own meditations, more persuasive and more enduring than ever flowed from human lips." After spending time by a grave site, "we return to the world, and we feel ourselves purer and better and wiser from this communion with the dead," for "what is a grave, to us, but a thin barrier

City Point, Virginia. Soldiers' graves near General Hospital, 1861–65.
Image courtesy Library of Congress, Washington, D.C.

dividing time from eternity and earth from heaven?" Widows, then, wanted their husbands in this type of resting place, close to home, not simply out of ritualistic obligation but for healing.[17]

In addition to satisfying the emotional needs of family members, getting the body home often fulfilled the requests of the recently deceased soldiers, too. Soldiers on both sides of the war wanted to be buried at home, for peace and rest. This feeling grew the more death they saw. As one South Carolinian wrote, "Some how I have a horror of being thrown out in a neglected place or bee trampled on as I have seen a number of graves here." During the war, a wife could not control how her husband died nor would she (most likely) have the opportunity to be present at his burial. But by gathering information about his grave site in letters from family, friends, and fellow soldiers, she could piece together a plan to get his body home to her, to bury him nearby, to visit, and to mourn. He would not be in a grave beside strangers but with his family, living and dead. Though they tried to get these bodies home, the majority of widows, especially those of working classes and fewer resources, would be unable to do so.[18]

Because casualty reporting was inconsistent, a woman was often at the mercy of the men who fought alongside her husband to learn not only the details of his death but even that the death had occurred. The arrival of a rumpled envelope addressed with unfamiliar handwriting might contain a message from a man such as William Fields, who wrote, "As you in all probability have not heard of the death of your husband and as I was a witness to his death I consider it my duty to write you although I am a stranger to you." Likewise, Rosa Delony, who was pregnant at the time, learned of her husband's death not from the hospital or even from a letter addressed to her. Instead, Rosa learned of Will's passing from two neighbors. William Church, a sergeant in Will's Georgia Troopers, informed Mrs. Pleasant Stovall of Will's death in a hastily written telegram. He told Mrs. Stovall, "On account of her condition break the news to Mrs. Delony as best you can. . . . William Gaston Delony . . . died on Friday afternoon from the effects of gunshot wounds he received on the left leg. His funeral took place on Saturday afternoon about four o'clock at Stanton Hospital where he died." Mrs. Stovall and Rosa worked together closely in the Ladies Aid Society. Church was a dear friend of the Delony family and a man whom Rosa affectionately called "Willie" in her letters. They knew that with the arrival of this slip of paper, Rosa's life would change forever. Even so, it contained a proof irrefutable.[19]

Widows' initial emotional responses to the news of death were as diverse as the widows themselves. Length of marriage, age of widow, and personality affected reactions. From shock to denial, depression to acceptance, wives came to terms with their new identity as widows in different ways and at different speeds. Disorientation was one emotion that seized widows. Tivie Stephens, for example, felt utterly befuddled by the new role and wrote her brother, "I know not how to write I am so bewildered." Though she had been told numerous times that her husband was dead, she felt, "I can not realize the whole truth, it seems dark and mysterious." Her other brother reflected, "I can offer no consolation now acceptable to such a grief as Tivie's, at present she can only realize the fact that he is lost to her, and see nothing in his death and the circumstances to console her." For Tivie, widowhood was a sadness incomprehensible.[20]

While some felt overwhelmed by sadness, others expressed anger. After the death of her husband to illness, one widow reflected, "God has seen fit to visit me with the sorest affliction the human heart could know," and she believed "God feels a peculiar compassion for the widow—knowing the utter desolation of her heart if her love is such as it should be for the one He has given her for a husband." She explained, "I am shut up in a selfish grief," and felt angry with herself that she could not say, "Thy will be done." Similarly, widowed Etta Kosnegary in Tennessee wrote, "It seems like I never can become reconciled to my fate." Her husband had died six weeks earlier. "I had his funeral preached last Sunday by our presiding elders," she continued, but it had not helped with her frustrations, for as she explained to her mother and sisters, "I hadent a relation in [the] world that I loved half as well as I did Lewis." Some widows felt this frustration and anger acutely, that God had seen fit to allow this trial, for days and weeks after the death.[21]

Some widows offered no reaction. One widow responded "unnaturally calm and has not shed a tear. . . . Poor girl, I fear the reaction when his body arrives—she had a sad and heavy responsibility left upon her and so young." For this type of widow, shock served as a temporary defense, sheltering the mind from the overwhelming and besieging emotions. But another young wife created such a scene of frantic grief that a nurse, Anna Holstein, felt the event was "graven as with an iron pen" upon her memory. Added to the fatiguing work of nursing, "there seemed to be no limit to the numbers who came looking after their dead and wounded, the loved and lost." According to Holstein, this particular wife "came hurriedly, as soon as she knew her husband was in a battle, only to find him dead and buried two days before her arrival." The young woman refused to believe that her husband had been laid "beside his comrades in the orchard." She insisted upon seeing him and could not contain herself as the shovels of earth slowly uncovered the grave. Consumed with an agonizing grief, the woman "clutched the earth by handfuls where it lay upon the quiet sleeper's form" unable to "wait the slow process of removing the body." When the "slight covering was removed, and the blanket thrown from off the face, she needed but one glance to assure her it was all too true." That was her husband's face. She went back to the hospital, "passive and quiet beneath the stern reality of this crushing sorrow." With this proof came a heavy certainty that brought no further immediate reactions from her.[22]

This widow was not the only one who craved the closure irrefutable proof could bring. One widow penned sorrowfully, "The last lingering hopes have all been crushed. None of us could mistake those pieces of cloth. I thank God that he had on clothes that we knew. Otherwise we never would have felt sure that they were his precious remains." Likewise, Barbara Ellen Huff only accepted the death of her husband when her brother-in-law sent her a lock of her husband's hair. One South Carolinian asked her sister, who had

"The Lost Found," by A. R. Waud, *Harper's Weekly*, February 3, 1866.
Image courtesy Library of Congress, Washington, D.C.

actually received a body, "O Mag you don't know how sorry I am about Kits dying I cant think of nothing else. . . . Did they open the coffin it looks like you all ought to have seen for certain whether it was him or not and how he was put away." Such evidence provided verification and a confirmation that the wife was now widow, destroying lingering hope and denial.[23]

Observers often felt unsure of how to handle widows' emotional reactions, writing things like "I cannot describe the grief of his widow & with sorrow I write these few lines." Others likened the sight to a physical destruction, often a crushing experience. When one mother's only son was mortally wounded, the woman who delivered the news recorded, "A sad task it was, but the poor bereaved old mother seemed to smother her own grief to comfort the poor crushed wife." Men struggled with the thought of denying wives one last look at their husbands. One deceased husband was so "dreadfully mangled in the face" that even though the widow had the body, "it was impossible to allow the family a last look. . . . How harrowing to their feelings to think those loved forms so near and yet unable to obtain one last agonizing look." While some widows knew where their husbands were buried, many women had no idea where their husbands' bodies lay. For Annie O'Hear, the arrival of letters only

The Horrors of War

added to "her overwhelming grief for her husband, whom there can be little doubt was killed in the fatal battle [in Virginia] which left desolation in so many other Charleston homes." This was the reality, and it was everywhere.[24]

The varied reactions of wives to this news of death offer a glimpse into varied emotional reactions, less filtered than traditional nineteenth-century etiquette. Before recent widows could live through the war, they first needed to find a way to survive the emotional turmoil within. In the first moments of widowhood, widows were allowed the most flexibility to react, grieve, and mourn. But as weeks stretched to months and years, pressure to conform to mourning etiquette mounted. A widow's behavior mattered not just to her family and her community but also to a Confederacy desperately fighting for recognition on a world stage.

"Women of the South! Do your spirits faint, or your hands falter?" asked one newspaper typically. "You, who so nobly urged this work, will you sustain it still? Are you not ready, if need be, to fill every possible post at home, and send the last man to the field?" Similarly, the *Arkansas True Democrat* lauded, "Thus it is with the glorious women of the South. . . . The laughing maiden, the busy mother and the mourning widow have vied in their efforts to advance our cause." When a wife received the news that her soldiering husband had died, certain prescriptions accompanied it. Relentlessly termed a sacrifice by newspapers, friends, and family alike, the death was by definition an offering, a gift provided for the greater good of the Confederacy. Once a widow, a war widow could never take the war off, in public. She would wear it, literally and figuratively, and own her victimization. As one woman penned of the performance in her diary after the war, "Now I'm a widow. Ah! That mournful word. Little the world think of the agony it contains!" Widows became walking embodiments of sacrifice for their communities, often struggling to contain these intense emotions of desperation and grief, emotions that affected their performances.[25]

Military leaders and politicians, in particular, emphasized the gallantry of deceased soldiers and the continued dedication of widows. Unity of all, including Confederate widows, was essential for the survival of the Confederacy, a theme that commonly appeared in speeches. Perhaps no one knew this better than the Confederate States of America's president. Jefferson Davis filled his speeches with sentiments such as this one, delivered to the Confederate Congress in May 1864: "Entire unanimity and zeal for their country's cause have been pre-eminently conspicuous among those whose sacrifices have been greatest." In other words, those that lost the most, or sacrificed the most, continued to support the cause above all else, he argued. One can think of few greater sacrifices than that of a husband. It was an *entire* unanimity for the cause, and an *entire* zeal for the cause, not limited to only those who had living husbands. Women had a special role to play in emotionally supporting, and legitimizing, the new Confederate project. "Wherever we go we find the heart and hands of our noble women enlisted. . . . They have one duty to perform—to buoy up the hearts of our people," Davis said in an 1864 speech. Again, widows were not exempt from this charge. They, too, must emotionally support the Confederacy, and those that did received accolades. It was their one duty, and that's what made them noble. This was needed to support the legitimacy of the Confederacy as it aspired to become a stable political regime.[26]

In January 1863, Davis shared the story of a Mississippi widow and her unwavering dedication to the Confederacy. U.S. soldiers took her only cow, then tried to force her to take an oath of allegiance to the United States. "She refused it, and when I last heard of her, which was before the enemy was driven from her home, she was living upon parched corn. May God bless her. She is worthy to be a Matron of the Southern Confederacy." This widow, though she financially struggled, refused to sacrifice her support of the Confederacy, even when faced with starvation. She would not take the oath. That made her a worthy exemplar in a speech of the president of the Confederacy. When Davis spoke of resolve in this speech, he spoke of the importance of unified resolve. When Davis spoke of an unconquerable spirit, he spoke of the necessity of that spirit existing in every person. "The mother who has given her son, the wife who has given her husband, the girl who has given her sweetheart, are not all their fingers busy making clothing for the troops in the field, and their words of encouragement a most animating impulse to the soldier? Whilst their prayers go up for the safety of a friend or relative in the field, always coupled with them is the earnest aspiration for the independence of our country." The encouragement of women animated the cause. According to Davis, women cared for the safety of their loved ones, yes, but they also sought Confederate independence—Confederate victory—with earnest aspiration. The two were intertwined, and if they could not have one, they must have the other. Davis believed it was this support, this emotional labor of women, that made soldiers in the field "invincible."[27]

In addition to politicians, throughout the war, newspapers, magazines, writers, and poets championed a particular version of a Confederate widow: the young wife who selflessly transferred her monogamous love from dead husband to the deathless cause for which he fought. In the immediate weeks after a soldier's death, etiquette books urged his widow to wear black, while families penned advice on a variety of topics in condolence letters. Just beyond her inner circle of support, newspapers and literary works also shared portrayals of ideal widowhood, while soldiers and Southern women added their opinions to the conversation. At a time when death was everywhere, so were opinions about death and mourning, manifested in superficial and substantive ways. A widow should wear black, accept advice, rely on religion, keep her eyes fixed on her husband's memory, be a good mother to his children, and most important, devote herself to the Confederacy. If a young widow could lose a husband and continue to support the war that killed him, what shouldn't other Southerners willingly give?

Mourning dress remained an important standard of public widowhood. Confederate communities expected Confederate widows to wear black dresses and black veils and progress into lavenders and grays over the course of two and a half years. Judith McGuire felt "it is melancholy to see how many wear mourning" clothes during the war. Similarly, when Lucy Breckinridge found herself surrounded by fourteen women dressed in black in December 1862, she remarked, "There were so many ladies there, all dressed in deep mourning, that we felt as if we were at a convent and formed a sisterhood." When describing a widow, especially a recent one, family members almost always remarked on her change in wardrobe. As one aunt described her niece, she "looked so sad in her deep black, so young and pretty, she touched all hearts." Though the prewar culture certainly wallowed in sentimental death, the rising death toll of this war doled a heavy dose of destruction. With supplies running low, and demand growing daily, the South developed a complicated mourning economy as widows tried to meet this wartime ideal. Strict mourning attire was more expected and achievable for women from wealthier backgrounds, but women with less money also received respect if they managed to meet the physical ideal. Even with the difficulties of war, the uniform remained an important aspect of ideal widowhood during the war.[28]

Condolence letters, which became a powerful source of guidance for young Confederate widows, arrived almost as quickly as the news of a death itself. While antebellum letters also contained religious sentiments, wartime condolence letters took on a more advisory tone in matters of religion. No longer written to similarly aged women, or older aunts and mothers, the letters were written to Confederate widows often much younger than the consolers. Most correspondents genuinely attempted to comfort a widow with the notion of reunion in the hereafter. Dallas Wood, after learning about the death of his brother-in-law, reminded his sister that "we all have the cheering assurance of a blissful home in Heaven where there will be no war and no parting again." Religious sentiments encouraged widows not to look to the past, for that could not be changed. They should instead look to the future. As one husband wrote before his death, "I want to meet you all in haven whear wores and fightings will be ore, whear wives and husbands part no more, whear parance and children each other greete, wheare all is joy and pleasure sweat." The idea that the separation was temporary, and that reunification in heaven was assured, comforted many widows.[29]

But living in the hopes of the future or memories of the past was impossible, so consolers urged widows to visit these places sparingly and, instead, look to Jesus as a daily source of strength. A recent widow should "lean you[r] head upon the bosom of your sympathizing Savior" and remember that "our Father reigns and in mercy remembers us." Consolers sympathized with promises that "God alone can sustain you while passing thru' these deep, deep waters" and assurances that "God will help you thro' your troubles." And yet letters urged widows to be patient and resigned, with such messages as "God love & bless you & bind up your broken, bleeding heart—give you patience under this heart-crushing sorrow, & resignation to His will" and "Now my dear friend, all that remains for us is to try to submit to His will." In addition to encouraging obedience and passivity in the wake of God's will, a fair number of letters encouraged widows to be cheerful in their situation. "I rejoice, as I know you do, that it [his death] has pleased our Heavenly Father, as we must believe," wrote one well-wisher, subtly encouraging a widow to celebrate in her husband's death. "Look upward, mourners, look above!" called yet another poem, "then trust in thy Redeemer's love." This form of religious sentiment could be read as distant and almost unfeeling, for instead of simply taking comfort in religion, a Confederate widow was also asked to rejoice, for her husband was in a better place. In the end, nineteenth-century Southerners did not understand mourning as a psychological process, exactly, but culturally they realized that religious sentiments offered a mental comfort for those grieving their husbands and urged widows to seek that comfort along the path to acceptance of the deaths.[30]

Quite unlike the antebellum widow, who was more likely to be beyond her childbearing years, a Confederate widow not only had young children but was often pregnant at the time of her husband's death. The many new wartime marriages brought many new babies. Condolence letters addressed this topic too, characteristically urging, "Take care of yourself for your dear children. Who can fill a Mother's place?" A widow's primary duty as a mother should not be overrun by her grief. As one mother-in-law urged, a widow "must not give up on your feelings my dear child, but think of those precious little

The Horrors of War

ones whose sole dependence is upon you, strive to cheer up." To the same widow, a cousin penned, "For the sake of the little ones depending upon you ... be calm and trustful." Even poems bestowed advice on grieving mothers to "not be by passion's tempest driven." Her husband's children must remain a priority.[31]

In addition to the directives of family and friends, wives also had the guidance of their belated husbands to consider. Asa V. Ladd, the Missouri soldier shot in retaliation for the Union men killed by a Confederate guerrilla leader, provided his wife with detailed instructions. "You need have no uneasiness about my future state, for my faith is well founded and I fear no evil. God is my refuge and hiding place," he assured her. As such, "I want you to teach the children piety, so they can meet me at the right hand of God," he wrote, echoing the sentiment of condolence letters in their religious instruction. He also wanted his wife to devote herself to her children by going "back to the old place and try to make support." "You are now left to take care of my dear children. Tell them to remember their dear father," he stressed. He did not want to be forgotten. Asa also included directions about closing up his business affairs and information to tell his friends. But to his wife, he only had assurances of love and a wish that "I dont want you to let this bear on your mind anymore than you can help. . . . I want you to meet me in heaven."[32]

When Stephen Dodson Ramseur died, he, too, left specific instructions that may have influenced his wife's decision to grieve all her life. On his deathbed, he ordered Maj. R. R. Hutchinson "to tell you [Nellie] that he had a firm hope in Christ and trusted to meet you hereafter." Ramseur hoped Nellie would remain faithful so that one day they would be reunited in heaven. Nellie obeyed and wore black until her own death decades later. Some believed Nellie was a true wife, for "the true wife, when widowed, remains a widow, till death re-unites her to the being—complementary to herself," as an antebellum etiquette book cautioned. This ideal, that "perpetual widowhood is alone consistent with our Ideal of woman; is alone worthy of a great heart, which love has filled," appears in hundreds of letters, as consolers encouraged young widows to remain dedicated to their late husbands.[33]

Confederate society became increasingly convinced that it was essential for war widows to remember their late husbands as honorable, another notion that would appear in condolence letters. The foundations for this idea came from the antebellum period, such as the etiquette book that insisted widows' "affections are in heaven, with the companions, whom, on earth they shall see no more." Patriotic Confederates built upon this. A war widow did not have just a dead husband but a "brave, gallant husband." A soldiering husband did not just die; he died "whilst gallantly fighting for his country." "Bless God that you had such a husband whose memory is honored and whose children will feel proud," wrote one consoler to a new widow. The pressure placed on widows to remember husbands stemmed in part from a fear that amid soaring death tolls, individual soldiers would be forgotten easily. In a letter to his sister, one soldier wrote that while he hoped she "may enjoy yourself this day and have a merry Christmas," there was "no doubt you could enjoy your self much more if dear Jimmy was alive." While this might be something that she had expressed to him previously, it might also be a subtle reminder to keep the soldier's memory alive, even in the midst of celebration. Wartime condolence letters urged widows to remain loyal to the cause that their husbands died defending, for nothing could be worse than to be remembered as "a hero in a broken cause" who was "pouring out his wasted life" and leaving "the land he loved to darkness and defeat." After the war, the white South wanted and needed someone to "strew the early flowers upon the soldiers' graves" and make sure that "no grave has been forgotten." But during the war, the Confederacy needed the support of widows to carry on, urging them on.[34]

In addition to condolence letters, newspapers also reinforced the ideals of devoted Confederate widowhood in the stories they printed. Rarely did they judge widows for emotional transgressions; instead, they relentlessly held up widows who supported the Confederate cause. Widows remained faithful to their husbands' memory, yes, but also to the Confederacy in these publications. An Arkansas newspaper described the speech of one Louisiana widow to her town. With "melting tones" she shared that she "wished she were a soldier herself, that she might prove her devotion to her beloved country on the battlefield." The death of her husband had not affected her devotion to the Confederacy. This was a cause worth great sacrifice. The article concluded with support of this widow, hoping that "the smile of an approving God rest upon her." Another reporter spoke favorably of a visit to a widow who "received me with great kindness, and spoke with deep emotion of the generosity of the Southern people towards herself and family." This widow was not hostile about her situation but kind. She did not let loss imbitter her. Poetry published in newspapers likewise reinforced the image of a selfless widow remaining tied to the Confederacy even after a death. When one widow lost her son, she fainted, then woke up and murmured, "Killed outright: It has cost the life of my only son; But the battle is fought and the victory won." Her husband was already dead and now her son. The victory, however, offered a silver lining: success for the Confederacy. In this way, newspapers also reinforced the image of a widow's devotion, not just to her family but to the Confederate cause.[35]

The *Southern Literary Messenger* also emphasized themes of political widowhood in its publication, affirming established notions of Confederate death culture. Take an 1863 poem titled "War Song." In it, the Alabama author urged husbands to war with "Should the God who rules above thee, doom thee to a soldier's grave, hearts will break, but fame will love thee, canonized among the brave!" Here, the brave died but the death meant something. Soldiers were men who would be missed. If they died, the loss would shatter hearts, but because of soldiers' actions, the poet assured men that they would be destined for fame. This death was preferable to survival and safety if that survival and safety was achieved by refusing to enlist. And just in case this driving message was somehow missed, the poem ended, "Rather I would view thee lying, on the last red field of strife, 'mid thy country's heroes dying, than to be a dastard's wife." Better to be the widow of a dead soldier, in this author's perspective, than to be the wife of a man who didn't go to war at all. The publication of this poem placed this sentiment into the hands of thousands of readers across the Confederacy and further tied the experience of widowhood to the Confederate political project. Widows had broken hearts but canonized the memory of their husbands. A woman ought to prefer widowhood over marriage to a man who chose not to support the cause.[36]

Fiction had the opportunity to work readers into a romantic frenzy while reinforcing the concept of a widow's eternal devotion to a Confederate soldier. During the war, one newspaper printed the following tale:

> An incident is related which affords a striking but sad illustration
> of the effects of civil war. The lady in question has resided with
> an only daughter for many years in Alexandria. About nine
> months since, a mutual friend introduced a young gentleman
> of Richmond to the family. The young people soon became
> intimately acquainted, and, quite naturally, fell in love. The
> parents on both sides consenting, the parties were betrothed,
> and the marriage date was fixed for the 4th of July. . . . The
> gentleman joined the forces of his state. . . . Matters thus
> remained till the 4th of July, when, exactly at the hour of the
> time originally fixed for the marriage, intelligence was received
> at the residence of the ladies that the young man had been shot

by a sentry two days before, while attempting to desert and join his bride. His betrothed did not shed a tear, but, standing erect, smiled, and then remarking to her mother, "I am going to desert too," fell to the floor, while the blood bubbled from her lips, as her soul passed back to Him who gave it.[37]

While the woman in this story was just one day short of marriage, this tale nonetheless described the high level of devotion Confederate culture glamorized in fiction. In a twist, though, this widow's alliance was stronger to her almost-husband than to even life itself.

Augusta Jane Evans, author of *Macaria: Altars of Sacrifice*, likewise explored wartime devotion in her popular novel. Published in 1864, the book sold more than 20,000 copies even before the war ended. "Oh, to this consecrated legion, stretching like a wall of flesh along the borders of our land, what a measureless debt we owe," exclaimed one of Evans's main characters, witnessing the death of a young boy, delirious after receiving a wound at the Battle of Seven Pines. "May we be constantly reminded of the debt of gratitude we owe to our armies," emphasized the text. Confederate society had a debt to the soldiers who died and, increasingly, to the widows they left behind.[38]

The pressure for widows to behave in a particular way affected more than the widows themselves; it spread to those who encountered them. Sarah Morgan regretted her behavior around a recently widowed woman and reflected upon it in her diary. "The thought of that little widow came often and often when we were playing our absurd games; I felt as though we were all doing her an injury. We grew shockingly undignified, playing Crambo. . . . We played too many ridiculous games; I for one am ashamed of myself," she decided. The mourning widow, wearing her black, turning to God, caring for her children, and devoting herself to her husband's memory and his cause, should not be bothered with such silly games. Her friends should have behaved accordingly. Her friends should rise to her level of devotion.[39]

Stories from soldiers reinforced the image of widows as devoted, not just to their husbands but to all Confederate soldiers. One soldier, while in Virginia, sat on the porch of a farmhouse with a soldier's widow who noticed that his coat was badly torn. The widow, "kindly offering to mend it," took the jacket and immediately sat down to fix the tear. This form of support, for the soldier and the uniform he wore, represented a continuation of her support for the cause as a whole. Another soldier, Robert Stiles, was so struck by a widow's actions at a funeral that he felt "it is strange how everything

The Horrors of War

connected with the burial, except the sad scene at the grave, seems to have faded out of my recollection." He described the funeral of James H. Beers, a Confederate soldier who died on May 3, 1863, from wounds he received at the Battle of Chancellorsville. Stiles acted as an escort for the family, riding "in the carriage with the widow and his two little girls." As Beers was laid to rest with military honors, Stiles reflected "that not a muscle of their pale, sweet faces quivered as the three volleys were fired over the low mound that covered him." He believed this incident to be "the most impressive instance I have ever known of trenchant, independent thought and uncalculated, unflinching obedience to the resulting conviction of duty—obedience unto death." Of all the memories, these three women, the widow and her two young daughters, remained fixated in his mind, and this was the story he publicly shared. They were obedient and they understood duty.[40]

White Southern women contributed to the creation of the image of the good Confederate widow as well. Upon arriving in Richmond in December 1861, Louise Wright, the daughter of a Confederate senator, described a Confederate army decimated by shot, shell, and disease. The "land ran red with blood and the wail of the widow above the roar and din of battle," she wrote. And yet she emphasized that no Confederate citizen cried, "Hold, it is enough." Despite the loss of husbands, "ultimate defeat was not contemplated." Louise went on to champion the plight of women and widows of the South. She described the women as "the most gentle and feminine," the ones "upon whom the suffering and sorrow of the time pressed most heavily." The women of the South, she continued, "were, if possible, more indomitable in their courage than the men!" Southern women, with "the tender fierceness of the dove," felt the pain of battle as their husbands did. "Into their own gentle breasts they received each wound by which a hero fell," she concluded. And yet they didn't call for the war to end, as Louise wrote it. They did not call for surrender or peace or the return of husbands. This description is typical of the idealized image Southerners crafted and pressured their women to embody. Widows who met the ideal were spoken of in this high language and championed as ideal women of the South.[41]

Similarly, Confederate supporters enjoyed stories like that of Madam Porter, a "war widow or otherwise" who bested U.S. officers with her wit and charm. William Wiley, a U.S. soldier from Peoria, Illinois, recorded the story on October 11, 1863, in his pocket diary. Madam Porter owned a large plantation in Franklin, Louisiana. Seemingly placing her property before her loyalties, she "was in the habit of entertaining some of our officers very nicely" with fine dinners in order to receive protection for her property. One night, when a lieutenant and several other young officers were being entertained at supper, one of Madam Porter's enslaved people "came running in and said, scuse me massa colonel but I guess you all had better look out a little I see a lot of fellers across ober de bayou in skifs and I think dey is rebels." The officers "left the table rather abruptly and mounted their horses and started for camp at the top of their speed supposeing that the widdow and the rebs had laid a trap for them." William was on picket at the time and watched as his esteemed officers "rode for dear life until they reached our picket line." This tale of a widow who tricked the occupying U.S. troops entertained the town for weeks.[42]

Emilie Todd Helm, a younger sister of Mary Todd Lincoln, is another example of a widow held up before Confederate society as an ideal. On September 20, 1863, Emilie's husband found himself in a "perfect tornado of bullets" at the Battle of Chickamauga. Amid the cutting storm of balls, dirt, and powder was one small lead mass that punctured his liver, ending his life before sunset and shattering Emilie's forever. A young captain from Kentucky received news of the Confederate victory and celebrated in his diary with "It is glorious news. It makes a fellow feel taller, stouter, fatter, better, lighter, heartier, saucier, braver, kinder, richer, and everything good & great. Hurra for hurra!!" He then turned to what the victory meant: "Gen Helm of Ky is killed. So the wail comes up with the shout of victory."[43]

This brings up an interesting point about the role of military victories, defeats, and Confederate widowhood. While some contemporaries might acknowledge a widow's grief alongside a great victory, as this captain did, for widows themselves it seemed almost inconsequential. When wives learned of their husbands' deaths, they did not ask whether the battle was won. Condolence letters rarely mentioned it to widows, particularly in the initial weeks of mourning. During and after the war, Confederate widows were defined by the death, not the particular cause of it. Whether by germ or gunshot wound, it did not matter how he died; a Confederate soldier was gallant in the grave.

As the news spread throughout the Confederacy, a steady stream of condolence letters came to Emilie, and like for many widows, they were filled with political language. "While my heart bleeds for you," wrote Mr. Halderman, "I also feel the deepest anguish at the severe loss sustained by the service and the Confederacy in the death of your husband." This was not just a loss for Emilie but a loss for the cause. "The sympathy so far as I can learn awakened in the breath of all Kentuckians," wrote H. M. Bruce, "is universal. Poor Hardin was a great favorite with the people of his native State; and has left behind a brilliant reputation and an endearing remembrance

The Horrors of War

which will die only with history." Likewise, Mrs. Halderman believed that all Kentuckians "feel that in the loss of your husband, Kentucky has been bereft of one of her best and bravest men." Even newspapers described her loss as Kentucky's loss, printing that her husband "still has a piece in our heart of hearts." Perhaps one wife put it best, writing Emilie plainly, "A great nation will bear on you its struggling heart . . . and millions of hearts will vibrate with your sorrow. Your loss has been theirs." Though her husband had died, because she was the wife of a Confederate officer, Emilie's loss would not simply be her own.[44]

Emilie wanted to return home, to Kentucky, from Georgia and worked through her connections to gain a pass. But after she boarded a boat to Baltimore, U.S. officials informed her that she would have to take an oath of allegiance to the United States before proceeding. Emilie refused. Her husband had just sacrificed his life in opposition to the United States, so how could she promise to uphold it? As her daughter would later explain, "It was treason to her dead husband [and] to her beloved Southland." Unable to persuade her, the U.S. officers telegraphed the White House for instructions. Abraham Lincoln, her brother-in-law, supposedly responded with one line: "Send her to me."[45]

When Emilie approached the White House in 1863, she was "a pathetic little figure in her trailing black crepe." Her trials had transformed the beautiful woman into a "sad-faced girl with pallid cheeks, tragic eyes, and tight, unsmiling lips." Reunited with Abe and Mary, Emilie wrote, "we were all too grief-stricken at first for speech. . . . We could only embrace each other in silence and tears." Certainly, the war had not been easy on the Lincolns either. The Todd sisters had lost two brothers, Mary had lost a son, and Emilie's loss of Benjamin gave them much to grieve over together. "I never saw [Abraham] Lincoln more moved," recalled Senator David Davis, "than when he heard of the death of his young brother-in-law, Helm, only thirty-two-years-old, at Chickamauga." When Davis went to see Lincoln on September 22, "I found him in the greatest grief. 'Davis,' said he, 'I feel as David of old did when he was told of the death of Absalom. Would to God that I had died for thee, oh, Absalom, my son, my son?'" Davis did not know how to respond. "I saw how grief-stricken he was . . . so I closed the door and left him alone."[46]

Emilie and Mary found comfort in each other's company, but their political differences divided them. "Sister and I cannot open our hearts to each other as freely as we would like," Emilie wrote. "This frightful war comes between us like a barrier of granite closing our lips." Not everyone who encountered Emilie would do so with a tongue thus tied. She was, after all, a widow of the enemy. "Well, we whipped the rebels at Chattanooga and I hear, madam, that the scoundrels ran like scared rabbits," jabbed Senator Ira Harris of New York when he visited the White House. Answering with a choking throat, Emilie retorted, "It was an example, Senator Harris, that you set them at Bull Run and Manassas." After a failed attempt to get a rise from Mary, Harris returned to prodding Emilie and informed her, "If I had twenty sons they should all be fighting the rebels." Forgetting where she was but not her Confederate loyalties, Emilie retorted, "And if I had twenty sons, Senator Harris, they should all be opposing yours." Longing for home, Emilie decided it was time to complete her journey to Kentucky. "You know Little Sister I tried to have Ben come with me," Abraham explained to Emilie before she left, reminding her of the position he had offered her husband with the Union. Emilie answered that her husband had followed "his conscience and that for weal or woe he felt he must side with his own people." In her actions, Emilie, too, was siding with her "own people" of the Confederacy. After embracing Mary and Abe, Emilie returned to Lexington to live with her mother, care for her children, and grieve. By refusing to take the oath of allegiance and refusing to denounce the Confederacy before U.S. officers, she began to cultivate a reputation of devotion to the cause, a reputation that would serve her well after the war. The broader political messaging was also useful to her community. If Abraham Lincoln's little sister, as he called her, could support the Confederacy even after the death of her husband, then who could doubt its worth?[47]

While some women, such as Emilie, would play the role of widowhood well from the very beginning, others would fail to wear the mask or accept the sacrifice. For widows who hid their emotions and wore their uniforms out of pride and necessity, the semblance of uniformity hid as much as it revealed. These darker reverberations of the Civil War expose much about the priorities of a society that created a role, built a stage, and applauded the performances of widows who played the role appropriately. Gone forever was the "most important character in our little home." How he died, what she initially felt, and the ideals of mourning were just the beginning for a recent widow. In the days to come, a widow's emotions would affect the way in which she saw the world and the way in which the world saw her. Her emotional expressions had political power, which she may choose to wield.[48]

4

A Dead Weight on My Heart

Surviving a War

We were among the first to arrive. Then came a faint flutter
and Mrs. Parkman (the bride's sister, swathed in weeds for
her young husband, who had been killed within a year of her
marriage) came rapidly up the aisle alone. She dropped upon
her knees in the front pew, and there remained, motionless,
during the whole ceremony, a mass of black crape, and a
dead weight on my heart. She has had experience of war.

Mary Boykin Chesnut

"Kiss me darling—Kiss me again," William begged his wife, after learning
that he was hemorrhaging once more. William Duncan Smith and Georgia
Page King had married just a year earlier, in June 1861, pushed to the altar by
weighty uncertainties of war and the desires of their hearts. "Oh Let me claim
you as my own! Let me have the right to protect you, and shield you by my
earnest love," William had begged, and as Georgia explained to her family,
"I feared that you all might not approve—but my heart relented." Now, they
were in Charleston, South Carolina, he was a brigadier general in the Confederacy, and it was the summer of 1862. When she discovered more blood

and he requested she kiss him again, they thought surely this would be their final kiss. It was not. He would suffer for sixty-seven days.[1]

William's fate, like that of thousands of others, "was not sealed amid the shock of battle but in the anguish and gloom of the sick chamber." On July 26, William became ill and was sent to his uncle's home. He was plagued by dysentery, an inflammatory disorder often caused by an infestation of parasitic worms. For William, the disease defied all medical treatment and was "painful and protracted." Georgia, even more glad she had claimed her independence and married him when she could, went to him in Charleston and devoted herself to his care. In a letter to her brother, she described this experience in excruciating detail. "About two weeks after the first hemorrhage my darling's appetite began to fail. . . . Nothing could check the constant action on his bowels—at least one day—oh God the agony!" she exclaimed. For the next two months, her new husband would remain bedridden, leaking blood and bodily fluids. "All night I watched—and by the clock gave the medicine and brandy and nourishment—fanning him all the time," Georgia recalled. William teetered continually on the brink of death.[2]

"For sixty seven days and nights he suffered—and I never left him night or day—thank God—instead of growing weaker I grew stronger and seldom felt the need of sleep," Georgia explained to her brother. She held William's head in her arms or lap while his body fought the disease. In his sleep, he spoke to Georgia, murmuring, "How dearly I love you how dearly I love you," again and again. Finally, after more than two months of debilitating pain, William died in the afternoon, on October 4, 1862. "At last—just before the angel came to take him from me . . . I bent down over him he raised his dying lips and kissed me twice earnestly," wrote Georgia. "I laid my head near his ear, and told him of my eternal love—and he was satisfied—it was what he desired. . . . My head was on his dear broad breast when the soul went out in a gentle breath." The first thought that came to her mind was "Oh God why did I not die! I dare not question thee."[3]

Throughout the Civil War, tears fell as husbands died and wives received the news. With the tears came a collection of societal expectations immediately dropped upon the new widows of the Confederacy. While the previous chapter explored the socially imposed and prescriptive dimensions of widowhood, this chapter cuts through the platitudes. These pages follow the voices of the widows themselves, how they bore and buried their grief, cried into their babes, and expressed the emotional effects of war. In spite of the pervasive guidance they received, not all widows mourned as society expected. Some mourned too much, some too little, and some could not afford the luxury of mourning. The reality of wartime widowhood, not surprisingly, deviated from the prescribed rituals and left many family members and friends without a template for behavior nor a guide for correction. This chapter gets more closely at how widows expressed emotion and how that matched (or did not match) what their communities expected.

"I have but one wish and that is to die," wrote Mary Vaughan, a Confederate widow in Mississippi, to her sister on February 22, 1863. Mary would not find peace in religion. "I cannot say 'thy will be done,'" she explained. Her anger toward God radiated in the letter. She confessed she had not read her Bible since learning of her husband's mortal wound. "Why am I so much more sinful than others?" she wondered. Mary would not find peace in her motherhood. Mary's sister attempted to bring Mary's attention back to her infant daughter, named Charlie, after her late husband. "You speak of my baby. Why Sister, will God smite me there too? Will he not darken my young life to the uttermost? I will crush back the love, welling up in the depths of my heart for the little one, so when God lays with chilling hand upon her limbs, it will not craze." Her heart, she believed, could not survive any other way. Mary would not find peace in her community. They did not understand her trials. She wrote, "I feel but one thing, I am alone, utterly desolate." And Mary would not find peace with the idea that her loss was worth it, for the greater good of the Confederacy. "Why am I selected from among so many who could so much better spare their husbands than I?" she asked. Mary ended her letter with a request for prayers "that I may become more reconciled to my great affliction." At the moment of this letter, she felt opposed to just about every aspect of proper mourning.[4]

Like a storm that couldn't be stopped, Emma Holmes believed a desperately grieving widow was the saddest of sights, and she hated to see "a young girl of beauty, talents, refinement & wealth, whose mind is so clouded by melancholy as to be oblivious of the realities of the present." Take this extended example of Octavia "Tivie" Stephens, a widow who succumbed to grief, plagued by a "broken, bleeding heart" and "heart-crushing sorrow." Twenty-two years old, Tivie was still grieving the recent death of her baby girl when a Union sniper picked off her husband, Winston, in March 1864. "We were side by side and tho' I was not looking at him when the fatal ball pierced him. I heard it and turned," her brother-in-law began in a letter to her, describing her husband's final breaths. "I dismounted and took him up and sit him on my horse. . . . That last look," the brother relived, carefully penning each word, "that last look was full of love. His lips moved but no word escaped. I see that look now and ever will."[5]

The tremendous grief Tivie felt after the loss of her daughter was nothing compared with the emotions that seized her after the death of her much-loved husband. Her brother Willie, who was also off soldiering for the Confederacy, knew that Tivie's grief would be nearly unbearable. He lamented to his mother that "I can offer no consolation now acceptable to such a grief as Tivie's, at present she can only realize the fact that he is lost to her, and see nothing in his death and the circumstances to console her." Little did he know that his mother, too, was dead, departing her earthly home just two days after Tivie learned of Winston's death. But even this does not encompass the whole story. In one week, Tivie became a widow, buried her mother, and gave birth prematurely to a baby boy. Tivie described her trials in her journal:

> March 15, 1864. With what a sad, sad heart I begin another journal. On Sunday Feb 28th, dear Mother was taken with a congestive chill. On Friday, March 4th, Davis came with the news of the death of my dear dear husband, he was killed in a battle near Jacksonville on the 1st of March. Mother grew worse and on Sunday, Mar 6th, she too was taken from us, between 12 and 1 o'clk she passed quietly away from Typhoid Pneumonia. At 7 o'clk p.m. I gave birth to a dear little baby boy, which although three or four weeks before the time, the Lord still spares to me. Mother was buried on the 7th. . . . Our relatives and new made friends have been kind in visiting. . . . I have named my baby Winston, the sweet name of that dear lost one my husband, almost my life. God grant that his son whom he longed for but was not spared to see may be like him.[6]

Relatives and friends quickly penned condolence letters to Tivie. "How shall I begin a letter to you, knowing how heart broken you are," asked Tina, a loving relative. "I declare I think about you and cry until my brain seems to be on fire. . . . Many wives have lost her Husband, but not such as yours, how short the time seems to look back when you were both so happy at Rose Cottage." Tivie's sister-in-law likewise assured, "I know that such affliction as yours there is nothing that can comfort but the hope of a reunion here after." An aunt explained, "My heart bleeds for you, dear—when I think of your trial in parting with him so suddenly and at that time," while her brother Willie shared, "I am happy in the belief that there are times when the spirits of those in Heaven hover around those whom they love on earth." Though they knew not what to say, these letter writers realized how difficult these losses would be for anyone and especially Tivie.[7]

A Dead Weight on My Heart

Of course, the letters also contained their obligatory pieces of solace and advice. "In a dream I had last night I thought you seemed quite reconciled and said you thought he was taken from the evil to come," wrote one cousin, subtly encouraging Tivie to accept Winston's death. Like other widows, Tivie received advice to "try to improve your health and spirits for the sake of your little ones." An aunt urged Tivie to "turn to the bright side and dont give up to grief." Religious sentiments laced almost every letter, as relatives recommended she "try and bear your afflictions with christian fortitude." Through these letters, writers tried to provide emotional support for Tivie, while simultaneously directing her behavior.[8]

Unlike plantation widows and widows in mountainous regions, who lived miles from loved ones, Tivie's physical proximity to a town provided her with physical support in addition to the written encouragements. Living near Thomasville, Georgia, at the time, Tivie received a multitude of visitors, including Aunt Caroline, Uncle Jared, Aunt Julia, Hattie, Henry, Lilla, Willie, and Lizzie in March 1864. These visitors allowed Tivie to "leave Rosa to make candy" and let her Aunt Julia watch the baby while she "went to the Court House." Though her family would be a source of aggravation at times, it also was a great support, offering temporary respite from responsibilities so she could grieve privately.[9]

But Tivie's family became increasingly concerned about the ways in which Tivie managed, or rather mismanaged, her grief. A couple of weeks after Winston's death, one brother wrote optimistically that "Tivie now is able to come to the table and will soon be around and attending to all the household duties, and before I leave her will be able to take interest in matters around her." The next week, Tivie described her progress in her journal with "I walked to the Pond with Willie . . . and the children, the first time I've been out for three weeks." Brother Willie praised her for her actions, writing that "your conduct through it all deserves the highest commendation, and has shown a character superior to most women many years older." But soon, Tivie seemed to regress. Willie worried "that you may allow yourself to sink into a state of melancholy. . . . Let me warn you against this and implore you my dear sister to strive to bear up under your terrible visitation with calmness and resignation." He wanted her to accept her fate. She needed to perform her "sacred duty to your helpless children." Willie explained that "I feel confident that after a time your life will not seem so gloomy and objectless to you." In another letter, Willie continued to advise her, recommending she bear her loss with meekness. In yet another, he implored her to "be patient and content." Tivie's aunt jumped to her defense, explaining that Tivie was simply misunderstood. She explained that Tivie was "peculiar but not cold, and has a great deal of character under that quiet exterior." In her aunt's opinion, Tivie was capable of settling into the appropriate role of a widow. Tivie may have looked sad in black clothing, but "she bore it all well."[10]

Despite the disagreeing opinions of her performance as a widow, her family knew that behind the performances, Tivie remained heartbroken. The death of Winston shattered Tivie's identity. "I know not how to write I am so bewildered. . . . My grief now is almost more than I can bear. . . . I have not the heart to do anything, all the pleasure of my life was wrapt up in Winston, he was almost my life," she explained. In her diary, she described mornings spent "reading some of my journals of the many happy hours spent with my dear husband" and evenings looking through old letters. While reminiscing about her newlywed years, she wished "oh that they could return." Her brothers became even more worried about her lack of progress as time passed. Willie insinuated that she was becoming "cold, gloomy, suspicious, irritable, and unhappy and making those around us unhappy. . . . I need only refer to you to your own feelings and experience for a confirmation of this." Tivie needed to learn how to pay her respects to her husband "without neglecting all else." Tivie was aware that she was not meeting expectations. In June 1864, she thanked her brother Davis for all his assistance and acknowledged, "I know it rests upon your minds, will I ever be able to take care of my children?" She didn't answer her question but simply informed him, "I always prayed that I might die first, that I might never have to mourn for him, I think I shall never become reconciled to his death." She could not seem to accept it. She could not seem to move forward. Tivie disappointed those who loved her most, in ways she could not seem to help, while lost in these depths of grief.[11]

Some widows felt condolence letters lacked true understanding because the authors typically had not experienced the same loss. Their spouses lived. How could they offer advice? E. A. Marshall, a widow in Abbeville, South Carolina, wrote, "Letters of condolence are often but formal proofs of sympathy, yet when they come from those who have drunk from the same bitter cup, we are induced to believe that they are prompted by more than ordinary sympathy." Ordinary sympathy was fine, but the authors could not appreciate the depth of a grief unless they, too, had husbands in the grave. Marshall had lost a husband. And so when she wrote a condolence letter, she spoke of feeling "the same crushing despair" that Sallie Fair Rutherford, a recent widow, must feel. Sallie had married William Drayton Rutherford in 1862. In October 1864, he died in battle. Marshall offered encouragement, writing, "Yes my Dear Sallie as one who has passed through all this, I write to you,

A Dead Weight on My Heart

"The Effect of the Rebellion on the Homes of Virginia,"
Harper's Weekly, December 24, 1864.
Image courtesy Indiana State Library Digital Collections.

not that I expect to alleviate your holy grief, for that, God and time alone can accomplish, but to offer you my sincere sympathy for your young widowed heart in its agony of grief." She reminded Sallie that they were in this grief together, as women without husbands, through her repeated use of *us*. For example, "Oh Sallie there is no sorrow like this but let us raise our eyes from the dark picture that surrounds us." After offering some religious encouragement, Marshall felt "it is useless My Dear Sallie for me to refer to the glorious death of your noble Husband." Referring to the glorious death of husbands of the Confederacy was a common trope for wartime condolence letters. But from one widow to another, Marshall believed referring to this particular sentiment was, as she put it, useless. Instead, she encouraged Sallie to place "your widowed head upon His loving Bosom" and seek her own peace.[12]

Another widow, Ellen Long Daniel of North Carolina, processed her grief through scrapbooking. Ellen lost her husband in 1865; Brig. Gen. Junius Daniel died from wounds received at the Battle of Spotsylvania Court House, Virginia. Ellen filled a scrapbook with poems, pictures, and newspaper clippings related to death. Through this scrapbook, readers gain tremendous insight into Ellen's grief. Early in the book appears a poem, which begins, "Gone!

Yes he's gone with no word of endearment," and continues on to discuss elements of widowhood, such as the blank life of a brokenhearted girl and that "the fabric of years was dissolved in an hour." The poem describes the bitter tears, stifled sighs, and the weariness of grief. The pressure of being a widow, to suffer in silence, is most apparent in the final stanza:

> Gone! Yes he's gone, and she'll nourish her sorrow,
> In silence and sharpness 'twill dwell in her breast;
> Sadness as weary to-day as to-morrow,
> The same mocking dreams ever haunting her rest;
> Man, in his anguish, may publish his sadness,
> And brazen it on by the force of his will.
> To woman 'ts given to laugh in her gladness;
> To suffer in silence—to weep and be still![13]

In addition to the poetry, Ellen's scrapbook also included a large picture of Mary Anna Jackson, the widow of Stonewall Jackson and a woman to whom she could relate. Imagining Ellen's scrapbooking process reveals the significance of the choices Ellen made in selecting material for her book. She had hundreds, possibly thousands, of print-culture elements before her. And yet she cut out these poems and glued these images to her limited pages. Together, themes of sadness, despair, and heartache emerge. Through Ellen's scrapbook, we see a community of grief, self-selected and sorrowful. [14]

The physical and emotional could not be separated. Widows lived in a world filled with tangible reminders, such as these scrapbooks, of the husbands they mourned. These items triggered feelings of melancholy long after the initial grief dissipated. Inconspicuous reminders haunted widows' homes—a pair of boots, an empty hat hook, a worn Bible—unsettling tokens of a man who no longer lived. The smells of firewood or freshly cut flowers carried with them memories of the man who used to complete those tasks. The quiet questions of children, about their father and what life would be without him, weighed heavily on mothers' minds. A lively fiddle tune might be all it took to transport widows to an earlier, happier time. Photographs and letters were not the only material reminders that held emotional power, affecting widows sometimes emotionally, sometimes physically.

Nannie Bierne Parkman's emotional reaction at her older sister's wedding illustrates how a place, an event, and a dress could affect a wartime widow. In 1862, Nannie cast "an indefinable feeling of gloom" over her older sister's wedding. Clad in deepest weeds, Nannie "glided through a side door just before the processional . . . tottered to a chancel pew, and threw herself

A Dead Weight on My Heart

Unidentified woman in mourning dress and brooch showing Confederate soldier, holding a young boy wearing a kepi. Photograph by Charles R. Rees, 1861–65. *Image courtesy Library of Congress, Washington, D.C.*

prone upon the cushions, her slight frame racked with sobs," according to one contemporary. Another recorded that Nannie "came rapidly up the aisle alone. She dropped upon her knees in the front pew. And there she remained, motionless, during the whole ceremony." Scarcely a year before, Nannie had been the bride floating down the aisle to a joyous wedding march. She had been "one of the gayest and most attractive of society's war brides," as graceful as she was beautiful. Her husband, a second lieutenant in the Seventh South Carolina Infantry, died at Antietam, leaving her to sit "in the cold ashes of her desolation" on her sister's special day. Not only was it in the same church, but the wedding dress the bride wore was none other than Nannie's, an evil omen that caused one attendee to shudder. These physical reminders brought physical reactions out of Nannie that she was unable to hide behind a frozen smile for her sister. Mary Boykin Chesnut summed her up well, as she often did, describing Nannie as "a mass of black crape and a dead weight on my heart. She has had experience at war."[15]

Wartime economic shortages added to the trials of widowhood, but they also reveal how physical items often fed an emotional need. The inability to purchase proper mourning garb plagued women of working classes early in the war and the majority of Confederate women by the end. Mourning was a luxury many women could not afford. Judith McGuire described "one sad girl" who was "too poor to buy mourning" due to fallen fortunes. But she wanted mourning dress and wanted it desperately. Another who could not afford to buy a mourning wardrobe dyed all of her clothes black in order "to make them suitable." A third widow, Etta Kosnegary, wrote to her sisters, asking how they dyed their dresses. She explained that she had the fabric for two dresses, but "I don't know how to get them black." Her husband had died six weeks earlier. Silk black dresses, heavy veils, and other features of antebellum mourning etiquette were expensive. Though they were priced out of respectable mourning rituals, many women, even those with very little money, often did the best they could to mimic these customs, even if it meant dyeing the only clothes they owned. At a time when there was so much out of their control, they could control the clothing they wore.[16]

With supply low and demand high, an economy of mourning flourished during the war. Southern newspapers, such as the *Daily South Carolinian*, announced triumphantly when shipments of mourning cloth arrived, often smuggled through Union lines. Proxy shoppers, often family members and neighbors, shopped for widows in urban areas, bringing back the necessary elements of mourning with them. As one proxy shopper wrote from Richmond in 1864, "The only mourning goods in town are merino and alpaca," "there is no very heavy crape," and "the milliner will make a crape bonnet and veil for $500." Signing off "with love and sympathy," the shopper awaited instructions from the war widow. The Southern Express, a company that transported bodies from battlefields to hometowns, enjoyed a booming

A Dead Weight on My Heart

business during the war. Embalming, though rarer in the Confederacy, was nonetheless advertised in Richmond newspapers, promising the return of bodies after the performance of disinfection, a process that would preserve a body in as lifelike a state as possible. While many women in the Confederacy could not afford such luxuries, advertisements targeted them in their grief and promised elements of a Good Death in a time when so much else was changing.[17]

While the widow who struggled within her mourning was a concern, a more problematic issue was the sexually promiscuous widow. In the antebellum period, the flirty, even sexually knowing widow had been something of a literary trope. During the war, such behavior was scandalous, suggesting that a Confederate soldier was easily replaced and his cause unworthy of honoring. "I was in hopes she would be more dignified than other widows," lamented one disappointed sister in her diary, while another Southerner, disapproving, reflected that while "gloom reigns in the hearts, and homes, of most of our people, widows and widowers are the only ones who are having a gay time." Widows were, after all, unmarried women with sexual experience, and when the average age of widows dropped dramatically during the war, they became difficult to categorize. At least one formerly enslaved man reported that his widowed mistress "ordered him to sleep with her, and he did regularly." Communities did not believe that young widows must remain single forever. But at a time of war, improper behavior or a hasty remarriage seemed implicitly unpatriotic.[18]

In a time when communities expected widows to cry, some widows simply did not. "Immorality sweeps over the land and religion burns dimly in the misty atmosphere," wrote Abbie Brooks in her diary. A reluctance to remain wedded to the memory of their husbands and to the Confederate cause was certainly a phenomenon not purely for widows but for many people across the South; the burdensome consistency of sorrow was simply too much to bear. As one resident of Richmond observed, "Some persons in this beleaguered city seem crazed on the subject of gayety. In the midst of the wounded and dying, the low state of the commissariat, the anxiety of the whole country, the troubles of every kind which we are surrounded, I am mortified to say that there are gay parties in the city." A number of elite Southerners, including widows, would rather "forget all our troubles," past and present. Social functions provided a distraction from mourning, death, and the constant supply shortages. Kate Stone wrote, "We can live only in the present, only from day to day. We cannot bear to think of the past and so dread the future." In a time of soaring death rates, Kate also mused that "one grows callous to suffering and death" and therefore people simply didn't mourn as they once did. To many, these parties seemed insensitive while soldiers, just 100 miles away, risked their lives. To others, these events served as critical coping mechanisms, providing a mental escape when bad news seemed to lurk around every corner.[19]

While it was difficult enough for some people to tolerate the fact that parties occurred during the war, it was even harder to stomach the idea that some widows attended these gatherings. One "gay young widow" shocked bystanders when seen dancing "a few months after the death of her soldier husband, with a long black veil on" and holding a handkerchief that "looked as if it had been dipped in ink." A disapproving observer remarked, "She should have dipped it in blood." In March 1864, a group including widows gathered for an oyster supper and "cleaned [the table] of all refreshments." When Sarah Kennedy learned of this, she haughtily remarked that "juveniles always cleared the table," insulting the widows in attendance. While most widows did not want to see their husbands' names on casualty lists, the finality of death did release them from the anxiety of the unknown that plagued many wives.[20]

For some men, young Confederate widows seemed to take on a certain peculiar attractiveness. Remarks by observers indicate that a level of sexual magnetism became associated with young Confederate widows. In September 1863, Mary Bell believed she had discovered "the secret attraction that widows seemed to possess." She supposed that their allure blossomed from their grief. "How much more the heart is touched by the tender beauty of a woman who has loved and suffered than by the gay shallow pink & white prettiness of a girl," she reflected to her husband. And when soldiering Ben Coleman wrote letters home to his parents, he casually instructed them to "tell that good looking widow (God knows I wish I could see her) to send me some wine." Even in mourning, their beauty remained.[21]

Although remarking on the physical attractiveness of a widow was not so scandalous, her supposed irresistibility proved more worrisome. Sexual assault did occur during the war, and victims included widows, as in the unfortunate case of Frances West, a widow living near Morrisville, Virginia. Thomas Dawson, a Union private with the Nineteenth Massachusetts Volunteers, entered her home at night, on September 9, 1863, and "did forcibly and violently and against her will have sexual intercourse." He hanged. Irresistible or not, widows without male protection were in a place of heightened insecurity.[22]

A Dead Weight on My Heart

Married men also remarked on the temptation of young widows. For example, one husband wrote his wife of a "young widow, real good looking," visiting his camp from St. Louis. "If you do not hear from me again you can guess 'what is the matter.' But unfortunately I was simple enough, when asked if I was married, to acknowledge the fact. Perhaps it will make no difference," he teased. His wife chose not to respond. Other women envied the magnetic draw widows seemed to possess. Miss Carrie, from Tennessee, remarked to a friend "that she almost wishes she had been born a widow. They are so fascinating and irresistible." Even James T. Ayers, a chaplain with the 104th Regiment of Colored Troops, struggled to resist the allure of a Tennessee widow. He described her in his diary as a "Little bewitching yong Blue Eyed fairskined widow tidy Enough for one to eat." "Seldom do I meet her Eaquals anywhere," he continued. "God bless the Little widow, them Blue Eyes that Little plump Rosy Cheek them Delicate Lilly white hands that Lady Like Smile." Ayers had visited her with the intention to recruit her enslaved man into his regiment. As he rode away, however, he realized "that Little woman had Caused me to forget" his purpose. Ayers shrugged off the loss, concluding that a "man would be A monster Could he Deny such an Angel as this" anyway.[23]

Public flirting, especially by widowed women who were supposed to be mourning the loss of their husbands, shocked and horrified traditionalists such as Mary Boykin Chesnut. On a train in November 1863, a smartly dressed woman sat beside her and "in plaintive accents began to tell her melancholy tale." Her husband had died recently in a battle near Richmond. When another man offered her a vacant seat beside him, the young widow left Chesnut and "as straight as an arrow she went in for a flirtation with the polite gentleman." In another scandal, Chesnut spoke with a man who witnessed "widows who brushed with their eyelashes their cousin's cheeks in the public cars." These actions did not pair well with the image of the proper widow, a heartbroken woman who sacrificed her husband to the Confederacy. Such liberties suggested a lack of dedication not only to their late husbands but also to the cause the husbands died defending.[24]

While flirting with other Southerners was bad enough, flirting with the enemy was simply unacceptable. For a widow to choose a Union man over a Confederate soldier represented an abandonment of her family, friends, and community and all her husband had fought to maintain. In Warren County, North Carolina, Mary J. White described one widow who "reaped the contempt of most her friends when she befriended a Federal officer." Some community members believed that she "had set her cap for the captain." The lack of respect this widow held for the Confederate cause infuriated Mary. "I wish he would take her off with him, but before she goes, I should like for her to be given a good coat of tar and feathers, for she richly deserves it," she steamed in her diary. This stereotype of a sexually promiscuous widow did not escape Union soldiers. Writing home from his station in Maryland, Union soldier Charles Johnson asked his wife to excuse the lewdness of the joke and informed her that the poetic line "Oh! for a lodge in some vast wilderness, amidst a contiguity of shade" had been paraphrased to "Oh! for a lodge in some vast widow's nest, amidst a contiguity of hair." He then explained that he had merely been trying to remember the poem, but "the two slipped into my idle brain together." He was not alone, for the joke appears in other wartime journals and letters of other soldiers such as Willoughby Babcock, who recorded in a letter that a friend of his "tantalizingly" asked, "How would you like a lodge in some vast widow's nest?" In small doses, young widows were fine. But as their ranks grew from the hundreds to the thousands and the tens of thousands, this trope became more worrisome for Confederate society. Confederate widows had the potential to challenge mourning customs and gender norms. And some, like the anecdotes above reveal, did.[25]

For families with widows who mourned too heavily, like Tivie, and families with widows who mourned too little, like these more flirtatious women, a widowhood like Georgia Page King's would have been much preferable. Like many widows, Georgia had a strong community. They advised her. And they watched her closely. Friends and family, aware of William's lingering sixty-seven-day illness, came to see the grieving widow. Georgia's letters are filled with names, including Molly, who "had come for me"; the Grants, who "are very near and kind as ever"; and Jenny, who would remain "until after frost." In addition to being grateful for this physical community, Georgia expressed thanks for her family, particularly her brothers, from afar. "God has been wonderfully merciful in sparing you beloved brothers," she emphasized. She may have lost her husband, but she still had them and chose to focus on the positive. Still, her life was difficult. "I do earnestly pray God in mercy to take me as soon as He, in his infinite wisdom, will consent to do it," she confessed, "but I know if I am left it is for some use to others." She would continue to strive to be useful. Though heartbroken, even in these initial days of grief Georgia tried to see the positive in her predicament.[26]

Certainly, Georgia felt the sorrow of losing a husband. She consistently wrote of her great love for William. Georgia believed, "God has seen fit to visit me with the sorest affliction the human heart could know." To her, nothing could be worse. In the early stages of her husband's sickness, she explained, "I did not feel that I could say 'Thy will be done.'" But through his sickness, her faith grew stronger and acceptance became easier. She believed God felt "a peculiar compassion for the widow—knowing the utter desolation of her heart if her love is such as it should be for the one He has given her for a husband." This was not a situation where a wife loved lightly and then mourned lightly. Georgia felt shattered by this loss, and while she remained faithful to her religious beliefs, she sometimes hoped that God might end her misery with her own death. But even as Georgia wrote, "I could have died with him—this separation is so hard," she finished the sentence with a reassuring "but I doubt not God's wisdom." Her grief was strong, but she would not allow it to overwhelm her.[27]

Georgia's determination to mourn her husband and accept God's will was exactly what those around her hoped she would do. Her mourning affirmed the worth of her husband. Her friend Lizzie Caperton wrote, "When I read yr letters, my precious one, I knelt down and offered Praise to god for the example to my simple desponding heart of your submission to His will and your great faith in His love." Georgia was a model because, as much as she grieved her loss, she did not succumb to depression. Instead, she mourned with grace and championed her husband's memory. She did not call her brothers home from the war but instead encouraged them to carry on in the fight. She followed the dictates of the etiquette books and the advice of her family. By mourning gracefully, she did not undermine the Confederacy but accepted that her husband was "a noble husband" called to give his life for a larger cause.[28]

Exploring the varied emotional responses of Confederate widows during the war, alongside the expectations placed upon them, reveals the complicated politics of mourning that lay beneath official tributes to women performing that work. "Your best earthly treasure has been snatched from you," read one condolence letter typically, "& I know you feel as if there was nothing left worth living for, but you must summon all your fortitude." Losing a husband was certainly "a great trial" for many Confederate wives. Some widows battled with too much grief, while others appeared to feel too little. For every Georgia that met expectations, there was a Tivie who grieved too much and a "gay young widow" dancing at parties. Some cried, some flirted, and some desperately attempted to live up to the ideals laid before them, dyeing the only clothes they owned black. But what widows may not have realized initially was that this emotional transition from wife to widow had political power, and the project of reconstructing a life began the moment a husband died. For a Confederate widow, her loss was hardly her own. For some, the performative expectations of widowhood became even more taxing in the weeks, months, and years after a husband's death. Even so, war widows had social capital, and the Confederacy was anxious to oversee how they spent it. After the marriage, after the death, and after the ideals, there were decisions to be made and a new Confederacy struggling to survive.[29]

A Dead Weight on My Heart

5

I Must Be Taken Care Of

Reconstructing a Life

Every Body say I must be taken care of by the Confederate
States they did not tell my Deare Husband that I should Beg
from Door to Door when he went to fight for his country.

Mary Jones to Mississippi governor John J. Pettus

"'Well, you have done a very gallant deed today, Sir,' I said, my wrath rising as
I spoke. 'As you belong to the Federal Army, no doubt you will be promoted
for burning the bread of a widow and her little children.'" Jane McCausland
Chinn's husband died in October 1862, and she had just given birth six weeks
before his death. When U.S. troops marched to her plantation outside of
Baton Rouge, Louisiana, to burn her grain stores in 1863, she met them with
wrath. "Were you ordered to burn all my bread? Could you not have spared
some for my little ones? Does the Yankee army make war on widows and
babies?" she accused the officer. Jane then dramatically shared the story of
her family; in addition to her recent widowhood, one of her brothers had
died at Manassas, another was a prisoner of war in New Orleans, and both
of their homes had already been burned. "I believe my family has paid a high
enough price for whatever crime you think we have committed but which

we consider our rightful way of life." She concluded her recounting of the encounter in her diary with lines that read straight out of *Gone with the Wind*: "'It could have been worse, Mistress,' said faithful Hillery. 'Yes, much worse,' I mustered the courage to reply. And, stiffening my back so that the frightened darkies around me could see that I was not defeated, I continued, 'We will manage somehow, Hillery. Tell your people I will see that they get bread. I will find a way.'"[1]

The work of reconstructing white widows' lives did not begin with the end of the war but with the end of a life. The death of a man triggered immediate and pressing decisions, beyond the varied grieving processes described in the last chapter. Widows negotiated complicated political and economic situations living in a war zone, leveraging their status as war widows when necessary. Widows not only were aware of the social capital they gained in widowhood but often used that capital for their own benefit during the war. Here, their ability to support the emotional regime of the Confederacy had real significance. Reconstructing a family also included the work of redefining households, as extended families discussed and debated who would retrieve a soldier's body, where the body should be buried, where his widow should live both during the war and after, who, wife or mother, should go through his earthly possessions, who would have what say in the raising of his children, and in some situations, who had the greater claim to grief. When death took away the man who had brought them together in the first place, grieving mothers and widows had to renegotiate who they would be to each other, now and in the future. For some widows, remarriage came quickly, opening new avenues of support and criticism. This varied work of reconstructing lives mattered, and it began right away.[2]

Of the many considerations on widows' minds, finances often weighed most heavily and most immediately. Antebellum custom and law allowed a widow her "dower thirds," or approximately one-third of her husband's estate, to support herself and her children. But for families already on the brink of economic disaster, this was of little help. Certainly, wartime financial hardships were nothing new. "If you could get up a concert in behalf of this poor Regt. it would be a good work for those who need it," wrote one officer to his wife in September 1861. "They are mostly poor men, some of them with starving wives at home. Wives and children crying to them for bread and they are unable to help them. What agony they must suffer," he concluded. When one of these wives became a widow, the temporary element of her financial hardships dissipated, replaced with a darker sense that this suffering could be permanent.[3]

I Must Be Taken Care Of

Many widows turned to extended family and friends for financial support. Rosa Delony learned of her husband's battle wound and subsequent death when she was eight months into her fifth pregnancy. She was thirty-one years old. Condolence letters flooded her home, and while words comforted Rosa, visits provided the physical support Rosa needed. Mary Ann Cobb visited Rosa within a week of hearing the news. She described the event to her husband as a visit with her "afflicted friend," who "is heart broken but endeavors to bear up under the weight of her affliction. It is double heavy. She will be confined next month, and had expected the return of her husband at that time." She also informed her husband that "I offered our sympathies and your assistance in every way you can serve her, especially in the matter of supplies." Rosa took advantage of this opportunity and requested pounds of meat, bushels of corn, and tin cans of lard. In a grateful letter to Mary Ann, Rosa claimed, "Had you not kindly offered to supply me with those things I scarcely know what I should have done. You must think of me this winter." Physical support, from family and friends, met not just emotional needs but financial ones.[4]

While many widows turned to a network of family and friends in times of financial insecurity, not all widows had this sort of social safety net. Sarah Gibbs and Lucy Fletcher found themselves in a problematic situation when they were arrested and investigated as "women of loose morals" in Richmond, Virginia. In her interview, Sarah claimed her husband had died near Richmond, fighting for the Seventeenth Georgia. Lucy believed her husband died at Gettysburg. The details imply a justification, an argument that they only turned to prostitution for economic reasons, as a result of their new status as widows. Prostitution (and sexually transmitted diseases) flourished during the war, especially in cities such as Nashville, New Orleans, and Richmond. Richmond's *Daily Dispatch* reported women "disporting themselves extensively on sidewalks" with "smirks and smiles, winks and . . . remarks not of a choice kind in a loud voice." While most widows would not take on this particular occupation, some did, by choice and necessity, highlighting one unexpected consequence of widowhood. The supposed widows, Sarah and Lucy, received releases from custody in Richmond, with the report concluding, "I see no reason why they, more than any other . . . be confined." To reconstruct their lives, these women needed money and turned to the oldest profession.[5]

For some widows, life in a war zone, with its shortages of clothing, food, and supplies, led to uncharacteristic political activities. Elizabeth Leeson begged the Confederate secretary of war James Seddon for her husband's

"Sowing and Reaping: Southern women hounding their men on to rebellion; Southern women feeling the effects of rebellion and creating bread riots," *Frank Leslie's Illustrated Newspaper*, May 23, 1863. *Image courtesy Library of Congress, Washington, D.C.*

return, writing, "Thare is no use in keeping a man thare to kill him and leave widows and poore little orphen children to suffer while the rich has aplenty to work for them. . . . My poor children have no home nor no Father." She believed her husband was of little good to the government but of great worth to his family. White women rarely negotiated or pleaded with government officials before the war, but many, desperate for assistance, took to petitioning secretaries of war and governors of Confederate states. While many women emphasized their positions as soldiers' wives in their letters, widows particularly used their status as a negotiation tool. "The ladies names in this petition are the names of widow ladies and soldiers wives," emphasized a petition from Stanhope, North Carolina, while the women of Upson County, Georgia, chose the descriptor "the wives and widows of deceased soldiers and mothers of soldiers in the Confederate army." They weren't just women living in the Confederacy. They were politically tied to and supporting the Confederacy through their husbands. They sacrificed their husbands to the cause. Because of this, they expected the Confederacy to take care of them.[6]

In individual letters, widows also made their connection to the state clear, signing things such as "wife of deceast soldier," "a poor widow," or "Mary

I Must Be Taken Care Of

Stilwell soldiers widow 6 childen" beside their names. Some widows, such as Mary Jones, were more pointed within the text of the letters themselves. "Every Body say I must be taken care of by the Confederate States they did not tell my Deare Husband that I should Beg from Door to Door when he went to fight for his country," she informed her Mississippi governor. She was from Natchez, but after her husband's death in the war, she traveled to Yazoo City in search of economic support for her three young children and herself. After being turned down by the officials in Yazoo, she concluded, "You ar all that I can call on for protection." Mary demanded support. She had given her husband to the Confederacy. Now, the Confederacy was obligated to support her.[7]

Newspapers also called for the support of widows, reminding readers that they had an obligation to help those who sacrificed to the Confederacy. On May 18, 1862, an Atlanta newspaper told of a "widow of a Confederate soldier who died in service and left a wife without a home, after she had been promised that the wealthiest secessionists about Nashville would support her." According to the article, a Union man had provided a home for her, but now, "Union men are turning the helpless women out of doors." The paper reminded the wealthy people of Nashville of their promise to the widow. The mayor and city marshal had also taken on this case and "determined that the rebel leaders shall fulfill their promise to the letter (to provide for this woman) or suffer the severest consequences." While unclear what the severest consequences would be, the public scolding in this article, published not just in Nashville but also in Atlanta, reminded all readers that they owed a special debt to Confederate widows such as this one. She had given a husband to the cause, and because of this, her community owed her support.[8]

Emilie Todd Helm, the younger sister of Mary Todd Lincoln who became a Confederate widow in 1863, also called for assistance. But instead of reaching out to the Confederate community, she reached out to family. What was not common was that her family was in the White House. When a bullet killed her Confederate husband at Chickamauga, she remained loyal to her husband's memory and, by extension, to the Confederacy. She was living in Kentucky in 1864 and her Georgia cotton had fallen within Union lines. Fearing it would be burned and seized, she again visited her sister and brother-in-law in the White House, to request a permit to sell her crop. At this point in the war, cotton was one of the most sought-after commodities in the country. Abraham Lincoln refused to grant her the pass. Of the many reasons for denial, perhaps one of the most pressing issues was that an election was just around the corner, and to the public, she was not "little sister" but the widow of a Confederate officer. Granting her an exception would not be viewed favorably by the press.[9]

On Emilie's disappointing return to Kentucky, she learned that one of her younger brothers had died of "want and destitution." Certainly, he had his own issues, but if he, an able-bodied man, could die in such a way, could this also be a possibility for her, a widow with three small children, no significant job skills, and no money? Fueled by this "dreadful lesson," Emilie wrote Lincoln again, to beg for a pass to the South, so she could attend to her cotton. "The last money I have in the world" was gone, she explained, before speaking of "the right which humanity and Justice always give to Widows and Orphans." Wrapping up her letter, she concluded, "If you think I give way to excess of feeling, I beg you will make some excuse for a woman almost crazed with misfortune." Emilie, as a Confederate widow, was not alone in this misfortune, especially of the economic sort. She refused to swear an oath of loyalty to the United States of America. She did not get her pass. The financial realities of widows' situations, even those of the upper class, could be quite precarious, as they sought financial security through family and, sometimes, the friends and former business partners of their late husbands. Protections, or rather connections, could make the difference between security and destitution, especially during the war years.[10]

Widows who supported the Confederacy in word and action were more likely to be supported by their Confederate communities. Much as a uniform helped to efface class distinctions (however partially) in men, widow's garb had the potential to lend even working-class women a certain social cachet. Judith McGuire described meeting one Mrs. Brown, a "wretchedly dressed woman, of miserable appearance," in 1864. Mrs. Brown shared that her husband had joined the Confederate army and was killed at the Second Battle of Manassas. She had left Fredericksburg with her three little children to find work in Richmond. When she could not get enough bread to feed her family, she "got turnip-tops from her piece of a garden, which were now putting up smartly, and she boiled them, with a little salt, and fed them on that." Judith, shocked by this story, asked, "But do they satisfy your hunger?" to which Mrs. Brown replied, "Well, it is something to go upon for awhile. . . . I am afraid to let the children eat them too often, lest they should get sick; so I tries to get them to go to sleep." Alarmed by this story, McGuire gave meat to the widow and wrote: "Poor thing, I promised her that her case should be known, and that she should not suffer so again. A soldier's widow shall not suffer from hunger in Richmond. It must not be, and will not be when her case is known." Mrs. Brown, as a soldier's widow who continued to speak well of her husband

and his cause, gained an elevated place in her community above other poor citizens. A widow had political and social standing because of this intimate connection to the Confederacy.[11]

When Confederate widows did not receive the respect they felt they were owed, they sometimes reacted violently, highlighted by this unusual snippet in the *Yorkville Enquirer*. In 1863 Virginia, a person who "had slandered the widow of a deceased Confederate soldier, was tied up by some half a dozen indignant women, and received twenty stripes." The brief report did not share what this person had said, but whatever it was, these women believed physical punishment was necessary. And while the clipping does not share exactly who these women were, it does offer one more detail, that "the women who administered this wholesome admonition were soldier's wives and widows." The inclusion of war widows twice in such a short article suggests that it was important and somehow related to the offensive language. The widow of a dead soldier was slandered, and because of this, other women, other widows, sought justice. Widowhood elevated her to a special status in Confederate society.[12]

Even in contested border states and divided Appalachian mountain communities, Confederate widows lobbied for and received support. In Missouri, a Confederate sympathizer recorded a secret party to support Confederate widows in her community. She wrote in her diary about "a supper given ostensibly for Fire Co. No. 2, but in reality for the benefit of the Southern widows and orphans, I cannot refuse anything pertaining to an act of charity for those I love." The widows had sacrificed husbands and remained Confederate, and because of this, the community should look after them. Similarly, an 1864 notice announced mass meetings in Adair County, Missouri, to provide widows necessities for the winter. Even in rural and politically divided communities, such as that of North Carolina's mountainous Caldwell County, widowed neighbors called on those they hardly knew. When Elizabeth Morrow's husband died of disease in 1864, she asked an elite neighbor, Ella Harper, for assistance. Ella's husband commanded Elizabeth's late husband's company. Elizabeth wanted her late husband's personal belongings and renewed her appeal to Ella again three months later. Ella passed the request to her husband. Elizabeth had limited resources, so she called on Ella, and though Ella reacted impersonally, she passed the widow's messages along nonetheless.[13]

Living in a border state brought its own unique challenges in reconstructing the lives of Confederate widows. In January 1861, Alexander H. H. Stuart believed if Virginia seceded, "brother would be arrayed against brother, and the whole land would be drenched with blood. The border country would be ravaged and laid waste with fire and sword. Firesides and fields would be desolated by invading armies, and the wail of the widow and the orphan would be heard in all our valleys!" Though many states held divided populations during the war, Virginia was the only state so divided that it physically split in two. West Virginia, which rejoined the United States on June 20, 1863, began calling for re-admittance to the North as early as 1861. The war was bloody for all, but for communities in Virginia and West Virginia, the conflict was particularly gory. Approximately 155,000 Virginia men served in the Confederate forces during the Civil War, 20,000 of whom came from the region which would become West Virginia.[14]

The experience of the men of the Second Virginia Infantry and their widows highlights the complicated nature of the Civil War in a contested and divided region. Shepherdstown resident Mary Bedinger Mitchell summed up the emotions of many well when she wrote, "We had been 'in the Confederacy' and out of it again, and were now waiting, in an exasperated state of ignorance and suspense, for the next move in the great game." While women in the deep South could publicly mourn their husbands and safely speak their hatred of the Union aloud, most widows of the Second Virginia Infantry did not have this luxury. Marching armies, frequent battles, and a divided local population affected the actions of Confederate widows of the Second Virginia Infantry. This regiment was primarily composed of soldiers from the Virginian counties of Jefferson, Berkeley, Clarke, and Frederick. When West Virginia returned to the United States of America as a new state in June 1863, it took the counties of Jefferson and Berkeley with it, while Clarke and Frederick remained Virginia counties. Women of Charles Town, Shepherdstown, Martinsburg, Hedgesville, Duffields, and Harpers Ferry became Confederate widows in a Union state governed by their husbands' foe. To the U.S. government and state officials, these women's late husbands were traitors and their own support for the Confederate cause was treasonous.[15]

To be an outspoken Confederate woman had consequences in contested areas, such as Jefferson County. On July 19, 1864, Henrietta Bedinger Lee's Shepherdstown home burned to the ground as a result of U.S. general David Hunter's orders. Henrietta was a Confederate sympathizer, her husband was a cousin of Robert E. Lee, and her household included "a widowed daughter, just risen from a bed of illness, [with] her three little fatherless children, the eldest not five years old." Furious that her home now lay in ashes, she wrote a fiery letter to Hunter to express her displeasure. "You name will stand on history's pages," she wrote, "as the Hunter of weak women, and innocent

I Must Be Taken Care Of

children; the Hunter to destroy defenseless villages, and refined and beautiful homes—to torture afresh the agonized hearts of widows. . . . Oh, Earth, behold the monster!" In her opinion, his actions were unforgivable. The agonized hearts of widows, even if they were Confederate widows, should be protected at all costs.[16]

Another relationship fraught with potential for negotiation, support, and conflict for widows was that with their mothers-in-law. In addition to creating an unprecedented number of young white widows, the Civil War created a substantial number of mothers who outlived their soldiering sons. The relationship between grieving wives and their grieving mothers-in-law was an interesting one. Mourning a common man, they still clashed over decisions about burial, religion, money, the (grand)children, and the degree to which the widow remained tied (and obligated) to her dead husband's family. Exploring the varied emotional responses of Confederate widows and mothers to the death of their husbands/sons—and their responses to each other—reveals the complicated politics of mourning that lay beneath the official praises to the "ever-living heroism of our women" and begins a larger process of seeing women as individuals.[17]

Of course, in the case of wives and their mothers-in-law, such tensions were even more fraught, particularly under the emotional, financial, and societal pressures of the war. When a soldier died, who had the greater claim to grief, his wife or his mother? Where should the widow go, who went through his things, where would he be buried, who would have what say in the raising of his children? Well-meaning mothers-in-law stuffed envelopes with innumerable pages of advice, writing out their own grief, even as they directed the grief of their daughters-in-law. Consumed with the pain and guilt of outliving their soldiering sons, many Confederate mothers quite naturally shifted their attention and energies to the lives of their late sons' wives. They had a common pain; they spoke a common female language. But the very closeness of their situations and relations could sometimes strain what was possible for two people to go through together. To be sure, some widows appreciated, even became dependent upon, the additional assistance, but others dreaded the arrival of another letter or, worse, the mother-in-law herself. Both supported and suffocated by this relationship, widows responded with gratitude, rehearsed civility, or, quite simply, rejection. The varied emotional responses of Confederate widows and mothers to the death of their husbands/sons, and their responses to each other, reveal a complicated politics of mourning.

Like wives who feared the death of a husband, mothers dreaded the possibility of losing a son and struggled with the absence of their boy(s), even if he had married and no longer lived at home. "By mother's request I write again to you," began one sister in Mississippi. "Mother's health is delicate, she pines to see her boy, her eldest, her hope stay and comfort, although she bears the separation from you with Christian resignation and fortitude," the sister wrote, with the addendum "Mother says, don't forget to read your bible." Soldiers typically followed letters to their wives with letters to their mothers during the war, creating large family correspondence collections. Even soldiers without mothers reflected on this relationship during the war, such as Nathaniel Dawson, who sought a wife to fill a void left by his deceased mother. He reflected to his fiancée, "It is ten years this morning since my good mother died, and I have been thinking of her virtues. I love to think of the dead, those treasures who have gone before to wean us from this world. . . . I was devoted to my mother and when she died, I felt all alone and yearned for the love of someone to supply her place." Many sons remained close to their mothers all their lives, even after they married. This sentiment became particularly visible in times of stress and instability.[18]

Not surprising given the closeness of many mothers to their sons, many mothers often felt emotionally shattered by their sons' deaths. Mary Patrick captured the emotions of many mothers in a journal entry after the death of her son in May 1862. "Hush poor heart! Beat not so wildly, stop let me tell it on this quiet page," she began, trailing on, "My Son. Oh my Son. Beautiful, noble, generous, Mother loving boy! Solace of my widowed years. . . . I would willingly die before the day goes out. Father forgive me," she grieved. Her entry included a poem, which told of a "mother's ceaseless moan" and the memories of teaching a young boy to walk, talk, and pray. Another mother shared her feelings with her son's wife, lamenting, "My son, my son, my first born, my pride, my hope—oh this wicked war of oppression—I know he died gloriously fighting for the freedom of his country but I can not feel that. . . . The loss of my child, my darling son, how can I out live him?" It wasn't natural, in their minds, to outlive their sons. This theme haunted the letters of many mothers who expected their sons to survive them.[19]

When the war began, many women chose to move in with, or at least closer to, their loved ones, combatting the loneliness, anxiety, and fear that often came when husbands left for war. "Well tomorrow is Williams birth day," wrote another soon-to-be widow typically. "O if we could only know if he be living or dead, if we knew he was still among the living we should hope some time to see him. And if we knew him to be dead than we should give up the last hope, and suspense would be at an end." This suspense was heavy and constant and motivated action. As historian Drew Gilpin Faust argued, many elite women "moved—sometimes long distances—to live with their parents or in-laws or even friends and acquaintances." Once the husband was dead, some wives hesitated, reconsidering which household they really belonged to. Those of younger ages, and shorter marriages, especially struggled in deciding between their birth families and their husbands' families. When the war began, Jorantha Semmes moved in with her husband's cousins in Canton, Mississippi. Even though her marriage was not a new one, and she was bringing her five children with her, Jorantha believed she was an unwelcome "nuisance" to the household. Further, she became furious when her host whipped her children alongside his own. Another woman, Emma Crutcher, moved to Vicksburg to live with her in-laws soon after her husband enlisted, but when her own parents rented a large house in a remote area to avoid the troops, she struggled with her decision. Ultimately, her desire to be near a railroad or post office, in order to communicate with her husband, won out. She stayed with her in-laws.[20]

After a son's death, a desire to be close to the widow—to comfort, mourn with, care for, or direct—increased for many in-laws. The death of a husband damaged a household structure, but it also offered the opportunity for a new kind of household to emerge. When one mother's only son was mortally wounded, the woman who delivered the news recorded, "A sad task it was, but the poor bereaved old mother seemed to smother her own grief to comfort the poor crushed wife." The author was struck by the mother's desire to place the wife's needs before her own. For others, such as Lucinda Helm, the solution was a bit less selfless. Her daughter-in-law must come to her to assuage her own great grief over her son's death. "I feel that the blow is more than I can bear. . . . Come home to us Emilie," Lucinda begged. Others decided to travel to the widow themselves, such as Emma Garnett's mother-in-law. Emma received a letter explaining, "Mother will go to you very soon. She loved you as her own child, and will do all she can to give your comfort." As for the desires of widows, not surprisingly, they varied, from those who desperately desired familial support in their time of grief to those who wanted to be completely alone. Some, such as Etta Kosnegary of Tennessee, could not make up their minds. Etta began a letter to family with "I think sometimes if I could be . . . with some body that loved him [her husband] as well as I did I would feel better." But she ended it by saying, "Company does me no good I had rather be alone." Widowhood and grief were hard. The additional decisions brought some widows comfort, as something to do, but threatened to overwhelm others such as Etta, who could not see clearly through her grief.[21]

Beyond sentimental desires, the difficulty of running a household without a husband worried many mothers-in-law. "I know it must have been hard for you to keep up & take that interest in your duties which your children & domestic cares call for, & I don't wonder that you yielded to these feelings," reflected one mother-in-law. Fathers-in-law also shared sentiments, such as how one "often wished that you were near us, that we might aid and encourage you in all your cares & responsibilities." Alice Harrison's mother-in-law counseled her to let her brother take care of her affairs after her husband's death. She explained, "Oh you know not enough of human nature to have such to deal with, and your life will become more and more labourious and miserable." Intrusive and honest, mothers-in-law often spoke more frankly to grieving widows, especially about their futures, than other members of the family. Many widows felt a continual pressure to move near, or into, the homes of their in-laws.[22]

If they could not be close physically, mothers-in-law often penned pages upon pages of advice to the new widows, remaining a mental presence. Mothers-in-law gave advice, opinions, directions, and consolations to widows. "We were thankful to see your hand writing," began one mother-in-law, before asking, "Do write often for we seldom receive more than 1 out of 10." She also instructed the young mother, "You must not give up to your feelings my dear child, but think of those precious ones whose sole dependence is upon you, strive to cheer up." In addition to messages about motherhood and grief, many letters contained religious advice, with lines such as "God will help you thro' your troubles." Clear messages about the proper way to live life, while mourning, came through to young widows through this handwritten medium.[23]

Without a son to care for, some mothers-in-law transferred their attention to their sons' children and desired to play a significant role in their rearing. "My poor child," began Lucinda Helm to Emilie, "my heart has yearned over you and Hardin's orphaned children." Contemporaries commonly took this view of children as "orphaned" when their father died, even though their mother lived. Even Abraham Lincoln, in his second inaugural address, invoked a deceased soldier and called for the nation to care "for his widow and his orphan." Lucinda assured her daughter-in-law that if she came back to Kentucky, "I will furnish you with a nurse soon as you get here." Further, Lucinda informed Emilie that if she came, "you shall be as a daughter and his children my children." In her own way, Lucinda hoped to replace her deceased son with Emilie as a daughter and her grandchildren as children.

I Must Be Taken Care Of

Just to be sure her message came through clearly, she added, "Oh Emilie I wish for you and your children every day," and signed the note "your affectionate Mother." Emilie would return to Kentucky but would not remain permanently.[24]

Similarly, widowed Cornelia McDonald, who had given birth to nine children and lived as a refugee in Lexington, Virginia, reflected on her own tragic wartime situation: "All thought that the children ought to be distributed among the older members of the family. . . . I listened, but was resolved no matter what happened not to part with my children; but was often pressed, and reminded how hopeless my condition was." In the end, Cornelia could not bear to part with her "poor little lonely ones. . . . That thought would nerve me for resistance." Like many widows, she found comfort in her role as a mother, especially after the loss of her societal position as wife. Though the support from extended family would lessen her load, it was a load she did not want to lose.[25]

In some situations, in-laws could understand grief better than any other. In 1860, Sallie Gray of Virginia married whom she considered to be "the best husband of the day." They had a daughter in 1861, and he left to fight for the Confederacy. In early 1862, Sallie's dear friend and sister-in-law, Lizzie, died. Then, Sallie's husband died at the Battle of Leesburg later that year. From Texas, Sallie's other sister-in-law tried to send her comfort: "As my dear Brother had to die, I am thankful that he had not to die in a hospital for I have a perfect horror of them—am so thankful that he was buried in a graveyard and I shall never cease to feel gratified to the Leesburg ladies that saw him buried and strewed flowers over his grave." They bonded over their shared grief, with lines such as "If I do mention my troubles to anyone they'll say 'everyone is losing friends now' and that is the last they think of it; but Oh! 'tis not the last with you and with me. 'Tis very true most persons are losing someone dear to them but that don't help me. It don't replace my loved ones." Sallie took comfort from this relationship, but then in early 1866, this sister-in-law also died.[26]

Sallie was not the only widow to take comfort from her in-laws only to watch them pass away too. In 1862, Charlotte's brother, John, died in the war. In 1864, her husband followed. "God bless and sustain you, my ever dear Sister, under this heavy stunning blow. We never heard the sad news until yesterday evening. Oh how my heart yearns towards you and your dear little ones and how I long to do something, to say something to comfort you—But I feel that I need comfort myself. I have lost my best friend and most devoted brother," wrote her brother-in-law. Charlotte decided to sell their plantation and move with her four children into the home of her father-in-law. But then, at the end of the war in 1865, he also died, to suicide.[27]

Of course, not all women had mutually supportive relationships with their in-laws; some relationships between mothers and daughters-in-law were rocky from the beginning. When Ann Marie Stewart Turner's husband left to fight, she and her children lived with his family in North Carolina. There, she penned pages upon pages of complaints to her mother, miles away in Texas, about her mother-in-law's "unhappy temper" and "unruly tongue." The mother-in-law was not simply upset that Ann married her only son. Ann wrote that the woman "said I had fondled around her husband till he cared more for me than any man might for any woman but his wife—that he had a passion for me & I encouraged by combing his hair." "I can't remember all the abuse she gave me," Ann explained to her mother. Ann's hardships further increased when a ball struck her husband at the Battle of the Crater. He was wearing "the same sweet smile he wore in life" when he died. "For your sake and my dear little ones I try to bear my loss as well as I can," Ann wrote her mother and sister, praying, "I hope that Heaven will after a while give me a spirit of resignation." Ann believed this final blow was retribution for her mother-in-law's "unkindness to me" and Ann's own heart. When reflecting again on her mother-in-law's unhappy treatment of her, Ann explained, "I have often wished to revenge myself and I feel now that I have been punished for this, for now a hand stronger than mine has struck her a blow which falls heavy on us both."[28]

For better or worse, widows and mothers-in-law did have a connection like no other, perhaps best illustrated by the final words of a dying soldier. Wounded between the first and second button of his shirt, William Lee would be one of 387 Confederate soldiers killed in the First Battle of Manassas. As he lay suffering, William's mind remained focused on his wife and mother, a detail not lost on his cousin Edwin. "He was still forbidden to talk," Edwin wrote to his aunt, "but he beckoned me to him and said, in a low whisper, 'Eddie, write to Lil and Mother.'" In his final moments, William's mind might have returned to his father, his brothers, or his comrades, but he seemed implicitly to understand that the real work of mourning him would belong to these women. And yet, even as female hearts reverberated with sorrow together, conflict arose within the work of reconstructing their lives in the wake of death.[29]

For some widows, a crucial part of the reconstruction of their lives continued to be getting their husbands' bodies home. While some succeeded

I Must Be Taken Care Of

View of the "Burnt District" in Richmond, Virginia, showing two
women dressed in mourning, walking together, April 1865.
Image courtesy Library of Congress, Washington, D.C.

in the early days of mourning, for others this project would extend into the
postwar years. Rosa Delony, the widow in Athens, Georgia, who was pregnant at the time of her husband's death, gave birth to Martha Roberta Delony
on November 8, 1863. Rosa's grandmother, aunt, and cousin were "thankful
to hear of the birth of your dear little girl and your doing well. . . . We were all
glad to hear that it was a girl." When Rosa held Martha, she held the last child
she would have with her late husband. Local families such as the Cobbs and
friends such as Mrs. Stovall and William Church continued to provide Rosa
with physical and emotional support in Athens through her pregnancy and
grieving. But what Rosa really wanted was to get her husband's body home.
"Your husband's body was buried in the Cemetery of the Soldier's Home, on
the hills to the north of Washington. The number of his Grave is 20; in Range

1; & lock 1. A Head Board marks it," shared a chaplain who was with Rosa's husband when he died. Because Rosa's husband was an officer, he received a burial that many men would not.[3]

During the war, Rosa was not successful in making much progress in her reinterment project. Then, on July 21, 1866, little Martha, age two, died of whooping cough. Rosa mourned the loss of the child her husband so early anticipated but never met. Two months later, Rosa buried another body—her husband's. On September 26, 1866, the *Southern Watchman* reported, "The remains of this gallant soldier and true patriot who died in Washington City in September 1863 from a wound received near Brandy Station, Va., reached this place on Monday, and were buried on Tuesday. Peace to his ashes. He was 'without fear and without reproach' and a grateful, loving people will enshrine his memory in their hearts and bequeath the story of his deeds and many virtues as a rich legacy to their children."[31]

In 1863, William had not been able to contain his excitement as he planned his trip home to Athens for Christmas and his daughter's birth. Now, he lay beside her in the Oconee Hill Cemetery. If Rosa could have chosen, she would not have planned for this chain of events. But at least now, in the midst of an uncertain future, one thing was certain. William was finally home.

By all accounts, Rosa managed her grief well, both publicly and privately, during and after the war. After she buried her husband in the local cemetery, she had a place to physically mourn him, and she could continue the project of rebuilding her life. But for some women, reconstructing a life did not mean allowing grief to fade. Some widows rebuilt their lives with heartache as a cornerstone. Though her marriage lasted just four years and four months, Tivie Stephens would mourn Winston's death for the rest of her life. To her brothers, it seemed she might finally be improving. Davis was "so much relieved to know that you are again able to attend to and take some interest in your domestic affairs." But in her diary, Tivie systematically reminded herself of her losses and continued to record her tremendous grief. With the rolling of each year, she marked anniversaries of their marriage and his death; Tivie immersed herself in a cycle of everlasting mourning. On October 21, 1864, she wrote, "My 23rd birthday, a sad one, so many changes since the last. My dear Husband and Mother both gone, beside many other changes." On November 1, 1864, "The 5th anniversary of my wedding day, but my dear husband is not with me to celebrate it, he is in a better world and how many years may pass before I meet him there I know not." Christmas 1864 was "a sad instead of a merry one." Christmas 1866 was also "a quiet and sad one to me, though the children happy." March 1, 1867, was "the third anniversary of my dear

Husband's death, a blue day with me." In 1873, "9th anniversary of Winston's death—I had a severe blind headache." Her grief proved immovable even with the passing of a new century. As late as November 1, 1904, she penned, "This is the date of my marriage 45 years ago."[32]

Some joy came to Tivie through the love of her two children, Winston and Rosa, but with that love came more grief. She named her son, who was born in the days following Winston's death, after his father. Yet she struggled to call him by name. Her cousin Tina lectured her, writing, "Dont call him Winnie it is a womans name and an ugly one, call him as you did the dear one after whom he is named." But Tivie could not bring herself to do this and would continue to refer to her son as Winnie well into his adulthood. When her daughter, Rosa, got married in June 1882, Tivie described it as "a real grief" and worried that a pregnancy could harm her "delicate" daughter. When Rosa became pregnant in late 1882, Tivie wrote a friend that "we all must be with her all we could." Tivie's motherly intuition proved accurate on February 24, 1883, when Rosa was fixing her hair and had a convulsion. She died later that afternoon. Tivie's darling son, Winnie, also left her, marrying and moving to Massachusetts to practice dentistry in 1894. Tivie visited him and his wife often but always returned home to the tiny town in Florida where she had fallen in love decades ago. In 1908, she finally died, ending her "share of the worlds trials," hoping to be reunited with the man she loved all her life.[33]

Tivie was not alone in rebuilding on a foundation of grief. For widows in this emotional predicament, reconstructing a life had little to do with the political projects of the Confederacy or the social possibilities of remarriage. Instead, some widows faced a lifelong struggle against depression and despondency. "This is the 50th anniversary of one of the saddest days of my life, and I've been all day fighting depression. I must talk to somebody," began Sallie in a letter to her grandson. Her daughter, she claimed, snapped at her whenever she tried to speak to her, so she instead turned to him. "But I haven't told you what the day is to me. It was the day your grandpa Spears bade me farewell for the battlefield, only three months before your mama's birth. . . . It was almost as bad as his death, for I felt I was giving him up for good." She wished that he could have known his grandfather and regretted spoiling her grandson's mother, who was her only child. "She was all I had and not only I but all the family indulged her in every wish, which is not good for any one. It was a mistake in my life and then in hers, she don't know how to stand adversity of which she has been called to bear. But I must stop this doleful strain and tell you what a comfort you've always been to me. Don't you let any body change you to your old Grandmother who wont be a trouble to any body long." She was seventy-six years old. She would live another seven years.[34]

While under public pressure to perform their new societal roles, some widows, quite unlike those caught in grief, could and did manipulate their single status to gain a peculiar attractiveness and power. Some widows were unable or unwilling to mourn thirty months before seeking a new husband. Upon seeing that flirtatious widow on a train, another stranger commented to Mary Boykin Chesnut, "Well, look yonder. As soon as she began whining about her dead beaux I knew she was after another one. . . . It won't be her fault if she don't have another one soon." The stranger watched a minute more and then remarked again, "She won't lose any time." Likewise, Southerner Naomi Hayes believed widows were even more impatient for marriage than maidens, for "those who already knew the pleasures of married life were less willing to live outside it." In a case study of Virginia, historian Robert Kenzer compiled statistical data suggesting that the younger a widow was, the greater the likelihood that she would remarry. Through an analysis of pension records and census data, Kenzer determined that 1866 was the most common year for remarriage and that widows who remarried had a median age of twenty-four years in 1860. Urban widows also appeared to have greater opportunities for new marriages. Kenzer concluded that "given the tremendous shortage of men after the conflict, the opportunity to remarry was quite restricted except for the youngest and wealthiest southern women." This shortage helps to explain why some young widows, when presented with an opportunity for marriage, refused to wait out the customary two and a half years of mourning.[35]

Not surprisingly, families—including those of the groom-to-be—worried about hasty remarriages. "Well I could fill a page," Emma Holmes of Charleston wrote in her diary in January 1863, "to express my astonishment at the news which arrived tonight, and which was like a thunderbolt." Her brother, Willie, had written "that he is engaged to Mrs. Ben Scriven, a widow with *five* children, & begs mother to please send his wardrobe as he will be married soon." That was all he said on the subject, leaving Emma perfectly dumbfounded, while "Mother burst into tears, frightening us." The age of the widow was particularly worrisome. "If it was a young lady, we would not have felt it so much—but the idea of marrying a widow, who must be at least five or six years, if not more, older than himself—an idea so repugnant to my feelings—then the five children—such a heavy responsibility for so young a man. She must have some property, for he certainly cannot maintain a family

I Must Be Taken Care Of

otherwise," she rambled. In the end, Emma decided to cheer up the house with laughter, for "indeed it seems preposterous and absurd in the extreme and I can scarcely believe the evidence of my senses. Of all the strange marriages & matches made by war, this takes the lead." The war made strange marriages indeed.[36]

Widows, and their suitors, were well aware of mourning etiquette with regard to remarriage, and some went to great lengths to hide their activities. Laura Cornelia McGimsey, who went by Corry, married in 1864, became a widow in 1865, and received at least four marriage proposals during her mourning period. She was widowed at twenty-four years old. One of her first suitors informed her that "my wife was very lively and I wish to get another of the same disposition." She apparently fit the bill. Corry objected to his proposal because of "the shortness of time" since her husband's death and her "inadequacies to the task of a stepmother." Instead of being discouraged, the suitor informed her that he would not "give up the pursuit at this state of the game, when the object is so alluring." As for the short length of time since her husband's death, he conceded, "You are right, it does take some time to heal," but still begged her to "marry me in a reasonable time, say six months." He also assured, "I will back it [the envelope] in a ladies hand." She declined his proposal. Similarly, another suitor wrote Corry, "I wish this to be kept a profound secret," and concocted an elaborate way in which they could exchange letters to "keep down suspicion." Ultimately, Corry would remarry, to the fifth suitor to approach her through the mail.[37]

Like Corry, Fannie Franklin Hargrave would also prove to be popular with her widowhood but with a bit less discretion. For Fannie, the war began when her father, Bright Williamson Hargrave, was shot outside of their Georgia home in May 1861. Perhaps Fannie was watching the argument, her face pressed against an upstairs window of their expansive plantation home, or perhaps her mother had banished her to the back of the house with the rest of her siblings, thirteen in all. Beard Williams, the man who shot her father, was Fannie's brother-in-law, the husband of her oldest sister, Olivia. Her father had recently returned from the Georgia Secession Convention, where he represented Carroll County and signed the secession ordinance. Why Beard Williams came to the house with a gun that day is unknown. Possibly it was politically inspired, possibly it was a culmination of a family quarrel, or perhaps it was merely a mishap in a heated argument. Either way, her father was dead. Fannie, eighteen years old and the oldest unmarried daughter, helped her mother gather up the ten younger children and take them to Atlanta. Her mother, while taking care of six children with the measles, contracted pneumonia herself and died in 1862. The family was scattered across the Confederacy. Fannie bounced back and forth between two guardians, Judge C. E. Long in Carrollton, Georgia, and David Clopton in Van Wert, Georgia. She would lose touch with several of her brothers and sisters in this time, unable to locate them again until she was elderly.[38]

In December 1863 or January 1864, twenty-year-old Fannie married James N. Carson. He was the co-owner of Carson-Brannan Cotton Brokerage in Pulaski, Tennessee, and a commissariat in the Confederate army. How they met, what their courtship was like, when exactly they married, and other details of their relationship are unknown, though one cousin of James's did exclaim, "I admit I was surprised, yes amazed, confounded, and astounded. I never dreamed of you marrying, I am glad indeed." James left his young wife in Carrollton, a town just west of Atlanta, when he returned to the war. Rumors of Gen. William Tecumseh Sherman's plans swirled throughout the South, causing Fannie to become nervous. "You hear all kinds of rumors— none however, in our favor," wrote Fannie to her "dear husband." In June 1864, she became "very uneasy about our falling in the Yankee lines. . . . I beg that you will come—if it is in the range of possibility & move me to a place of safety." Whenever she traveled, Fannie hid the money James left her, $6,000 in gold, around her waist, afraid to leave it at home. In the midst of all the uneasiness, she informed James, "How much I miss you, you can't imagine." Judge Long, with whom she was staying, told James, "Do come if possible very soon, and take Fannie away from here—she had been deeply sad for the past few days. I cannot realize that she is the same frolicsome, lively creature that she was when you were with her." Her sadness would only increase in the coming months.[39]

On July 3, 1864, James was in Cedartown, Georgia, purchasing supplies for troops. He was visiting a friend's home when "Yankees dashed into town before any one had any notice of their coming." James raced out the back door of the house and "attempted to get to the Plum orchard but they killed him just as he jumped the fence." James was shot in the bowels and brought into the house with blood streaming from his wounds. For his friends, this was traumatic. "If I live a thousand years I can never get over seeing him shot," Mrs. Darden, a friend, recalled. In a letter to Fannie over a year after the incident, she added, "You can imagine how I feel standing here looking at the floor with blood all over it. We have had it scoured three times but it is perfectly plain now and never will come up."[40]

Like many, Fannie had to adjust to not only life as a widow but also life as a mother. Shortly after James's death, Fannie gave birth to a little boy. She

I Must Be Taken Care Of

named him James N. Carson Jr. in honor of her late husband and affectionately called him Jimmy. This baby, however, would only be in his mother's world for about nine months before he died, bringing more loss into the twenty-one-year-old widow's life. "We all loved your sweet little cherub and mourn for him as if he were our own," remarked her sister. Sympathizing with Fannie, she claimed, "I too can never forget his heavenly eyes—his bright sunny face." Death seemed to follow Fannie, seizing those she loved most and heaping tragedy upon the young widow.[41]

And yet just one year and seven months after her husband's death, Fannie was married again. Her choice was Hiram King Brannan, Fannie's late husband's business partner in their cotton-brokerage business and his second cousin. In November 1865, Fannie left for Pulaski, Tennessee, with the intention of marrying him, despite the fact that she was still in the midst of her mourning period. Fannie wrote her friends, "Now don't go scolding because I didn't tell in my other letter for I didn't think then it would come off so soon." Fannie's sister, while full of compassion for Fannie, wrote, "I can hardly help from hating Mr. Brannan for stealing you from us. Poor Jule cried for three days and nights after you left." Fannie's friend Mollie remarked, "I was quite surprised when I heard you were going to marry." Another flatly told her, "O I wish you were not married." In a fleeting moment of introspection, even Fannie doubted her decision, writing, "I hope I made my choice with considerable deliberation." She knew it was quick. And she knew she was still supposed to be mourning. But after the double loss of husband and baby, she saw an opportunity to rebuild and took it. Fannie's new sister-in-law was happy about the development and felt her brother was "quite fortunate to have him a fine looking, captivating, rich" new wife who could produce "a dozen little Brannans—dear little red headed pug nosed babies they will be." Fannie's age, wealth, and beauty outweighed her widowhood.[42]

Beyond her decision to remarry, it also appears that Fannie was a popular widow in Georgia. After she left for Tennessee, her sister complained that "every time I go out, or see anybody 'have you heard from Miss Carson' is dinged in my ears." In fact, she explained to Fannie, "I have been questioned by some of your admirers until I have grown almost tired." To pacify one eager suitor, Fannie's sister played quite a trick. After days of being tormented by a certain captain, Fannie's sister went home to get him a lock of Fannie's hair. Giving a man a lock of hair was a sign of nineteenth-century affection. "I came home and clipped a tress from old yellow oxen tail, perfumed it highly and sent it to him with the request that he should wear it next to his heart and not expose it to the vulgar gaze of anyone. The last time I saw him he drew it out of his breast pocket and pressed it tenderly to his lips," wrote the trickster sister. Wealthy, beautiful, and only twenty-one years old, Fannie appears to have made quite an impression. The literary tropes and stereotypes of irresistible widows likely added to her allure as well.[43]

On February 21, 1866, three months into her second marriage, Fannie received an important letter describing "all the particulars of the death of your much loved husband." This letter did not describe the death of her current husband, Hiram, but her late husband, James. Unaware of Fannie's new marriage, the writer of the letter tried to tell all the messages of love that James had left her. Additionally, the letter writer remarked that "we have so often thought and talked of you and wondered where you were or what had become of you." They likely did not imagine that the young woman was already remarried, and to her late husband's business partner at that. The lack of a family and home, combined with her youth and personality, led to a different type of widowhood for Fannie. This case study highlights how it was not just societal status or finances that affected widows' journeys through reconstruction; it was personality and emotion, too. For Tivie, described as young, wealthy, and beautiful, perpetual mourning was the only solution. For Rosa, similarly young, wealthy, and beautiful, her energies focused on the reinterment of her late husband. But for Fannie, a different path emerged, and she ultimately built her new identity around wifehood, not widowhood. Each woman was pregnant, each lost a husband, and each had to rebuild her life. But even as they experienced the same loss, the reconstruction of those lives looked different for each one.[44]

Remarriage, reinterment, reconstruction—for most widows these decisions could not be put off until 1865. Reconstructing a life came not with the death of the Confederacy but with the death of a husband. His societal position had been clear. He was a soldier of the Confederate States of America. His familial status had been clear. He was a son of his parents. But what was a widow's relationship to these institutions and to this family? Negotiations began in an emotionally charged environment, and widows quickly recognized emotional expression could be used as a currency for respect and support, even as they worked through their personal grief. And when the war did end, and the rest of the nation turned to this project of reconstruction, some widows, particularly elite ones, recognized just what could be gained with this emotional currency.

6

Beautiful Tributes Were Paid to Her

Reconstructing a Nation

Mrs. Helm is "Mother of the Orphan Brigade," and her portrait
appeared on the badges of red, white and blue, worn by the veterans
of the Brigade. Her husband commanded the Brigade, and after
his death they gave Mrs. Helm the honorary title. In the addresses
made during the reunion beautiful tributes were paid to her.

Bourbon News, *October 5, 1920*

"What evidence have we that the cause has died out? But when we see widows wail or hear an orphan cry, I feel then the cause has indeed died out. If you let one of them wail, you may well say the cause is dead. It shall be to your cost," lectured Gen. Henry A. Wise before a church in Richmond, Virginia, in January 1867. Newspapers across the country picked up his speech and printed it under the title "Relief for the Widows of Confederates—Addresses by Generals Wise and Rosser—They Declare the Cause of the South Not Lost." It had been nearly two years since the final shots of the war, but Wise called for action. The action, however, might not have been what readers expected. He called not for guns or weapons. He called not for eulogies or monuments. "Leave the noble memorials you have begun which are only vanity. The Confederate dead all, all sleep well, thank God," Wise continued. He instead called for support for Confederate widows. This, he believed, is what the deceased soldiers would want above all else. While men lay in graves, their wives were very much alive and very much suffering. "We must provide an asylum for both widows and orphans," Wise argued. This was where the true Confederate cause lay, not in marble but in mourning women.[1]

At the conclusion of the war, all widows made decisions about work, home, and possible remarriage. But in the former Confederacy, personal grief combined with communal mourning as memorialization became a central concern for many white Southerners. Not everyone had lost husbands, but most white Southerners had lost something and were left living in a nearly apocalyptic region of destroyed railroads and mass food shortages. This chapter explores the act of reconstructing a nation more broadly and the part widows played (or rather did not play) in this project. While some elite widows, such as Emilie Todd Helm, played starring roles, the majority of widows did not. Economic class mattered; the widows of officers had more opportunities to stand on veterans' association stages and speak in ways that the widows of privates did not. Many war widows, too busy, tired, or emotionally spent, chose not to participate in formal memorialization organizations such as Ladies Memorial Associations (LMAs). They also had nothing to prove. As Confederate widows they, by definition, had supported and sacrificed to the cause in ways that intact families had not. They already had cultural standing. Together, this diversity in postwar mourning reveals that white women did not seamlessly work together to create a Lost Cause ideology and suggests that those the war hurt most had the least left to give. While some elite widows did play an essential role in the formal creation of the postwar Lost Cause narrative, it is important to realize that the majority of widows did not.

For many widows of the Confederacy, life continued to be extremely difficult after the close of the war. As Susan Cooper put it, "Has any of my splendid castles ever reached the summit I anticipated they should? No, no, not one." The struggles of widows were of no surprise to the people of the former Confederacy. Newspapers, in particular, were filled with stories about the hardships of Confederate widows during Reconstruction. In September 1866, Atlanta's *Daily Intelligencer* printed the following plea from a Southern woman: "The widows of the Confederate dead appeal to you with broken

Beautiful Tributes Were Paid to Her

hearts and tearful eyes. They say to you, 'Give to us of your abundance; you are spared, with loved ones and plenty.'" The war had not spared widows; they lost their spouses and they lost financial security. For them, there was no plenty, and therefore the former Confederacy owed them support. The author reminded readers that many of them still had families and economic stability. Meanwhile, she described widows left with nothing but broken hearts and tearful eyes. She also drew attention to the fact that these Southern widows would receive no pensions from the U.S. government and begged for action from the community. For widows, the war disrupted the structure of the domestic sphere, and they needed financial support from their cities and states.[2]

A year later, in September 1867, the *Georgia Weekly Opinion* reported that thirty Confederate widows were starving in Montgomery, Alabama. The widows had published a card in the newspapers to make their case known, for they could "get no work with which to support themselves and their helpless children." They appealed to their community for help because they were unable to find someone to hire them. "This certainly is a piteous appeal," the Georgia reporter concluded, as "these women are the widows of the Confederate soldiers who perished in battle or died from diseases of the camp." All widows deserved sympathy, but war widows, in particular, must be supported. They were owed as much. The author "hoped the citizens of Montgomery will not disregard a cry of distress so full of agony—literally the wail of the widow and the orphan."[3]

An 1867 paper in Richmond, Virginia, tells another story, of a table with two beautiful wax dolls. "The larger one of the two is neatly dressed as a widow, and the smaller is arrayed as her orphan." The two figures sat over a basket. People who walked by should "drop just a penny for those whom the dead of the South left behind them." For those who chose not to donate, the article offered harsh words. "The man who passes by this without giving something to those to whom we owe a sacred duty, has no heart, is without sympathy." Again, the language of owing something to the widows of the Confederacy is central. It was a sacred duty to support the women who lost their husbands in the war.[4]

In short, sympathy could sell, and Confederate widows used this to their advantage. When facing financial difficulties, many widows highlighted their connection to the Confederacy, even in brief advertisements. Employment was one category in which widows highlighted their particular situation. For example, in Texas's *Weekly Democratic Statesman*, one widow attempted to find a teaching position. She described herself as "the widow of a Confederate major general, who fell on a Virginia battlefield, would gladly have employment as a teacher in Austin or in Southwestern Texas." Likewise, another woman led with the description that she was "a respectable white woman without children, the widow of a Confederate soldier," when she placed a job advertisement in a Virginia paper. She sought a position as a housekeeper or cook. Of all the details she could highlight, such as experience, she instead chose to emphasize her connection to the Confederacy in her effort to gain employment.[5]

Widows also used their standing to draw audiences to lectures, productions, fundraisers, and performances. When Laura Webb, an author, prepared for a reading, the local paper included the following descriptor: "Mrs. Webb is the widow of a gallant Confederate soldier, and is entitled to our sympathies and support." Again, the use of *gallant* affirms a positive memory of the Confederacy, and the use of *entitled* reminded members of her community that they owed her for her sacrifices. When describing a "grand gala day" in May 1867, a different advertisement shared, "When it is remembered that the proceeds will be appropriated toward the relief of the distressed widows and orphans of the Lost Cause, no other incentive should be necessary to draw together thousands of our people." Supporting Confederate widows was incentive enough, according to this Memphis, Tennessee, paper.[6]

Widows even used their standing when negotiating housing arrangements. "A respectable widow (relict of a Confederate Soldier) of small means, occupying one large room, wishes to take a lady into the house with her for companionship, and to lessen her expenses. No objection to one child," wrote one Tennessee widow in her search for a roommate. Similarly, an 1868 advertisement in the *Alexandria Gazette* read, "Attention is called to the advertisement of Mrs. Gray, in to-day's Gazette. The widow of a Confederate soldier, Mrs. G. has come among us to earn a livelihood, and has opened a first-class boarding house. The table is unsurpassed, the house is well and comfortably kept, and the terms moderate." This woman had enough money to maintain a home, but even so, she needed work to sustain herself. Her widowhood justified her foray into the public sphere and the opening of her home as a boardinghouse.[7]

Even those who were not widows recognized the potential power in the social standing of Confederate widowhood and used it to their advantage. In one 1866 scandal, a woman claimed to have an original signature of George Washington. "She represented herself as the widow of a confederate officer on her way back from Europe and in great need," West Virginia's *Wheeling Daily Intelligencer* reported. In the letters she mailed, the fraud attempted

A FEMALE SWINDLER.—A person with the address and appearance of a lady has recently been in
the habit of stopping persons on King-street and
begging them for assistance for a friend, the widow
of a Confederate soldier. She first asks directions
for some place in the city, and after she has succeeded in engaging the attention of the person addressed,
she commences to beg. Some ladies offered, a day
or two ago, to accompany her to the residence of her
distressed friend, and she became greatly offended
and left them immediately.

"A Female Swindler," *Charleston Daily News*, January 18, 1869.
Image courtesy University of South Carolina Libraries Digital Collections.

to have twenty-five dollars sent to her. "Autograph collectors should be on
their guard against frauds like this," the article concluded. Another "female
swindler" would stop people on the street, "begging them for assistance for
a friend, the widow of a Confederate soldier." Once she had their attention
and sympathy, she would proceed to beg. With all the language of Confederate society owing a debt to its widows, it is not surprising that others might
attempt to use this moniker for their own financial gain.[8]

Children added additional responsibility to the struggles of poverty and
looming starvation of many Confederate widows. In October 1868, one particularly heart-wrenching newspaper notice began with the title "Two Little
Girls Offered for Adoption." The notice ran for three consecutive days. "A
very respectable lady of Southern birth, the widow of a Confederate soldier,
being in destitute circumstances, offers for adoption her two little daughters,
one seven and the other eleven years of age." Necessity induced her to make
this sacrifice, as the notice calls for a respectable family to support her. After
eleven years of motherhood, she could find no other way to move forward.
As a Confederate widow, she hoped someone would come to her assistance.[9]

This widow was not alone in her plight. One orphans' home, run by the
Methodist Episcopal Church, South, in Georgia, showed a dire situation.
"The Home was quickly crowded to overflowing," a newspaper reported.
It was unable to welcome more children due to lack of space and unable to
create more space due to lack of money. "It would grieve you, Messrs. Edi-
tors, and your thousands of readers, to hear widowed Confederate mothers

in their tearful appears on behalf of their homeless and destitute children." The author requested more money to support the home. What is notable here is that these children still had a living parent, a mother, and yet found themselves in a home such as this because she could not financially provide. Stories such as this reveal the tragic and desperate situation many Confederate widows found themselves in after the war.[10]

Some poor Confederate widows did keep their children with them, only to meet tragedy a different way. In Milton County, Georgia, there was a "poor but industrious widow of a Confederate soldier; like many of that class, she had a hard struggle to keep want from her door and raise her orphan children." She had two little boys. One day, they went to the millpond to bathe. Later, a man noticed the clothes of the boys on the bank but no children. He became alarmed, gathering neighbors to help find the young boys. They searched in vain, ultimately finding the two bodies at the bottom of a stream, next to each other. The paper reported, "It is supposed that one of them got into deep water and the other went to his assistance and both sank down to a watery grave." The report concluded by returning to the widow, hoping that God would "sustain the distressed mother in this sore calamity." For this widow, who lost a husband in the war, then two children while struggling to support them, there were likely no words that could bring comfort.[11]

And yet while widows struggled with these kinds of financial strains and emotional wounds after the war, stone monuments rose across the former Confederacy. Some considered this to be utter foolishness. "A sensible Virginian suggests that marble monuments to the Confederate dead will not feed starving Confederate widows and orphans," reported North Carolina's *Carolina Watchman* in July 1867. Another author, from South Carolina, agreed, arguing that Southern communities must support widows, not monuments. "The South owes a deep debt of gratitude to the soldiery that maintained her cause in the Confederate struggle. And we would ask in what better way than *this* could that debt be in part discharged?" the author asked. The "this" he referred to was a home for Confederate widows. If soldiers could be consulted from the grave, he believed they would not want prestige or eulogies; they would want this home for widows. "Better indeed than any eulogium—better than costly monument—better than starry-pointing pyramid is the Home," he concluded.[12]

"Remember the Living," urged another newspaper in Columbia, South Carolina, in June 1866. The lengthy article described a letter received from an "accomplished widow of a gallant officer," who lacked both food and clothing. Her husband was a gentleman, by birth and education, and a man of ample

Beautiful Tributes Were Paid to Her

means before the war. "And yet since his death his widow and children have been reduced to such terrible straits that his widow was forced to appeal to us for assistance. We do not mention this as an isolated case," revealed the article. Famine stood "like a wolf" at the doors of these Confederate widows. Like in the previous articles, the attention shifted to the present project of honoring the dead. "We trust that the work of decorating and honoring the graves of the dead will go on; but the noblest tribute which we can pay the memory of a dead soldier is to take care of those desolate loved ones. . . . Let us not commit the melancholy error of expending all our sympathies upon those whose quiet slumbers no earthly honors can disturb," the paper argued. Financially caring for the living was the best way to honor these soldiers, not placing flowers on their graves. It would be an error to forget the living while memorializing the dead, they argued.[13]

Other community leaders, such as Rev. Charles Wallace Howard, offered more extensive arguments against expensive memorialization efforts. "When our poorer soldiers enlisted," he said in an address in Charleston, South Carolina, "we told them if they fell the survivors would take care of their families. It was a promise carrying with it the sanctity of an oath. Have we kept it? Do we remember that the widows of hundreds of these brave men are now suffering from want of the common necessaries of life, pinched with hunger and cold?" Howard believed communities had not remembered these widows. They failed to uphold the promises made to the Confederate soldiers. Howard then turned to the actions taken by the former Confederacy. "Inscriptions on coin and monumental marble have sometimes a great value. We have erected monuments to the Confederate dead," he said. That sentiment was noble, he admitted, but he bluntly concluded, "The dead can wait. They rest quietly in the cold grave; that grave will become no colder." But the living, he argued, the living widows of these men, could not wait. Hunger and vice threatened widows of the Confederacy. The Charleston home for widows and orphans of Confederate soldiers needed financial support, and it needed it now. This was more important than the memorialization efforts.[14]

For some men, widows were not more important than monuments but were monuments to the cause themselves. Gen. Thomas "Tex" L. Rosser gave remarks at a church before a large assembly of people in Richmond, Virginia, on January 17, 1867. "We are entirely at the mercy of the conquerors, in whose hands is our fate, and who, instead of being magnanimous, are bitterly oppressive," he began and received much applause. Rosser wished he had died on the battlefield instead of living through the postwar era. "But if we could ask the brave men who died for us what they would require, they would say, 'give our wives and our children bread.'" They did not want monuments or eulogies but financial support for their wives. "The cause lives," Rosser argued, not in the men who died but in "the noble women and children who have lost husbands and fathers." Gen. Henry A. Wise spoke next, building on these themes. "What evidence have we that the cause has died out?" he asked, before answering his own question. "When we see widows wail or hear an orphan cry, I feel then the cause has indeed died out. If you let one of them wail, you may well say the cause is dead." Here, widows and the late Confederacy are one. Here, widows represent the war, and the Confederate cause, itself. "Leave the noble memorials you have begun which are only vanity. The Confederate dead all, all sleep well, thank God," Wise continued in front of the crowd, before drawing their attention back to the widows and again calling for financial support. For these two Confederate officers, this was how the cause could live on, through its widows. Confederate widows, not Confederate monuments, represented the late Confederacy.[15]

But in spite of this argument, and these stories of financial and emotional woe, monuments continued to rise, and a larger political project was underfoot. Former Confederate leaders and politicians continued to call for unity from white Southerners and continued to call for emotional support for the cause by its widows. In one speech, Maj. Gen. Henry R. Jackson said to veterans in Georgia, "The world has been told that the people of the South made war to perpetuate African slavery. This is false." He instead shifted the focus to a Confederacy "red with the blood of Confederate heroes, moist with the tears of Confederate widows and orphans." The Confederate heroes had done their part by dying, but the Confederate widows needed to continue to play their part, in mourning, to uphold this image.[16]

Just like during the war, in Reconstruction newspapers continued to publish stories of widows who championed the late Confederacy. For example, a young man moved from Massachusetts to Atlanta to become a schoolteacher for formerly enslaved people. "He had casually made the acquaintance of a Southern lady of two score and ten, whose husband had fallen under the Confederate flag, leaving her a widow of handsome estate," an article described. The Confederate widow informed the schoolteacher, in front of a large number of people, "that she'd rather be buried alive than marry a Yankee." The man, completely humiliated, returned to Boston, and the paper concluded that this "one occasion especially convinced us that the lava of secession still burned in the Southern bosom." This was February 1866. For elite white widows like this one, who had the time, emotional energy, and

Beautiful Tributes Were Paid to Her

Richmond women, in mourning veils, walking to receive government
rations. One woman says, "Don't you think that Yankee must feel
like shrinking into his boots before such high-toned Southern ladies
as we!" Sketched by A. R. Waud, *Harper's Weekly*, June 3, 1865.
Image courtesy Library of Congress, Washington, D.C.

financial ability to play a political role championing the former Confederacy,
there lay a possibility to gain an almost celebrity status.[17]

Some widows engaged in the memorialization project by writing memoirs and biographies of their late husbands. In this way, they shaped their
husbands' legacies while also championing their belief in the legitimacy of
the Confederate cause. Doing so brought both financial support and the adoration of thousands. An infamous example would be the work of Mary Anna
Jackson. In 1892, she dedicated *Life and Letters of General Thomas J. Jackson* to
his grandchildren, with the hope that he might be an example to them. But by
publishing this account, rather than simply handing it to them, her intention
was also to share her recollections of her husband with the world. This was
not a project Anna could have attempted during the war. In the preface, she
explained that in her initial years of mourning, "the shadow over my life was
so deep, and all that concerned him was so sacred, that I could not consent

to lift the veil to the public gaze." But time had eased her sorrow. Filled with personal anecdotes and reflections, this book shared intimate details about her husband, subtly reminding her audience that she knew General Jackson best. She was his widow, an identity that loomed even larger as the years passed, as fewer wives, widows, soldiers, and officers remained. When she republished it, with additions, in 1895, the new title reflected her identity: *Memoirs of Stonewall Jackson, by His Widow*. The war had taken his life, but the cause was worth it, and she would mourn her husband evermore. Veterans adored her, inviting her to reunions and events across the South.[18]

Confederate widows, in particular, could connect with this famous widow. In 1863, Anna became a thirty-one-year-old widow with a five-month-old baby. Her elite status and officer husband contributed to her initial prominence. Numerous Southern women, particularly widows, clipped newspaper articles about Anna and her "hero-husband," as Anna called him, pasting the clippings into their scrapbooks. After the war, Anna remained one of the most popular women associated with the former Confederacy, in part because of the way she polished the image of Thomas "Stonewall" Jackson. In addition to writing about him, she donated his things to the newly established Confederate Museum, sent relics to Confederate bazaars throughout the South, attended dozens of veterans' reunions, and authorized numerous biographies before writing her own. In writing her memoirs, she explained, "It has been my aim, up to this period to keep myself in the background as much as possible; but in what follows, my own life is so bound up with that of my husband that the reader will have to pardon so much of self as must necessarily be introduced." The book ends with seventeen tributes to her husband, which she offers as "evidences of the love and veneration in which his name and memory are enshrined in the hearts of his countrymen," even decades after his death. This was a man worth venerating, she argued. Anna would die in 1915, at the age of eighty-three, after a lifetime of public mourning.[19]

The widows of well-known officers were not the only ones who penned memoirs and biographies; other widows felt inclined to record their stories for future generations. In 1921, Eliza Jane Kendrick Lewis Walker finished her memoirs. Her twenty-year-old husband had been a recent graduate of the University of Georgia when he had marched off from Russell County, Alabama, to war more than five decades earlier. One day, a sheet of pale blue paper arrived at her home, with penciled words from her husband. Noticing every detail, she remarked that her husband had written the note with a hand that must have been very weak. "My darling wife," he began, "I am getting along just as well as I could." He assured her that he would be up in a day or two, that many were ill, but he received good care. Concerned for his wife's emotional well-being, he cautioned Eliza, "Don't be distressed," and promised her that a "telegraph will be resorted to when I get low down." Eliza recalled that the letter had scarcely reached her when she suddenly heard the clatter of a horse at twilight. "Instinctively I knew that the mission of that rider would be over when he saw me," she wrote. Eliza received the alarming telegram and left immediately by carriage and train, trying to get to her husband. She made it, but three days after she arrived, her husband was in a plain pine coffin. "If only the graves could have given up their dead," she lamented after the war when reflecting upon the loss of the Confederacy.[20]

Eliza's daughter transcribed the entire manuscript just a few years after Eliza finished it. "As I now write, the days that follow seem dim to me," Eliza had admitted, "but can bear witness that Lincoln's proclamation, freeing the slaves, seemed nothing in comparison to the anguish in the homes from here had gone forth the soldiers of the Confederacy, thousands never to return." For Eliza, the dead, including her husband, were more important than the political project of abolition, or so she claimed after the war. She subtly suggested that this was not the cause of her war, as she saw it in the 1920s. By writing these memoirs, she again reaffirmed the worth of her late husband and the value of his bravery and took part in the construction of a larger Lost Cause narrative.[21]

Other elite, wealthy widows honored their late husbands not with writing but with action. Flora Cooke Stuart is another elite woman who found an identity in war widowhood, wearing mourning attire for fifty-nine years. Like many families, the Stuart family divided during the war; Flora's father remained in the U.S. Army, while her husband joined the Confederacy. Flora struggled emotionally with this, and ultimately she and her husband would rename their son, who had been originally named after her father. Flora traveled with her husband for much of the war and wrestled greatly with grief when their daughter died of typhoid fever in November 1862. Flora wore mourning attire, honoring this child, until April 1864. The following month, she received a telegram informing her that her husband, J. E. B. Stuart, had been wounded at the Battle of Yellow Tavern in Virginia. She immediately went to see him, but she was too late by just a few hours. The *Richmond Whig* reported that she "plunged into the greatest grief." For the rest of her life, she preferred to be called Mrs. General Stuart and worked as an educator for young women. She did not write a memoir for the public, but she did participate in the many projects commemorating her late husband. In June 1888, Flora returned to the battlefield where her husband received his mortal wound and stood before a crowd, watching as the veil fell away from the monument marking the spot. In 1907, Flora again stood before a large crowd of veterans, this time with her granddaughter, as the Veteran Cavalry Association of the Army of Northern Virginia dedicated a monument to her husband in Richmond. Flora kept mementos from her husband around her home and publicly worked with a number of memorial groups; in 1905, she served as the honorary president of the Virginia Division and the General Division of the United Daughters of the Confederacy. She raised her children in the South, as her husband had requested, and was buried beside him in Hollywood Cemetery in Richmond. Veterans approved of her actions and in return granted her public commendations and platforms.[22]

Eliza Maney Cook is yet another officer's wife who stood on stages as a widow of the Confederacy. She had married Ed C. Cook, a lawyer and member of the Tennessee legislature, in 1861; he died at the Battle of Culps Farm in Georgia in 1864. "God bless you and home and spare me to see you again in health is my comfort prayer. Write often," Ed asked approximately a month before his death. After the war, Eliza would not remarry and would turn to rebuilding a life for her infant son, named after his late father. The men who fought with Eliza's husband continued to hold her in high esteem, inviting her to reunions in the decades after the war. "It is most proper that the widow of the brave, gallant chivalrous Col. Ed Cook should grace our reunion with her presence on the 18th inst and we therefore beg you to come," began one such invitation. "The gallant dead of our state are our pride and we delight to do them honor. Among the many from Williamson who sacrificed themselves in the 'Lost Cause' none achieved a more undying fame and certainly no one would be more welcome than his dearly loved wife," they assured Eliza. When she sent him to war, she sent him with a battle flag made from her wedding dress. In his death, she remained publicly wedded to his memory, achieving an "undying fame" as his widow. Six decades may have passed, but she was still lauded as the good wife, then the good widow, who accepted his sacrifice to the Confederacy.[23]

Elite widows' devotion to memorial activities and veteran organizations was unique when compared with the experiences of many other more impoverished war widows. In May 1865, women in Winchester, Virginia, began to gather the scattered dead and inter them in a single graveyard. This group of women formed the first LMA, and by the end of 1866, the former Confederacy contained more than seventy similar organizations. Historian Caroline Janney argued that women who physically supported the war, through acts such as sewing battle flags and volunteering in hospitals, joined LMAs to "continue to express their Confederate patriotism" and "deploy gender in the interest of Confederate politics." By honoring the soldiers of the Confederate nation, women claimed a right to mourn the dead and began "to engage in civic life as never before." As women, the threat they posed to the U.S. government and Southern white patriarchy appeared minimal in the years immediately following the war. Janney concluded that LMAs "were responsible for remaking military defeat into a political, social, and cultural victory for the white South."[24]

But the most active members of the LMAs, and the United Daughters of the Confederacy (UDC) to come, tended to be married women or women widowed after the war, not widows who lost husbands during the actual war. The mourning of those participating in LMAs was often more impersonal or of a distant connection. They mourned the loss of members of their community, not necessarily direct kin relations. And they especially mourned the Confederacy's loss and the loss of their cause. For example, in Virginia, the women who participated in LMAs overwhelmingly did not lose male relatives in the war. So why did war widows choose not to participate in these associations, particularly those of middle and working classes? Perhaps it was too painful to honor a cause that killed their husbands. More likely, given the other evidence, perhaps war widows were simply too busy caring for young babies and running households. Perhaps the members of LMAs unconsciously felt that they needed to prove their commitment to the cause since their families remained intact. After all, members of LMAs could decorate a grave or organize a monument dedication, but at the end of the ceremony, they returned home to their fathers, brothers, and husbands, many of whom had not served in the Confederacy's military. Alternatively, many widows did not have the money or the time to attend memorialization events. They had already proven themselves. They did not need to decorate miscellaneous graves; they already had a grave to decorate. And on at least one occasion, the political motivations of the LMAs overshadowed the desires of a grieving family. Jubal A. Early, a veteran general of the Confederacy, accused members of the Lexington group "of taking advantage of Mary Lee's grief to secure the burial" of Robert E. Lee, even as Early "continually pressured the widow to reinter her husband's remains in Richmond." White women did not seamlessly work together to create a Lost Cause ideology.[25]

But even so, a handful of elite widows did devote their lives to public mourning and, in doing so, received a tremendous amount of social, cultural, and financial acclaim. Emilie Todd Helm, the widow of Confederate brigadier general Benjamin Hardin Helm and little sister of Mary Todd Lincoln, was

"Hollywood Cemetery, Richmond, Virginia—Decorating the graves of the rebel soldiers." Sketched by W. L. Sheppard, *Harper's Weekly*, May 31, 1867. *Image courtesy Library of Congress, Washington, D.C.*

a widow who performed almost perfectly and, in doing so, made a postwar career as a Confederate widow. While her quick tongue, famous family, and stint as a visitor in the Civil War White House make her a fascinating figure, Emilie's experience as a young widow in a war-torn Confederacy is a broadly typical example of an elite Confederate widow. "Mother" to her husband's "Orphan Brigade," organizer for the UDC, author of unpublished Lost Cause fiction, and unswerving puffer of her husband's memory, Emilie achieved a kind of professional fame as a widow—and through her we can more clearly see the society that created her role, built her stage, and applauded her performances. Seven years married, she would be for almost seventy years the public widow of Benjamin Hardin Helm. She is worth an extended case study because suffering like hers would be rewarded, not merely by her region but, ironically, by her nation, which found room not only to pity and thank her for her sacrifice but also to erect on the foundation of such Southern suffering a narrative of *national* reconciliation.

A lifeless slip of paper had delivered the news. "Atlanta, Ga.," the telegram read. "Mrs. General Helm is in Griffin. Find her and send her up in train today. The General is dead." After receiving the message, Emilie felt so

Beautiful Tributes Were Paid to Her

heartbroken that, she recalled, the "days and weeks after I scarcely remember at all." She was a twenty-six-year-old mother of three children under the age of six. Eighteen months later, lingering wartime hostilities also made a widow of Emilie's older sister, Mary Todd Lincoln. Mary's husband famously died in April 1865, when an actor slipped behind him in a theater, raised a gun, and pulled the trigger. In the crowded back room of a boardinghouse, Mary's heart broke before a hushed assembly as she wailed for her husband to "take her with him."[26]

The Todd sisters were but two of 200,000 white women widowed by the war. Mary, somewhat infamously, became a diva of grief, inconsolable and insufferable after the war. Unlike Mary, as a widow Emilie did not retreat to the gloomy confines of her mind or home; she remained active in her community and state. Her papers are filled with invitations and announcements. She joined bustling crowds in 1883 for the gubernatorial inauguration, continuously crisscrossed Kentucky visiting friends, and often stayed with extended family. She joined clubs, such as the Filson Club, to "share in gathering, from original sources, historic matter relating to Kentucky." And Emilie remained an integral part of Elizabethtown, Kentucky, in her position as postmistress. On January 14, 1891, the *Pittsburg Dispatch* reported that Emilie, the "widow of a Confederate General," was reappointed for yet another term, her third. Newspapers across the nation reported on her movements, announcing her arrival to various locales. In July 1895, she ran unsuccessfully for state librarian, but still the newspapers heaped praise upon her. "Mrs. Emily Todd Helm, the late postmaster of Elizabethtown and widow of the gallant leader of the Orphan Brigade," reported a paper in Stanford, Kentucky, "is the latest entry and we will wager dollars to doughnuts that in the final count the excellent and deserving lady will be there or thereabouts." As time went on, when newspapers reported on Emilie's activities, it seemed less important that she was Helm's widow, specifically, and more important that she was a Confederate widow, generally. Newspapers that stopped using his name continued to identify Emilie as a Confederate widow. As a widow of the Confederacy and not of a specific man, she had broader representative appeal, especially as death thinned the aging ranks of Confederate veterans and widows.[27]

Though many in the public loved Emilie, her late husband's Orphan Brigade nearly worshiped her. During the war, she had cared for, camped with, and verbally defended the men. In 1863, her husband not yet two months dead, she wrote a letter to Cdr. John C. Breckinridge after some Kentuckians felt hurt by his reported remark that their Orphan Brigade "was one of the worst and but a band of thieves and robbers." He assured her that "I never uttered such language." After the war, soldier George W. Quarles, who hoped to become the deputy warden of his county, asked for Emilie's aid and influence. He did not want others to know he solicited her support, he explained, so "write as though unsolicited and having known me through your husband." In addition to writing recommendations, Emilie also sent pictures of her husband to those who requested them, such as Frank Lyon, who promised, "I shall treasure it very highly and place it among my collection of those other heroes who went down in the lost cause." In 1868, Edwin Porter Thompson approached Emilie to gather information about her husband for his history of the Orphan Brigade, feeling it a duty to communicate with her, vowing that "when I get a copy of the General's biography, I will take time to transcribe and send you a copy for examination and approval, or suggestions." He hoped to please her in his commemoration efforts. Additionally, the Elizabethtown Volunteers company changed its name to the Helm Guards, not in honor of her husband but "in honor of Mrs. E. T. Helm, the widow of the late General Hardin Helm."[28]

Veterans formally invited Emilie to reunions of the Orphan Brigade, which began in 1882. While her status as the widow of their general earned her a place on the invitation list, her relationship with the brigade caused men to genuinely desire her attendance, for she was "especially invited." In 1884, the reunion committee not only consulted Emilie about its plans to move Benjamin's remains but forwarded the program for her for approval or amendment. The chaplain wrote to Emilie for advice about the eulogy, because he wanted the eulogy "to be precisely what will gratify you." He urged her to employ her ready pen and tell him "frankly and fully what manner of allusion I should make to you and the dear little fatherless children who were just entwined about my heart near twenty-one years ago." At a later reunion, Emilie announced her desire to shake hands with every member of the command, and the veterans, in turn, voted to bestow on her the title "Mother of the Brigade." In the 1920 reunion outside of Paris, Kentucky, Emilie's own portrait "appeared on the badges of red, white and blue, worn by the veterans of the Brigade," and tributes were paid to her, not her husband. As a part of the brigade's yearly ritual, Emilie symbolized all that the veterans hoped a wife and woman could be. Faithful to her husband and his cause decades after his death, her actions suggested that a Confederate soldier, and his cause, was worth the postwar hardships.[29]

Emilie also served in Kentucky's UDC. "We meet in session," she insisted, "not for the purpose of keeping alive the prejudices, acrimonious feeling and hatred of the past," but rather to "cherish the memory of our dead heroes, to devise ways and means to make their graves, to re-entomb as many of them as possible in their native state," and to "prevent a fake record of our heroes deeds being brought down as History." Emilie called for a history without passion and prejudice for Kentucky's schools. Union veterans might not approve of her version of the truth, but Confederate veterans would. Emilie believed and repeatedly wrote that "the men of the South fought for a just cause and that in an unequal struggle they were the bravest of the brave." Histories that wrote of Southern men as rebels did not please Emilie. Kentucky's UDC grew rapidly and gained thousands of white middle- and upper-class members across the South, encouraging Emilie in what she believed to be a "sacred duty."[30]

To create her version of history, Emilie urged members to gather up letters and preserve all war relics of Confederate soldiers. She hoped "to perpetuate the glorious memories of the most unselfish devotion to home and country." Additionally, she called for women to conduct interviews with soldiers. Women should be gathering details from survivors, because they were the "noblest and bravest people that ever suffered." For her work with the UDC, a chapter was named after her husband. When the organization met in 1901 to decorate graves, "a life sized portrait of Gen. Ben Hardin Helm occupied a conspicuous place." Emilie thus continued to shape the memory of her husband, bringing recognition and honor to him decades after his death.[31]

The longer Emilie lived, the more organizations clamored for her attendance and participation. The Chickamauga Park Commissioners, the *Confederate Veteran Magazine*, and the *UDC Historian* all sought her. In addition to the yearly Kentucky reunions of the Orphan Brigade, Emilie was invited to reunions across the South. In 1898, the Louisiana division of the United Confederate Veterans encouraged her to attend their ceremonies and promised her "a seat upon the platform" and the opportunity to "make any remarks you may see fit." Despite the many invitations, Emilie remained closest with her husband's command. Forty years after her husband's death, she still served as a living representation of their general. A letter from her, even in the twentieth century, was, as one veteran put it in 1901, "like a message of approval from Gen Ben Hardin Helm."[32]

Emilie also devoted time to writing fictional and nonfictional accounts of the war and postwar era. While she would never become a published author, Emilie's pieces provide insight into her thoughts on racial tensions in the South. In one story, a widow was seemingly abandoned by her formerly enslaved nurse, who later discovered that the newly freed woman was washing clothes to support them. "Now Old Miss," said the Black woman in Emilie's narrative, "whar is [it] I got to go—I am gwine to stay right whear I is—my white chillen expects me to stay and tak car of you. . . . I aint gwine to leave you." The widow, "endeared to her by so many ties," believed the woman to be a member of the family and allowed her to remain "on her own terms." This happy slave narrative conformed to the Lost Cause themes developing throughout the South.[33]

Similarly, in a second story, Emilie described an African American woman who wanted "an occupation." "Walking over the white and melancholy snow," the piece began, "watching the clear yellow tones of the sunset as they faded into steely blue and slate gray haze I was accosted by a negro girl of about twenty years." The young woman, Jennie, asked for the white woman to sign her name to a piece of paper as a reference of Jennie's character. The white woman repeatedly asked what occupation she sought, and Jennie repeatedly replied, "Can't you see, I want an occupation!" unable to describe it further. They circled round and round in this conversation, until ultimately an African American man walked by and clarified that Jennie "wanted to sell things around." The story emphasizes the patience of a white woman and ignorance of a Black woman about the ways of the world, a theme that fit neatly into the stereotypes of the time.[34]

It is important to pause here and point out that there were exceptions to this racial project. In Mississippi, one Confederate widow was physically punished by the Ku Klux Klan in September 1869 for undermining their attempts to retain the racial order of the late Confederacy. The men visited the "widow of a confederate soldier, who had been teaching a colored Sabbath school, for which they took her out and beat her." The article reports that the Ku Klux Klan believed her conduct to be disgraceful. But even so, this widow was an exception, while Emilie fell much more fully within the standard racial beliefs of the era.[35]

As a living relic of the Todds, who had all passed away by the early 1900s, Emilie represented them and shaped how they would be remembered. Better yet, Emilie's siblings could not undermine or challenge her efforts from their graves. She worked tirelessly to salvage the image of her sister Mary, who passed away in 1882. In 1898, the St. Paul Daily Globe reported that Emilie denied there had ever been two marriage ceremonies arranged for Mary and Abraham and rejected "the existence of that inharmony to which so many allusions have been made." The paper concluded, "It would be better for the world to accept these statements, bury rank gossip in the dark pit in which it belongs and henceforth regard Mrs. Lincoln only as the honorable and honored helpmeet of the greatest American of the century." Of course, as Emilie knew, Abraham and Mary had two engagements (but the first ended prior to choosing a wedding date) and marital discord, but this was not the image of the Todds or the Lincolns that Emilie wanted remembered.[36]

While Emilie strove to shape the memory of the Todds, another project was taking place. In 1909, "while ten thousand people stood in reverence with bared heads . . . a veiling of the stars and stripes fell gracefully away" to reveal a statue of Abraham Lincoln in Hodgenville, Kentucky. One paper reported that the "canopy that hid the statue from view was drawn away by the hand of Mrs. Ben Hardin Helm, a sister to the wife of Lincoln, and cheer after cheer went up." "Your Minnie bullets have made us what we are," Emilie had written bitterly to Abraham in the final years of the war. Now, she honored him before a crowd of 10,000 Americans, as a widow of the war and nation, not simply of the South. Instead of rehashing the political divisions of the Todd family, reporters instead emphasized their familial ties. It was as Emilie had written, "We should revive no memories that may embitter the future." To the nation, the reunification of the Todd family represented the reunification of white America, and Emilie's suffering had redeemed them all. Union widows had lost husbands but won a war; Confederate widows had lost it all. If a Confederate woman could honor the man responsible for the death of her husband and two brothers, could not the nation also become one again?[37]

The Civil War existed as a transformative force in many women's lives, but this was especially true for widows. Widows like Emilie did not seamlessly work together with impoverished widows to create a Lost Cause ideology. The majority of widows struggled significantly after the war, facing extreme poverty. These women did not lead the charge for memorialization; in fact, many argued that money should be given to them instead of memorialization. But they would largely be the ones forgotten while others, such as Emilie, had a specific role to play—bound not merely to patriarchy but to nationalism, first to Confederate nationalism and then to national reconciliation. Through Emilie, we see how the emotional, human experience of losing a husband could be channeled, contained, and reinvested. Through her loss she earned social capital, which she spent wisely, shaping the terms of reunification. Instead of an embarrassment, the Todd family became a sacrifice; instead of traitors, they became national heroes. Emilie herself became Southern pride and American patriotism personified in one little widow. She served as the unelected spokesperson of the Todds and a symbol of reunification, and as the years marched on Emilie increasingly became a living monument to the official American past. In short, she succeeded in doing what the Confederacy failed to do—she survived and shaped the nation, until her heart finally stopped on February 20, 1930, sixty-six years and five months after her husband's. "We ought not to grieve over anyone who has to live until they are feeble and unable to enjoy life," wrote Emilie, adding, "I hope every one will feel this if I live to be old." After devoting a lifetime to the cultural politics of mourning, this widow did not want anyone to grieve over her.[38]

Conclusion

Here she sat like a crow with hot taffeta to her wrists and buttoned
up to her chin, with not even a hint of lace or braid, not a jewel
except Ellen's onyx mourning brooch, watching tacky-looking
girls hanging on the arms of good-looking men. All because
Charles Hamilton had had the measles. He didn't even die in a
fine glow of gallantry in battle, so she could brag about him.

Margaret Mitchell, Gone with the Wind

In 1939, Scarlett O'Hara waltzed across the silver screen and flirted her way
into American hearts. When her first husband died, she was just seventeen
years old and believed that she was far too young to be a widow, for as she
said in the book, "widows should be old—so terribly old they didn't want
to dance and flirt and be admired." But the Civil War changed lives, even fictional ones. Scarlett's mother cautioned her to "never chatter vivaciously" and
always "wear hideous black dresses without even a touch of braid to enliven
them." Scarlett felt trapped, forced to "go on making a pretense of enthusiasm
and pride in the Cause which she could not feel, acting out her part of the
widow of a Confederate officer who bears her grief bravely, whose heart is
in the grave, who feels that her husband's death meant nothing if it aided the
Cause to triumph." Of all the mourning requirements, to Scarlett the most
dreadful of all was the expectation that she "could in no way indicate an interest in the company of gentlemen." Under the weight of these expectations,

Scarlett discovered "how easily a widow might get herself talked about" and concluded that "widows might as well be dead."[1]

Sixty years later, a real-life widow, Alberta S. Martin, captured the attention of millions of Americans as "the Oldest Living Confederate Widow." With a "yeah, reckon so," Alberta had kissed William Jasper Martin and married him. The year was 1927. William was eighty-one years old and a Confederate veteran. She was twenty-one. Decades later, when asked about her unusual marriage, Alberta explained that it was "better to be an old man's darlin' than a young man's slave." In 1996, Dr. Kenneth Chancey, a member of the Sons of the Confederacy, discovered the elderly Alberta nestled in Elba, Alabama. Poverty and obscurity may have haunted her past but becoming the belle of Confederate history buffs changed her life. "I ain't the oldest livin' Confederate widow," she exclaimed, "I'm the onliest one. The last of the livin'." She attended conventions, reenactments, and rallies across the South dressed in the colors of the late Confederate flag. The Alabama governor's office bestowed on Alberta the title of honorary lieutenant colonel aide-de-camp in the state militia, while another Confederate group named her an honorary cannoneer. Over ninety years of age, she laughed, "And I ain't never shot a peashooter!" Alberta became the matriarch of a large family and was surrounded by people who would hold her hand, "crying and thinking about their family that suffered greatly in the past." She would play this part even in death. When Alberta died on May 31, 2004, Memorial Day, planning began for an elaborate funeral. Men marched in Confederate uniforms, her casket was draped in a Rebel flag, and people gathered to watch the half-mile parade.[2]

When the term *Confederate widow* is typed into an internet search, these women appear. One old, one young, both harkening back to an era lost. As icons, both Scarlett and Alberta represent a much larger population of women, whose contemporaries, in turn, expected them to be icons. Margaret Mitchell produced a piece of fantasy and yet, when it comes to widowhood, she unearthed something painfully real. Some young widows, like the fictional Scarlett, felt they had given enough to the cause and refused to be buried with it. The Confederacy was simply asking for too much—too much from the human heart. Alberta, as the last Confederate widow, was neither young nor beautiful like Scarlett but similarly lived as a spectacle, a stately ruin of the Confederacy. Civil War buffs could visit with her for a moment or an afternoon, but at the end of their tour, they returned home safely, family intact. She could be gazed upon, but they did not themselves have to crumble. Cultural phenomena like Scarlett and Alberta have shaped the image and legend of the Confederate widow, revealing both the strength of the patriarchy and the power of performance.[3]

We see the takeaways of *Love and Duty*—that women mourned differently, that emotional expressions had political implications, and that war created a stage upon which widows could be seen and heard—hold true even in these two widows' lives decades later. But the unifying argument of this book—that the emotional expressions of widows carried new political meaning amid the crisis of war and the battle to establish the Confederacy's legitimacy—begs the question of why. Why was Scarlett not written differently? If it was so essential for widows to invest in the emotional regime of the Confederacy, why then is Scarlett not an Emilie Todd Helm or a Georgia Page King? The answer, I believe, lies in the timing. When author Margaret Mitchell turned to craft the experience of Confederate widowhood in her novel, she did not turn to the same widows that nineteenth-century politicians, newspapers, ministers, and veterans held up as exemplary. Mitchell did not turn to those who bolstered the Confederacy in word and action through their mourning. She did not turn to them, in part, because she did not have to. By the 1930s, the late Confederacy no longer needed its widows to invest their emotional support and legitimize the Confederate cause, because by this time, that was a project already won. The Lost Cause, with all its heroes, monuments, myths, and textbooks, had succeeded in establishing the late Confederacy as just and honorable in white popular culture. The majority of the white South already believed it.

Mitchell remembered growing up perched "on the bony knees of veterans and the fat slippery laps of great aunts," listening to their stories of the American Civil War. "I heard so much when I was little about the fighting and the hard times after the war that . . . I was about ten years old before I learned the war hadn't ended shortly before I was born," she would later recall. Born on November 8, 1900, Mitchell grew up in Atlanta, among literal ruins of the conflict. "Sherman's sentinels," lone chimneys that rose above ruins of wooden homes, captured her imagination. But more than the landscape of her backyard, people inspired Mitchell. As she grew older, she spent her leisure time riding horses with Confederate veterans. In 1926, when an ankle injury limited her mobility, twenty-six-year-old Mitchell began work on what would become *Gone with the Wind*. To supplement what she had learned about the war from the people she knew, she read old diaries, newspapers, and her grandparents' letters. Mitchell wanted her account of the Civil War to be "air tight so that no grey bearded vet [can] rise up to shake his cane at me and say, 'But I know better.'" On June 30, 1936, more than a decade after beginning the project, the book was released. American readers purchased it in droves, breaking publishing records. In six months, more than 1 million copies sold. "A first novel does well if it sells five thousand copies in a lifetime," wrote one *New York Sun* reviewer to emphasize the popularity of this work. The novel won the American Booksellers Association's National Book Award for Most Distinguished Novel in 1936 and the Pulitzer Prize for Fiction in 1937. Mitchell could hardly believe her success, confessing, "I invited my husband to pinch me so often that he now refuses, saying the black and blue spots on a new author do not look well and may, justifiably, lead to talk."[4]

Mitchell's starring character, Scarlett O'Hara, a young, demanding, and spoiled Southern belle, was hardened and transformed by the war. Scarlett played various roles throughout her life, including that of a flirty war widow. When Scarlett's first husband died of disease while off fighting for the Confederacy, she believed she was far too young to be a widow, for "oh, it wasn't fair that she should have to sit here primly and be the acme of widowed dignity and propriety when she was only seventeen." Mourning customs irritated Scarlett, "but she was a widow and she had to watch her behavior." She hated it all, from the "grave and aloof" behavior to the veil that "had to reach her knees." The worst part, of course, was that she could no longer be doted upon by potential suitors. "Oh, yes, thought Scarlett, drearily, some widows do remarry eventually, when they are old and stringy. Though Heaven knows how they manage it, with their neighbors watching." And watch they did, especially the young Scarlett.[5]

With the encouragement of Rhett Butler, Scarlett decided to dance. "I have always thought," Rhett shared with her, "that the system of mourning, of immuring women in crepe for the rest of their lives and forbidding them normal enjoyment is just as barbarous as the Hindu suttee." He explained the custom to Scarlett, of Indian wives climbing on the funeral pyres of their deceased husbands, to burn with the body, as an alternative to life as a widow. "How dreadful," remarked Scarlett, to which Rhett replied, "Personally, I think suttee much more merciful than our charming Southern custom of burying widows alive!" Scarlett balked, and Rhett continued, "How closely women clutch the very chains that bind them." Ultimately, Scarlett danced the night away with him. The following morning she declared to her family, "I'm tired of sitting at home and I'm not going to do it any longer. If they all talked about me last night, then my reputation is already gone and it won't matter what else they say." Of course, when her mother's letter expressing concern about Scarlett's conduct arrived, and her father visited to share that "everybody knows of our disgrace," she more fully realized the consequences of her actions. Even so, traditional widowhood did not suit Scarlett, for she, like thousands of other women in their teens and twenties, was not a traditional widow.[6]

The exact inspiration for Scarlett's widowhood is unknown. It is possible this portrayal was inspired by Mitchell's conversations with the elderly veterans and neighbors who lived through the conflict. Historian Darden Asbury Pyron, for example, writes, "When Mitchell moved to 179 Jackson Street, nothing separated their yard from the oak-dotted property of the Captain's widow." It is likely that Mitchell gleaned stories from women such as this, but as Mitchell did not record these conversations, we will likely never know how this influenced her take on war widowhood. Shortly after publishing her book, Mitchell wrote, "If the novel has a theme, the theme is that of survival." Perhaps Scarlett's actions as a widow represented coping mechanisms Mitchell could relate to through hardships and heartbreak. "What makes some people come through catastrophes and others, apparently just as able, strong, and brave, go under? We've seen it in the present Depression," remarked Mitchell, while reflecting on her theme. "I don't know," she concluded. "I only know that the survivors used to call that quality 'gumption.' So I wrote about the people who had gumption and the people who didn't."[7]

Even before the formal release of the book, Mitchell's publisher began negotiations with Hollywood producers, who hoped to transform the novel into a movie. Though Mitchell did not want to assist in the writing of the screenplay, she did want to have some say in the final version, to be sure that the script did not include outrageous adjustments, like having "Scarlett seduce General Sherman." On July 30, 1936, just one month after the publication of *Gone with the Wind*, producer David O. Selznick acquired the screen rights. The adaptation closely followed Mitchell's text, and filming for the movie began and ended in 1939. Clark Gable quickly secured the part of Rhett Butler, and English actress Vivien Leigh eventually earned the role of Scarlett. While the choice surprised some, those who knew Leigh felt she could handle it. British director Victor Saville, when in Hollywood, called Leigh and said, "Vivien, I've just read a great story for the movies about the bitchiest of all bitches, and you're just the person to play the part."[8]

A highly anticipated film, the movie premiered in Atlanta on December 15, 1939. Georgia's governor Eurith D. Rivers declared the day a statewide holiday, while William B. Hartsfield, Atlanta's mayor, proclaimed a three-day festival in the city. "To Georgia it was like winning the battle of Atlanta 75 years late," reported *Time* magazine, adding, "Mayor Hartsfield urged every Atlanta woman and maid to put on hoop skirts and pantalets, appealed to every Atlanta male to don tight trousers and a beaver, sprout a goatee, side-burns and Kentucky colonel whiskers." Confederate flags flapped from "every building" and the Rebel yell echoed through the town. Notably absent from many of the events was Margaret Mitchell, who was described as shy. After the movie, "most of them [viewers] were dabbing their eyes, and for those who were not the impact of the picture was too powerful to talk about." After seeing the film, Mitchell remarked, "It was a great thing for Georgia to see the Confederates come back." Despite the film's success in Atlanta, some realized that "though delighted Georgians clapped, cheered, whistled and wept at the historical sequences, Northerners might not." Certainly, many African Americans were not pleased with the portrayal of enslaved people, including Malcolm X, who responded, "I was the only Negro in the theater [in Mason, Michigan], and when Butterfly McQueen went into her act, I felt like crawling under the rug." Even so, producer Selznick felt he had "a sure fire Rebel-rouser for the South, a sure fire love story for the rest of the country." He was right. Breaking box office records, the movie was also nominated for fifteen Academy Awards, winning eight of them, including a Best Actress in a Leading Role Oscar for Leigh.[9]

The movie mirrored Mitchell's version of Scarlett as an unconventional widow. Leigh became, as one reviewer wrote in 1939, "the very embodiment of the selfish, hoydenish, slant-eyed miss who tackled life with both claws and a creamy complexion, asked no odds of any one or anything—least of all her conscience." Perhaps one of the most memorable scenes from the film is Scarlett's direct challenge to the etiquette of the antebellum South. To raise money for the Confederate cause, men who wished to lead the opening dance with a lady were urged to bid for her. As he did in the book, in the movie Rhett bid $150 in gold for Scarlett, amid a number of gasps. "Mrs. Hamilton is in mourning," the auctioneer explained, urging him to make another choice. Rhett refused and the auctioneer informed him, "She will not consider it, sir." Gathering up her skirts, Scarlett exclaimed, "Oh yes I will!" soliciting another chorus of audible gasps. As they began to dance, Rhett smirked and said, "We've sort of shocked the Confederacy, Scarlett." "I don't care what you expect or what they think, I'm gonna dance and dance. Tonight I wouldn't mind dancing with Abe Lincoln himself," replied Scarlett. And dance and dance she did, her swirling black dress amid a mass of brightly colored costumes. A photograph of the scene appeared in *Life* magazine's visual spread entitled "High Spots in 'Gone with the Wind.'" In the following scene, Scarlett, still in her mourning attire, nearly kisses Rhett. Holding her face in his hands, he utters one of the most famous lines of the movie: "No,

I don't think I will kiss you. Although you need kissing badly. That's what's wrong with you. You should be kissed, and often, by someone who knows how." With lines like this, the defiant widow, in Scarlett, won out in popular culture.[10]

Though the majority of widows died off by the early twentieth century, long before the oldest living Confederate widow, Alberta Martin, died in 2004, Confederate widowhood never disappeared from the American cultural scene. Stories such as *Gone with the Wind*, more than materials in archives and libraries, shaped the way thousands of Americans imagined Confederate widowhood and the late Confederacy. As Scarlett, the South was not a threat but a spoiled girl stamping her feet, in need of a good kissing. As Alberta, the South was not a defiant or murderous Confederate slaveholder threatening to dissolve the Union but a cute little old lady from a nursing home, giggling with all who kissed her hand. They outlived the Confederacy in ways their husbands could not. And they offer a feminine representation of the white South, rendering it practically harmless, and almost humorous, once again.

Confederate widows, real and imagined, lost husbands but gained a tremendous amount of attention. For these women, reconstruction began not with the death of the Confederacy but with the death of a husband. And when the war finally came to a close, they did not seamlessly work together to create a Lost Cause ideology. The dynamic and diverse ways white Southern women mourned reveal a complicated relationship between emotional expressions and politics. Studying these experiences amplifies our understanding of how the white Southern household functioned during the crisis of war. Grief, and grieving rituals, could be simultaneously compliant and oppositional. And grief caused many to behave in unpredictable ways, not always in complete alignment with the dominant culture. Even so, widows gained social power through their loss and through their grief, which stood as valuable currencies in a stubbornly patriarchal society.

Acknowledgments

As you are now well aware, this is a book about death. It would be easy to slide into this darkness and sit in worlds of grief for far too long if it weren't for the people in my own life. Below is a long, winding, surely incomplete list of wonderful people.

My family has heard me talk about this project for far too many years. My parents, my parents-in-law, my siblings, my siblings-in-law, my extended family of all kinds—thank you. I could fill pages upon pages with all the ways I appreciate each of you and your support. My mother deserves extra appreciation, for joining me on early research trips, proofreading nearly every word I have ever written, and encouraging me each step of the way. James, we miss you.

When I was a student, the Department of History at the University of Georgia became such a home away from home that I decided to stay for three degrees—triple Dawg, as they say. Dillon Carroll, Kathleen Clark, Jim Cobb, Laura June Davis, Benjamin Ehlers, Andrew Fialka, Katie Fialka, Kylie Hulbert, Matt Hulbert, John Inscoe, Luke Manget, Sam McGuire, Leah Richier, Kathryn Tucker, Trae Welborn, and more, I appreciate the many conversations and classes. I took my first undergraduate history course with Steve Nash and have felt grateful for his mentorship ever since. Dave Thomson used to be just an office away. Now he is just a text away, a privilege I surely overuse. And Steve Berry once said kind things about my writing at an award ceremony, which I only half heard because I had a noisy toddler on my lap (and perhaps another beside me, I can't even remember at this point). Throughout this academic journey, he has been a steady and quiet encouragement. Thank you.

In a postdoctoral position at Virginia Tech, I found a helpful department of new mentors and colleagues. I benefited tremendously from conversations with Mark Barrow, Melanie Kiechle, Dan Thorp, and Peter Wallenstein. Paul Quigley (and family), thank you especially for the warm welcome in Virginia. From dinners to conferences to Civil War Weekend adventures, we are lucky to have you in our lives.

Academic colleagues and friends continue to be a steady support system. I have workshopped and conferenced this project in so many pieces, and I cannot fully acknowledge my deep gratitude for co-panelists, chairs, and commentators. The Society of Civil War Historians, Southern Association for Women Historians, Southern Historical Association, and St. George Tucker Society are particularly appreciated. Of course, organizations are only as good as the scholars within them, and here, my cup truly runs over. Caroline Janney's support and wisdom helped shape this book in many ways, and I am inspired by her. Lauren Thompson continues to encourage me with her generous spirit. Comments and discussions with Judkin Browning, Catherine Clinton, Mandy Cooper, Melissa DeVelvis, Niels Eichhorn, Kristen Epps, Allison Fredette, Hilary Green, Anya Jabour, Ryan Keating, Kelly Kennington, Erin Mauldin, Brian Craig Miller, Julie Mujic, Barton Myers, Megan Kate Nelson, Tom Okie, Tore Olsson, Otis Westbrook Pickett, Holly Pinheiro Jr., Angela Riotto, Christine Rizzi-Davis, Anne Rubin, Rachel Shelden, Diane Miller Sommerville, Matt Stanley, Amy Murrell Taylor, Katie Thompson, Ann Tucker, Michael Woods, and Ben Wright have strengthened this project, to be sure, but also made conferences so much more enjoyable. Lorri Glover, I am grateful for your generosity and advice. John Jeter and Jim Farmer, our conversations have been a true gift. Jim Broomall, I am already looking forward to the next time I am in Shepherdstown, to visit the center and all the great things you are doing there.

One of the reasons this book is finally published, and not still on my computer, is my Civil War writing group. Megan Bever, Laura Davis, Jonathan Lande, Laura Mammina, Lindsay Privette, and Evan Rothera are fantastic scholars, yes, but more important, fantastic human beings who motivated me in the midst of pandemic teaching and homeschooling. My writing has also benefited from the anonymous readers of University of North Carolina Press, whose suggestions strengthened this project tremendously. I want to also express appreciation for Mark Simpson-Vos, for walking me through this publication process with kindness and generosity, and for the whole team at the press, including María Garcia and Erin Granville. Iza Wojciechowska, thank you for the thorough copyedits.

Acknowledgments

When I began teaching at Converse, I met colleagues who were always willing to lend an ear and, when I needed it, an opinion. Joe Dunn, Jeff Poelvoorde, John Theilmann, Melissa Walker, and Eddy Woodfin have offered tremendous encouragement and insight these past few years. Outside of my department, I also discovered dear colleagues, and I might as well print the faculty roster to fully account for all who inspire me both inside and outside the classroom. Doug Bush, Gabriel Ford, Meg Hanna-Tominaga, Emily Harbin, Jenn Hawk, Chandra Hopkins, Stefania Licata, Danielle Stone, Erin Templeton, and Abree Williams-Jones, thank you for all your support, up to and including brainstorming titles for this book. Students, you too have challenged me to become a better professor and better at expressing myself and my ideas. I am lucky to have you in my classrooms.

Like most historians, I owe a great debt to archivists, librarians, and researchers across many states. It can be a hard thing to spend time away from family, but when the ghosts called, you helped bring their voices to the light. I discovered just how generous and gracious an archival staff can be. I am thankful for the research funding I received from Converse University, Duke University, Filson Historical Society, Amanda and Greg Gregory, the George Tyler Moore Center for the Study of the Civil War, Louisiana State University, University of Georgia, University of North Carolina at Chapel Hill, and Virginia Tech. Published essays provided an opportunity to explore my research, and I appreciate my editors Tom Appleton, Lisa Tendrich Frank, Melissa McEuen, Natalie Starostina, and LeeAnn Whites. I also appreciate the University of Georgia Press for granting permission to publish revised and reorganized pieces of that research here.

I have wonderful friends and neighbors who have provided essential mental breaks and clichéd cups of sugar when only a cookie break would do. Church friends, school friends, soccer friends, friends who somehow fell into our lives and we just can't seem to let you go, I appreciate you for keeping everything in perspective. Lauren Costley, Beth Crowley, Diana Sargent, Jenna Sargent, Valerie Thomason, Megan Upton, and many others—thank you for the dinners, the distractions, and the constant supply of laughter. Sam and Heather McGuire, *kindred souls* still captures it.

Nathan, this project began when it was just "us." There are no words to convey my appreciation for your support. Noah, Levi, and Chloe, we are so blessed that you have joined us along the way. I will never forget receiving the final approval of this book manuscript. The email came through on my phone, I had icing in my hair (we had been making a birthday cake), our youngest was on my hip, and there was noise and chaos everywhere. It took many late nights, early mornings, and Disney movies to get this project wrapped. I love you and I am so overwhelmingly grateful for each of you.

And it's probably my turn to do the dishes.

Notes

1. This book keeps all spelling and phrasing quoted from documents in its original form without including the intrusive "[*sic*]" notation, except for occasions when punctuation has been converted for clarity.

2. Longstreet, *From Manassas to Appomattox*, dedication; Alexander, *Military Memoirs*, dedication; Davis, *Rise and Fall*, dedication.

3. The number of women widowed by the Civil War is difficult to determine. J. David Hacker suggests that approximately 750,000 men lost their lives in the Civil War, and that if 28 percent of the men who died in the war were married at the time of their death, 200,000 widows would have been created; Hacker, "Census-Based Count." A map illustrating the tremendous number of widows created by the Civil War can be found in Hacker, Hilde, and Jones, "Effect of the Civil War," 65. Other valuable discussions of mortality statistics include Faust, *This Republic of Suffering*; and Vinovskis, "Have Social Historians Lost." "A Sketch of General Ben Hardin Helm," June 1867, Helm Papers, KHS.

4. McCurry, *Confederate Reckoning*; Faust, *This Republic of Suffering*, xiii; Glymph, *Women's Fight*, introduction; Edwards, *People and Their Peace*; Stanley, *From Bondage to Contract*; Ott, *Confederate Daughters*.

5. Reddy, *Navigation of Feeling*, 129.

6. Reddy, 124–25.

7. Jefferson Davis, speech, December 26, 1862, Jackson, Mississippi, transcript, Davis Papers, RU; example of the speech printed in an Atlanta newspaper at "Our Special Richmond Correspondence," *Southern Confederacy*, January 17, 1863.

8. For more on the centrality of the household, see Frank and Whites, *Household War*. This idea, that mourning is not universal, is also beautifully highlighted in Hodes, *Mourning Lincoln*. Blair, *Cities of the Dead*, x; Varon, "Southern Women and Politics," 19.

9. Sommerville, *Aberration of the Mind*, 71–72; John G. McDermott to Isabella McDermott, March 14, 1862, as quoted in James M. McPherson, *For Cause and Comrades*, 154; Sommerville, *Aberration of the Mind*, 13.

10. Other historians, such as Caroline Janney and Karen Cox, also lay this essential foundation on the complex female participation in the reconstruction of Southern society after the war. "Are We Defeated?," *Savannah Republican*, July 19, 1863, in Coopersmith, *Fighting Words*, 189; "Confederate Loan," *Arkansas True Democrat*, July 25, 1861.

11. Smith-Rosenberg, "Female World."

12. Gabriel Ford (assistant professor of English at Converse College), conversations with author, February 2020; Garrison, "Attitudes toward Suicide."

13. E. H. Tulman to Emilie Todd Helm, November 13, 1863, Helm Papers, KHS.

14. In his first inaugural address, on March 4, 1861, Lincoln said, "Physically speaking, we can not separate. We can not remove our respective sections from each other nor build an impassable wall between them. A husband and wife may be divorced and go out of the presence and beyond the reach of each other, but the different parts of our country can not do this." Chesnut, *Mary Chesnut's Civil War*, 25; Adams, *Education of Henry Adams*, 99.

15. Davis, *Rise and Fall*, dedication.

16. For the purpose of this book, I define an emotion as a feeling elicited by an external event, which in turn affects perception and thoughts, which often inspire bodily reactions or facial expressions and often lead to action tendencies. Like Stearns, Prinz argued that "palpitations, pangs, and twinges in the gut" contribute to reasoning and ultimately action.

This definition is discussed in more detail in Prinz, *Gut Reactions*, viii; Stearns, *American Cool*, 14; and Reddy, *Navigation of Feeling*, xi. Lystra's *Searching the Heart* also persuasively argues that romantic love shaped the contours of American history as surely as technology or finance did throughout the 1800s. Susan J. Matt is another example of a historian who uses emotion as a lens: "The history of homesickness recovers the story of how Americans learned to manage their feelings, but beyond that, it reveals how Americans learned habits of individualism that supported capitalist activity." Matt, *Homesickness*, 7; Sommerville, "Will They Ever," 321–39; Sommerville, "Burden Too Heavy," 487, 486, 470; Silkenat, *Moments of Despair*.

17. Eustace, *Passion Is the Gale*, 12.

18. Susan Heiskell McCampbell to William McCampbell, August 14, 1858, as quoted in Stephan, *Redeeming the Southern Family*, 95; Rosa Delony to William Delony, January 1, 1862, Deloney Papers, UGA. (In the text, I use the spelling "Delony" (without the e) as William/Rosa spelled it.)

19. Brimmer's *Claiming Union Widowhood* is a powerful study of African American widowhood and the U.S. pension system. Confederate widows were not eligible for pensions from the U.S. government in the decades immediately following the war. Wood's *Masterful Women* includes one chapter on widows in the Confederacy, persuasively arguing that a "slaveholding widow developed a distinctive version of mastery" upon which the Civil War had a "devastating impact." The financial aspects of Confederate widowhood are more thoroughly explored than the emotional aspects, particularly by Jennifer Lynn Gross in "'And for the Widow and Orphan.'" Gross discussed the financial aspects of a widow's family wealth, property, and "shift from a reliance on local resources to a reliance on the state." She briefly referenced the emotional experience of widowhood, with women becoming "increasingly loud and active" because they "believed they were sacrificing too much for the cause." Another important article on the financial implications of widowhood is Kenzer's 2002 essay, "The Uncertainty of Life," which examined nearly 3,000 of Virginia's widows and determined their likelihood to rely on relatives for support. When the Civil War ended, Virginian widows "could not look to a national Confederate government for assistance" and therefore depended on kinship ties during periods of financial difficulty. The majority of material discussing widowhood in the Union also remains wedded to the pension system. For excellent articles on that topic, see Amy E. Holmes, "'Such Is the Price'"; McClintock, "Civil War Pensions"; and Richard F. Miller, "For His Wife." In addition to Faust, in 2008 Schantz published a book on religion, death, and the American Civil War. Like Faust, he refers to widows tangentially. Schantz, *Awaiting the Heavenly Country*; Faust, *This Republic of Suffering*, 146–47, 148.

CHAPTER 1

1. Winston will die in the war.

2. Bryant to Stephens, October 12, 1856; and Stephens to Bryant, June 17, 1859, both in Stephens-Bryant Family Papers, UF.

3. Eighth Census of the United States, 1860, Slave Schedule I, Population Schedule, Putnam County, as quoted in Blakey, Lainhart, and Bryant, *Rose Cottage Chronicles*, 14.

4. Jabour, *Scarlett's Sisters*, 90; Octavia Bryant diary, October 21, 1856, Stephens-Bryant Family Papers, UF.

5. Loula Nannie Nottingham to Olin Davis, August 13, 1858; Loula Kendall Rogers diary, July 21, 1855; Sallie Collinson to Anna Louisa Norman, 1860; and Loula Kendall Rogers diary, July 3, 1857, all as quoted in Jabour, *Scarlett's Sisters*, 74–75, 73, 75–76, 80–81.

6. The twenty-three-year-old referenced, Laura, will marry, quite unhappily, and die eight years and four children later; Laura Wirt to Louisa Cabell Carrington, June 13, 1826, as quoted in Jabour, "'It Will Never Do,'" 193. Telfair to Mary Few, July 24, no year, as quoted in Carter, *Southern Single Blessedness*, 1. It is hard to determine how many white women remained single in the antebellum South. Some historians believe between one-fifth and one-fourth of adult white women remained unmarried for life; others argue the number hovers around 7.5 percent. Carter, *Southern Single Blessedness*, 3; Ann Reid to William Moultrie Reid, June 2, 1848, as quoted in Carter, *Southern Single Blessedness*, 1; Mary Francis Page Cook to Lucy Carter, March 13, no year, as quoted in Jabour, *Scarlett's Sisters*, 134.

7. For more, see Jabour, *Scarlett's Sisters*, chapter 4. Richardson to James Screven, January 21, 1821, as quoted in Clinton, *Plantation Mistress*, 70; Amanda Jane Cooley diary, June 30, 1850; Mary Cooke to Martha Hunter, January 19, 1840; Laura Margaret Cole Smith diary, n.d.; "Willie" to Mary Virginia Early, August 19, 1844; and Mary Hawes to Virginia Peal, August 26, 1850, all as quoted in Jabour, *Scarlett's Sisters*, 89, 131, 129, 130–31, 136.

8. Lebsock, *Free Women of Petersburg*, 18, 28.

9. For an excellent discussion of law and marriage, see Bynum, *Unruly Women*, 59–87. Blackstone as quoted in Salmon, "Equality or Submersion?," 94.

10. Telfair to Mary Few, January 7, 1828, as quoted in Carter, *Southern Single Blessedness*, 1; Laura Margaret Cole Smith diary, October 1, 1833; and Elizabeth Ann Cooley McClure diary, November 9, 1845, both as quoted in Jabour, *Scarlett's Sisters*, 94, 163; Shealy to Burson, March 23, 1859, and January 17, 1859; and Burson to Shealy, January 14, February 3, 1859, both in Shealy Letters, LSU.

11. Theocritus Jr. (pseud.), *Dictionary of Love* (New York: Dick & Fitzgerald, 1858), 146, as quoted in Lystra, *Searching the Heart*, 12.

12. Stephens to Bryant, June 27, 1859; and Bryant to Stephens, February 15, 1858, both in Stephens-Bryant Family Papers, UF.

13. Bryant diary, June 5, 1858; Bryant to Stephens, December 11, 1858; Bryant diary, July 5, 1858; Bryant to Stephens, January 29, 1859, all in Stephens-Bryant Family Papers, UF.

14. Bryant to Stephens, September 2, 1858, January 1, 1859, Stephens-Bryant Family Papers, UF.

15. Bryant to Stephens, February 13, 1859; Bryant diary, February 20, 1859; and Stephens to Bryant, February 20, 1859, all in Stephens-Bryant Family Papers, UF.

16. Stephens to Bryant, April 10, July 31, 1859; and Octavia Bryant to James W. Bryant, September 6, 1859, all in Stephens-Bryant Family Papers, UF.

17. Susan Heiskell McCampbell to William McCampbell, August 14, 1858, as quoted in Stephan, *Redeeming the Southern Family*, 95; Anne Eliza Pleasants Gordon diary, June 22, 1857; and Elizabeth Ann Cooley McClure diary, March 15, 1846, both as quoted in Jabour, *Scarlett's Sisters*, 184, 185.

18. Schlesinger, *Learning How to Behave*, 18; Kasson, *Rudeness and Civility*, 45; Samuel G. Goodrich, *Recollections of a Lifetime* (New York: Miller, Orton & Mulligan, 1856), 388–89, as described in Kasson, *Rudeness and Civility*, 47.

19. Famously, Child would edit the memoir of Harriet Jacobs, which would later become *Incidents in the Life of a Slave Girl*. Leavitt, *From Catharine Beecher*, 10; Child, *American Frugal Housewife*, 95; Beecher, *Treatise on Domestic Economy*, 39, 246–49.

20. Leavitt, *From Catharine Beecher*, 17; Neal, "Constant."

21. Andrew, *Family Government*, 35, 34–35. See Stephan, *Redeeming the Southern Family*, for an excellent, and more thorough, exploration into religious ideals and realities in antebellum courtship and marriage. Rogers, "Woman's Proper Sphere," 676–77.

22. Andrew, *Family Government*, 31, 34, 30–31; Lund Washington journal, 1789, as quoted in Clinton, *Plantation Mistress*, 34; John Bayley, *Marriage as It Is and as It Should Be* (New York: M. W. Dodd, 1857), 131, as quoted in Buckley, *Great Catastrophe*, 178.

23. James Madison, "Advice from a Father to an Only Daughter," *Watchman of the South*, November 21, 1839, as quoted in Buckley, *Great Catastrophe*, 177.

24. William T. Barry to Susan, August 1, 1824; John Crittenden to Ann Coleman, November 18, 1831; Nancy Thomas to Sally Gillet, December 5, 1824; and Anne Izard to Mary Manigault, all as quoted in Clinton, *Plantation Mistress*, 19, 68, 59; Fitzhugh, *Sociology for the South*, 214–15.

25. For an excellent book on this story, see Schoenbachler, *Murder and Madness*. Beauchamp, "Confession," 12, 14, 33.

26. Schoenbachler, *Murder and Madness*, 226.

27. This autobiography is more of a representation of reality rather than reality itself, shaped by both Edward Isham and the lawyer who penned it. The editors of the published edition, after an external and internal review, concluded the autobiography to be "essentially honest and largely true" with a few caveats. Isham, *Confessions of Edward Isham*, 4–5. For more on gender roles, and Edward's relationship with his mother, see Bynum, "Mothers, Lovers, and Wives," 83–100.

28. Isham, *Confessions of Edward Isham*, 5.

29. McMillen, *Motherhood*, 32–33; Price to Betsy Blanks, January 5, 1839; Leonidas Polk to his brother, March 2, 1835; Henry Bedinger to his sister Susan, January 22, 1842; MMLB to Mildred, May 9, 1844; and William Elliott to his mother-in-law, Ann Smith, August 7, 1829, all as quoted in McMillen, 108–10.

30. Charles A. Hentz obstetrical records, December 2, 1858; *Recorder*, October 30, 1842; and tombstone in Providence Presbyterian Church Cemetery, Mecklenburg County, North Carolina, all as quoted in McMillen, *Motherhood*, 44, 83, 82; McMillen, 81.

31. Fischer to Anna Hoskins, June 1, 1839, as quoted in Jabour, *Scarlett's Sisters*, 231; Sarah Scott to Elizabeth Lewis, May 2 [no year], as quoted in Clinton, *Plantation Mistress*, 46; Turner, Little Jesse's diary, August 29, 1857, as quoted in McMillen, *Motherhood*, 111; Lucy Taylor Wickham to Elizabeth Kane, February 2, 1847; and Penelope Skinner Warren to Thomas Warren, August 28, 1840, both as quoted in Jabour, *Scarlett's Sisters*, 204, 205.

32. Anna Matilda Page King, *Anna*, introduction. A story similar to King's can be found in Delfino, "Susan P. Grigsby." Susan Grigsby's husband will fight in the war but survive it; Grigsby Family Papers, FHS.

33. Anna Matilda Page King to Jane, January 27, 1827, in Anna Matilda Page King, *Anna*, 8.

34. Anna Matilda Page King to "My Dear Sir," March 3, 1842, in King, 17.

35. Anna Matilda Page King to Thomas Butler King, June 2, 1842; and to Jane, December 2, 1839, both in King, 19, 13.

36. Anna Matilda Page King to Thomas Butler King, June 26, 1849, in King, 62.

37. For an excellent study on the topic, as well as on the social implications of divorce for those women who successfully received them, see Buckley, *Great Catastrophe*, 170. See also Fredette, *Marriage on the Border*; Hansley v. Hansley, 32 N.C. 365 (1849), as described in Bynum, *Unruly Women*, 71–72; and the petitions of Jane Godwin, Rollins, and Ball, petition and court order of Roberts, and petition and court record of Hutchings, all as quoted in Buckley, *Great Catastrophe*, 170–73.

38. Eliza Thompson to Sally W. Griffith, n.d., as quoted in Buckley, *Great Catastrophe*, 171; Thomas Buckley, ed. "'Placed in the Power of Violence': The Divorce Petition of Evelina Gregory Roane, 1824," *Virginia Magazine of History and Biography*, 1992, 50, as quoted in Buckley, *Great Catastrophe*, 171; State v. Preslar, 48 N.C. 417 (1856), as described in Bynum, *Unruly Women*, 82–83; statement of Huldah Heiskell, Heiskell v. Heiskell, and Ferdinand Heiskell to Huldah Heiskell, September 22, 1849, in petition of Ferdinand S. Heiskell, as quoted in Buckley, *Great Catastrophe*, 171–72.

39. Louis Bourne divorce petition, Louis County, Virginia, December 16, 1824; Louis Bourne divorce petition, Louis County, Virginia, January 20, 1825; Thomas Culpeper divorce petition, Norfolk County, Virginia, December 9, 1835; and Elizabeth Walters v. Clement Jordan state supreme court manuscript record, all as quoted in Hodes, *White Women, Black Men*, 69, 74.

40. Chesnut, *Mary Chesnut's Civil War*, 29; Hervert A. Kellar, ed., "Diary of James D. Davidson," *Journal of Southern History* 1 (1935): 348, as quoted in Clinton, *Plantation Mistress*, 212; Philip Thomas to William Finney, July 28, 1859, as quoted in Walter Johnson, *Soul by Soul*, 113; Jacobs, *Incidents in the Life of a Slave Girl*, 27.

41. While difficult to determine, most scholars believe that Americans coming of age before the Civil War expected to live into their midforties. Schantz, *Awaiting the Heavenly Country*, 10.

42. Floride Calhoun to Anna, as quoted in Schantz, *Awaiting the Heavenly Country*, 33; Charlotte Verstille to Nancy Verstille, October 29, 1821, as quoted in Stephan, *Redeeming the Southern Family*, 198. For a more extensive discussion of the Good Death, see Faust, *This Republic of Suffering*; and Andrew, *Cross of Christ*, 74–77.

43. *How to Behave*; Coffin, *Death in Early America*, 197–98.

44. Thornwell, *Lady's Guide*, 217.

45. Torrey, *Ideal of Womanhood*, 129–32.

46. Douglass to Henry Taylor, September 15, 1837; E. G. Plumer to Douglass, September 12, 1837; Drury Lacy to Douglass, October 26, 1837; and W. M. Atkinson to Douglass, September 13, 1837, all as quoted in Stephan, *Redeeming the Southern Family*, 205–7.

47. Andrew, *Cross of Christ*, 109. Schantz argues that while major lithographic firms were established in the North, his evidence suggests that they were tapping into a national market as early as the 1830s and 1840s. See Schantz, *Awaiting the Heavenly Country*, 166, 169–71, for more examples of these images.

48. This study offers a masterful and extensive analysis of widows' wills in Massachusetts, Maryland, and South Carolina before 1750. Conger, *Widows' Might*, 10; *Art of Good Behavior*, 108–10.

49. *Records and Files of the Quarterly Courts of Essex County, Massachusetts* (Salem, Mass.: Essex Institute, 1911–75), 8:99, 259–63, 288–89, 296, 308, 433, as quoted in Ulrich, *Good Wives*, 96–97; Behn, *Widow Ranter*, 369–432.

50. William Gilmore Simms, *The Sword and the Distaff: or, "Fair, Fat, and Forty"* (Philadelphia: Lippincott, Grambo, 1852), as quoted in Tracy, *In the Master's Eye*, 126–34.

51. Edwards, *Scarlett Doesn't Live Here*; AL to R. Motte, June 11, 1840; and Mary Poindexter to Jane Clingman, February 10, 1831, both as quoted in Clinton, *Plantation Mistress*, 77, 170.

52. While widowers almost always married women younger than them, and sometimes younger than their first wives, widows often matched with older suitors, increasing the likelihood of being widowed twice. For more on the economics of slaveholding widows before the Civil War, see Wood, *Masterful Women*. Burge, *Diary*, 46, 59, 95–96.

53. Trice v. Trice, fall 1839–fall 1842, divorce records, Orange County, North Carolina, as described in Bynum, *Unruly Women*, 75–76.

54. Petition of Norman; extracts from depositions, Acts of the General Assembly of Virginia (1848–49), chaps. 322, 247; and *Richmond Whig*, February 2, 1849, all as quoted in Buckley, *Great Catastrophe*, 146–47, 169.

55. Information from this paragraph is from the fantastic biographical essay by Crawford, "Martha Rutledge Kinloch Singleton," 15–26.

56. Ann Gray to Ann Thomas, April 22, 1835, as quoted in Clinton, *Plantation Mistress*, 77; Bumpass diary, November 16, 1854, as quoted in Stephan, *Redeeming the Southern Family*, 209–10; Brevard, *Plantation Mistress*, 8, 10.

CHAPTER 2

1. This is the same widow who appears in the previous chapter, whose husband spent the majority of their marriage in a "Lunatic Asylum." A surprising number of reluctant secessionists mourned with her and expressed sorrow over disunion, as highlighted particularly well in the final chapter of Woods, *Emotional and Sectional Conflict*. Brevard, *Plantation Mistress*, 114–15.

2. For more information about marriage trends in the Civil War, see Hacker, Hilde, and Jones, "Effect of the Civil War." Fondren to Robert Mitchell, May 14, 1862, as quoted in Ott, *Confederate Daughters*, 44; McGimsey Papers, SHC; Ramseur, *Bravest of the Brave*.

3. Douglas, *I Rode with Stonewall*, 271, 325; McGuire, *Diary*, 341; Harrison, *Recollections Grave and Gay*, 203, 205; Jane Cary to Mr. Riccards, May 14, 1865, as quoted in Griggs, *General John Pegram*, 118. See also Carmichael, *Lee's Young Artillerist*.

4. Additionally, for elite white women, Confederate loyalty and service replaced many other qualifications, such as wealth, manners, and family lineage, in evaluating the worth of a suitor, according to historian Anya Jabour's "Days of Lightly-Won and Lightly-Held Hearts." Certainly, not all women sought marriage during the war. Jabour persuasively argued that many young women also used the war to actively delay marriage. The shortage of marriageable men offered them an acceptable alternative to marriage and an excuse to remain single. Brown to Cynthia Blair, May 20, 1863, as quoted in Jabour, *Scarlett's Sisters*, 270; McGuire, *Diary*, 329; Mother to Jane Sivley, December 5, 1864, as quoted in Ott, *Confederate Daughters*, 114; Alden as quoted in Simkins and Patton, *Women of the Confederacy*, 188; Faust, *Mothers of Invention*, 151; Hacker, Hilde, and Jones, "Effect of the Civil War," 42.

5. Schaller, *Soldiering for Glory*, 44.

6. Smith to King, January 20, 1861, King-Wilder Papers, GHS.

7. Smith to King, April 10, 1861, King-Wilder Papers, GHS.

8. To read more about the family dynamics of the Kings, see Berry, "More Alluring." Smith to Georgia Page King, April 10, 19, 1861; Anna Page King to Thomas Butler King,

August 15, 1842; and Georgia Page King to Thomas Butler King, April 18, 1861, all in King-Wilder Papers, GHS.

9. Georgia Page King to Henry Lord Page King, July 1, 1861; and to John Floyd King, July 8, 1861, both in King-Wilder Papers, GHS.

10. Henry Lord Page King to Georgia Page King Smith, July 15, 1861, King-Wilder Papers, GHS.

11. Henry Lord Page King to William Duncan Smith, August 3, 1861; and William Duncan Smith to Georgia Page King Smith, December 22, 1861, both in King-Wilder Papers, GHS.

12. Jabour, *Scarlett's Sisters*, 13.

13. Nutt, *Courageous Journey*, 82.

14. Emma Crutcher to Will Crutcher, January 4, 1862, as quoted in Faust, *Mothers of Invention*, 115; Winston Stephens to Octavia Stephens, May 4, 1863, Stephens-Bryant Family Papers, UF; William Pender to Fanny Pender, March 4, 1863, in Pender and Pender, *General to His Lady*, 201.

15. Mary Bell to Alfred Bell, July 27, 1862, as quoted in Faust, *Mothers of Invention*, 123; Malinda Waller Averett to Harris Hardin Averett, September 11, October 1, 1863, Averett Papers, ADAH.

16. Robert H. King to Louiza A. Williams King, valentine, n.d.; and to Louiza A. Williams King, November 8, 1861, both in King Papers, Library of Virginia, Richmond.

17. It would not "turn out right." William died in 1863. For more on camp life, particularly homesickness, see Carmichael, *War*. William Delony to Rosa Delony, March 16, 8, 1862, Deloney Papers, UGA.

18. Ramseur, *Bravest of the Brave*, 250, 262, 261; Ebenezer B. Coggin to Ann E. Coggin, January 20, 1862, Coggin Papers, ADAH.

19. William Duncan Smith to Georgia Page King Smith, July 9, 1862, King-Wilder Papers, GHS.

20. A portion of this letter collection is available via Berry and Elder, *Practical Strangers*. Dawson to Todd, June 26, 1861; and Todd to Dawson, May 9, 1861, both in Dawson Papers, SHC.

21. Dawson to Todd, August 21, 1861; and Todd to Dawson, May 15, 1861, both in Dawson Papers, SHC.

22. This concept, of the importance of emotional ties with family members as a political project, is more fully argued in Aaron Sheehan-Dean's book. For example, "because Confederate soldiers participated fully in both the battlefront and the home front, they did not distinguish the political nation from the domestic nation"; Sheehan-Dean, *Why Confederates Fought*, 2. Dawson to Todd, December 18, 1861, Dawson Papers, SHC; William Pender to Fanny Pender, March 26, 1861, in Pender and Pender, *General to His Lady*, 12; John Cotton to Mariah Hindsman Cotton, August 3, 1862; and Mariah Hindsman Cotton to John Cotton, August 21, 1862, both in Cotton and Cotton, *Yours Till Death*, 14, 16.

23. Samuel Sanders, "Letters of Dr. Samuel D. Sanders," *South Carolina Historical Magazine* 65 (July 1964): 129–35, as quoted in Ott, *Confederate Daughters*, 46; Sydenham Moore to Amanda Moore, May 24, 1862, Moore Family Papers, ADAH; Berry, *All That Makes*, 183.

24. James J. Nixon to Louisa A. Nixon, December 19, 1861, Nixon Letters, UF; Commodore Decatur Epps to Catherine Epps, December 30, 1862, Epps Papers, SHC; Ramseur, *Bravest of the Brave*, 166.

25. Editor M. Jane Johansson published the letters between Harriet and her husband to document the "intimate and emotional" lives "of one couple and their ultimate tragedy." Too often, the tale ends as this published narrative does. When Theophilus died in battle, just over four years after his marriage to Harriet, the book ends. The editor includes a half page informing the reader that Harriet moved to North Carolina and remarried in 1872 but nothing more. Theophilus Perry to Harriet Eliza Perry, July 17, 1862; Harriet Eliza Perry to Theophilus Perry, August 3, 1862; Harriet Eliza Perry to Mary Temperance, October 22, 1862, all in Perry and Perry, *Widows by the Thousand*, xv, 1–2, 5, 10, 45.

26. Lucy Wood diary, May 24, 1861, as quoted in Jabour, *Scarlett's Sisters*, 251–52; Emma Crutcher to Will Crutcher, February 1, April 8, 1862, as quoted in Faust, *Mothers of Invention*, 121–22; Fitzhugh, *Sociology for the South*, 214.

27. James J. Nixon to Louisa A. Nixon, December 5, 1861, Nixon Letters, UF; James E. Rains to [Ida Yeatman Rains], January 3, 1862, Rains Family Papers, TSLA; William Pender to Fanny Pender, April 11, June 6, May 30, 1861, in Pender and Pender, *General to His Lady*, 14, 30, 25.

28. John Cotton to Mariah Hindsman Cotton, June 17, December 26, 1862, January 19, February 2, August 18, October 5, 1863, in Cotton and Cotton, *Yours Till Death*, 6, 40, 45, 47, 79, 87.

29. Commodore Decatur Epps to Catherine Epps, August 3, 1862, Epps Papers, SHC; Petty, *Journey to Pleasant Hill*, 103; Morgan Callaway to Leila Callaway, August 28, December 20, 1863, as quoted in Faust, *Mothers of Invention*, 123; Octavia Stephens to Davis Bryant, June 11, 1864, Stephens-Bryant Family Papers, UF.

30. Historian Stephanie E. Jones-Rogers's remarkable work complicates this narrative, highlighting the vast social and economic power many white women gained through their personal ownership of enslaved people, and reveals how many mistresses did, in fact, have much experience with the management of enslaved persons prior to the war; for more, see Jones-Rogers, *They Were Her Property*. *Macon Daily Telegraph*, September 1, 1862, quoted in Mohr, *On the Threshold*, 221; Mary Bell to Alfred Bell, January 30, May 22, 29, September 21, December 16, 1862, as quoted in Faust, *Mothers of Invention*, 71; James J. Nixon to Louisa A. Nixon, December 19, 1861, Nixon Letters, UF; Lizzie Neblett to Will Neblett, August 18, 1863, as quoted in Faust, *Mothers of Invention*, 66; Mrs. W. W. Boyce to W. W. Boyce, April 12, 1862, in Akin, *Letters of Warren Akin*, 4–5.

31. Lizzie Neblett to Will Neblett, letter fragment [1864]; and Mary Bell to Alfred Bell, November 24, 1864, both as quoted in Faust, *Mothers of Invention*, 70, 72; Chesnut as quoted in Muhlenfeld, *Mary Boykin Chesnut*, 109; Stephens, "Slavery the Cornerstone," 288–90. The historiography of mistresses and masters is deep. Some essentials include Elizabeth Fox-Genovese, *Within the Plantation Household*; Clinton, *Tara Revisited*; Clinton, *Plantation Mistress*; Faust, *Mothers of Invention*; and Ott, *Confederate Daughters*.

32. William Pender to Fanny Pender, June 25, 1860, in Pender and Pender, *General to His Lady*, 5.

33. William Pender to Fanny Pender, April 3, May 30, June 2, 9, 23, 26, 30, 1861, in Pender and Pender, 14, 25, 27, 31, 39, 40, 42.

34. Fanny Pender to William Pender, June 30, 1861, in Pender and Pender, 42–44.

35. William Pender to Fanny Pender, July 2, 1861, in Pender and Pender, 45.

36. William Pender to Fanny Pender, July 11, 1861, in Pender and Pender, 47.

37. William Pender to Fanny Pender, December 5, 1862, February 25, 1863, August 27, 1861, October 7, 1861, in Pender and Pender, 193, 197, 51, 77.

38. William Pender to Fanny Pender, September 11, 1861, March 6, 1862, in Pender and Pender, 57–58, 118; Pender and Pender, 262. Many widows had to deal with the loss of other family members, in addition to husbands, during the war. Fanny's younger brother, Jacob Shepperd, was sixteen at the outbreak of war, became William Pender's aide, and was killed at Fredericksburg.

39. James E. Rains to [Ida Yeatman Rains], July 1, 1861, Rains Family Papers, TSLA.

40. McDonough, *Stones River*, 211.

41. "For the Standard," *Semi-Weekly Standard*, January 24, 1865; McGuire, *Diary*, 249–50; Octavia Stephens to Winston Stephens, August 5, 1863, Stephens-Bryant Family Papers, UF; Mariah Hindsman Cotton to John Cotton, July 16, 1863, in Cotton and Cotton, *Yours Till Death*, 77.

42. Union wives, too, had similar fears. Septima Collis, after fruitlessly searching a nearby battlefield for her husband, felt overwhelmed by questions. "Was I widowed? Was my husband lying in the trenches suffering from some horrible wound, and I not near him? Oh what an anxious night!" she penned. The next day, Septima gratefully discovered that her husband was alive, though "literally covered from head to foot with cakes of mud." Collis, *Woman's War Record*, 50–55; McClatchey, "Georgia Woman's," 212–13; Rosa Delony to William Delony, June 15, 1862, August 2, 1863, January 1, 1862, Deloney Papers, UGA; Octavia Stephens to Winston Stephens, March 19, 1862, Stephens-Bryant Family Papers, UF; Emma Crutcher to Will Crutcher, January 22, 1862, as quoted in Faust, *Mothers of Invention*, 115.

43. William Pender to Fanny Pender, September 26, 1861, in Pender and Pender, *General to His Lady*, 68; James J. Nixon to Louisa A. Nixon, December 5, 1861, Nixon Letters, UF; William Stilwell to Molly, September 18, 1862, in Lane, *Dear Mother*, 186.

44. At the start of the war, most Americans believed the conflict would be short. Commodore Decatur Epps to Catherine Epps, October 13, August 17, 1862, Epps Papers, SHC; William Delony to Rosa Delony, October 11, 14, 1862, Deloney Papers, UGA; Ebenezer B. Coggin to Ann E. Coggin, July 14, 1862, Coggin Papers, ADAH.

45. Wainwright as quoted in Faust, *This Republic of Suffering*, 59; William Delony to Rosa Delony, June 23, 1862, and Rosa Delony to William Delony, January 4, 1863, Deloney Papers, UGA; *Southern Confederacy*, September 28, 1862, in Kreiser, *Marketing*, 152; John McCorkle to Martha Stallings McCorkle, July 14, 1864, McCorkle Correspondence, GHS.

46. Harris Hardin Averett to Malinda Waller Averett, September 10, 1863, Averett Papers, ADAH; John F. Davenport to Mary Jane Davenport, August 20, 1862, June 1, 1864, Davenport Civil War Letters, ADAH.

47. John Cotton to Mariah Hindsman Cotton, August 1, October 2, 8, 1862, September 24, 1863, February 1, 1865, in Cotton and Cotton, *Yours Till Death*, 13, 24, 26, 85, 128; Cotton and Cotton, vii.

48. McGuire, *Diary*, 254–55.

49. McGuire, 254–55.

CHAPTER 3

1. For more on death and Richmond, see Ash, *Rebel Richmond*. McGuire, *Diary*, 310–13. The epigraph at the beginning of the chapter is from Norman S. Fields to Abigail, January 5, 1863, Fields Papers, MDAH. Norman, too, would die during the war.

2. McGuire, *Diary*, 310–13.

3. Missing records make it quite difficult to pinpoint the exact number of Confederate soldiers who died in the Civil War, making 250,000 probably a low estimate. Some wives would not be as lucky as Catherine Epps. For example, Rebecca Jane Cary Edwards retrieved her husband in Virginia, but he was too weak to make the trip back to South Carolina. They had to disembark from the train in North Carolina. He died, but his body finished the journey home and is buried in the local cemetery; for more, see Edwards Diary, Spartanburg County Public Library, Spartanburg, South Carolina. Freemon, *Gangrene and Glory*, 48; Alexander, *Fighting for the Confederacy*, 291; Commodore Decatur Epps to Catherine Epps, November 13, 1863, Epps Papers, SHC; Catherine Epps widow's application, 1891, Murray County, Georgia, ancestry.com.

4. Another powerful example in this "death surrounded by strangers" trope is that of William Butler, who was killed at the Battle of Natural Bridge in Florida. As a Black man, he fought for the Union, and a letter from his wife was discovered in a knapsack next to a body. For more, see Butler Letter, GHS. Ebenezer B. Coggin to Ann E. Coggin, October 17, 23, 1863, Coggin Papers, ADAH.

5. When U.S. troops occupied New Orleans in April 1862, Charles Didier Dreux's widow left the Confederacy and sought refuge in Havana, Cuba. While there, her only child died. Solomon, *Civil War Diary*, 62; Grace Elizabeth King, *Creole Families*, 66.

6. Mothershead was a Confederate soldier from Haynesville, Missouri. It is unclear which battle or skirmish he is writing about on June 13, 1862. He died August 6, 1864, in Atlanta. Mothershead Journal, March 7, June 13, 1862, TSLA.

7. For another example, see Vige Letters, LSU. James J. Nixon to Louisa A. Nixon, Nixon Letters, UF; U.S. Bureau of the Census, United States Federal Census Population Schedules, Chattahoochee, Gadsden, Florida, 1860; Lt. F. L. Boathby to Ann E. Coggin, October 23, 1863, Coggin Papers, ADAH; Goodbar, "Mrs. Richard Ledbetter," 36; Richard Boies Stark, "Surgeons and Surgical Care of the Confederate States Army," *Virginia Medical Monthly* 88 (October 1961): 604, as quoted in Green, *Chimborazo*, ix.

8. When John A. Harris became ill, he stayed with his mother-in-law in Alabama in March 1864. Unfortunately, he would be killed outside Atlanta. For more, see Harris Letters, LSU. W. H. Channing to Rosa Delony, November 28, 1863, Deloney Papers, UGA; Freemon, *Gangrene and Glory*, 50; W. W. Keen, quoted in Green, *Chimborazo*, 136.

9. B. B. Oneal to Nancy Gilliam, June 2, 1862, Gilliam Papers, ADAH; Rutkow, *Bleeding Blue and Gray*, xiii; Green, *Chimborazo*, ix.

10. Malinda Waller Averett to Harris Hardin Averett, October 2, 1863; and P. Zimmerman to Malinda Waller Averett, October 27, 1863, both in Averett Papers, ADAH; U.S. Bureau of the Census, United States Federal Census Population Schedules, Reeltown, Tallapoosa, Alabama, 1870.

11. Ella Gertrude Clanton Thomas diary, April 17, 1862, Thomas Papers, DUKE.

12. Acts of retaliation performed on unarmed prisoners of war remain the "most incredulous and least known aspect" of the Civil War, according to Speer, *War of Vengeance*. The number of men who died in these situations is unknown. A similarly fascinating situation is that of David O. Dodd, executed for spying (but who did not leave a widow behind). Ladd to wife, October 29, 1864, Ladd Papers, TSLA; Speer, *War of Vengeance*, 7–8.

13. For another Johnson's Island example, see Morgan Letters, LSU. While Andersonville is infamous for the high casualty rates and miserable conditions, other prisons in the North could prove to be just as hazardous to a soldier's life. New

York's Elmira, for example, recorded a 24 percent mortality rate, which is not unlike Andersonville's mortality rate of 29 percent. However, it is important to note that the majority of Andersonville's deaths were due to neglect, while Elmira deaths were tied to disease. See Mee Papers, SHSM. The Union prison system was more stable and had a lower casualty rate than the Confederate prison system; Cloyd, *Haunted by Atrocity*, 1. William Speer, "A Confederate Soldier's View of Johnson's Island Prison," ed. James B. Murphey, *Ohio History* 79 (Spring 1970): 109, as quoted in Cloyd, *Haunted by Atrocity*, 15; Cloyd, *Haunted by Atrocity*, 14; Brownlow Letters, ASA; Emma Holmes, *Diary*, 375.

14. William Pender to Fanny Pender, March 30, 1862, in Pender and Pender, *General to His Lady*, 129–30.

15. F. Lay to E. L. Harris, October 11, 1864, E. L. Harris Papers, DUKE. For more on a Good Death, see Faust, *This Republic of Suffering*, 6–11.

16. Maj. Gen. Earl Van Dorn, dubbed "the terror of ugly husbands" by one reporter, provides yet another unique story of how a husband might die at war. Though married, Van Dorn had a reputation for adultery before and during the war. Dr. James Bodie Peres, who believed that Van Dorn had had an affair with his wife in 1863, shot him in the back of the head and killed him. What might widowhood have felt like for Van Dorn's wife, Caroline Godbold? Channing to Rosa Delony, November 28, 1863, Deloney Papers, UGA.

17. For more on Union families' attempts to bring home husbands' bodies during and after the Civil War, see Giesberg, "Work That Remains," 39–45. Gray to Frances Douglass, October 7, 1840, Douglass Papers, DUKE; Frances Jane Bestor Robertson journal, September 17, 1854, as quoted in Stephan, *Redeeming the Southern Family*, 215; McGuire, *Diary*, 310–13; Joseph Story, *An Address Delivered on the Dedication of the Cemetery at Mount Auburn* (Boston: Joseph T. Edwin Buckingham, 1831), as quoted in Wills, *Lincoln at Gettysburg*, 65.

18. William F. Vermilion of the Thirty-Sixth Iowa wrote his wife, "You have often asked what I want you to do if I should not get home." He had come to a conclusion: "Get me home if you can," he penned, "bury me on some nice loyal spot of ground, plant flowers over the grave." Most important, "don't forget to go to that spot Dollie." "I don't want to sleep in the land of traitors," he explained. "I couldn't rest well." For more on the burying of dead in the Civil War, see Faust, *This Republic of Suffering*, chap. 3. William Vermilion to Mary Vermilion, June 30, 1863, in Vermilion, *Love amid the Turmoil*, 150; Sutherland, *Seasons of War*, 274.

19. Fields to Mrs. Fitzpatrick, June 8, 1865, as quoted in Faust, *This Republic of Suffering*, 15; Church to Stovall, telegram, October 6, 1863, Deloney Papers, UGA; Stegeman, *These Men She Gave*, 99, 149–50.

20. Stephens to Davis Bryant, April 4, 1864, in Blakey, Lainhart, and Bryant, *Rose Cottage Chronicles*, 334; Willie Bryant to Rebecca Bryant, March 8, 1864, Stephens-Bryant Family Papers, UF.

21. Georgia Page King Smith to Henry Lord Page King, October 30, 1862, King-Wilder Papers, GHS; Kosnegary to family, November 12, 1862, Kosnegary Letter, LSU.

22. Octavia Stephens to Davis Bryant, April 4, 1864, in Blakey, Lainhart, and Bryant, *Rose Cottage Chronicles*, 334; Emma Holmes, *Diary*, 179; Holstein, *Three Years*, v, 13.

23. Louis P. Towles, ed., *World Turned Upside Down: The Palmers of South Santee, 1818–1881* (Columbia: University of South Carolina Press, 1996), as quoted in Faust, *This Republic of Suffering*, 146; Kenzer, "Uncertainty of Life," 120; Flora McCabe to Dearest Maggie, January 26, 1862, as quoted in Faust, *This Republic of Suffering*, 86.

24. David Todd to Emilie Todd Helm, April 15, 1862, as quoted in Berry, *House of Abraham*, 116; McDonald, *Woman's Civil War*, 211; Emma Holmes, *Diary*, 70; Augustina Stephens to Octavia Stephens, March 21, 1864, in Blakey, Lainhart, and Bryant, *Rose Cottage Chronicles*, 330.

25. Faust, *This Republic of Suffering*, xiii; *Savannah Republican*, July 19, 1863, in Coopersmith, *Fighting Words*, 189; "Confederate Loan," *Arkansas True Democrat*, July 25, 1861; Perry Diary, November 30, 1867, ADAH.

26. Jefferson Davis, speech to Congress of the Confederate States, May 2, 1864, Richmond, Virginia, transcript; and Jefferson Davis, speech, September 23, 1864, Macon, Georgia, transcript, both in Davis Papers, RU.

27. Jefferson Davis, speech, January 5, 1863, Executive Mansion, Richmond, Virginia, transcript, Davis Papers, RU.

28. McGuire, *Diary*, 250; Breckinridge, *Lucy Breckinridge*, 88–89; Blakey, Lainhart, and Bryant, *Rose Cottage Chronicles*, 336.

29. For more on condolence letters, see Mays, "'If Heart Speaks Not,'" 377–400. For a powerful collection that includes condolence letters to a Union widow, see Vanvalkenburgh Papers, FHS. For another Confederate example, see Koger Collection, MDAH. Wood to Louisa A. Nixon, December 25, 1861, Nixon Letters, UF; John F. Davenport to Mary Jane Davenport, September 7, 1862, Davenport Civil War Letters, ADAH; Martha D. D. to Rosa Delony, October 13, November 6, 1863, Deloney Papers, UGA.

30. Martha D. D. to Rosa Delony, October 13, November 6, 1863, Deloney Papers, UGA; sister to Nellie Ramseur, November 8, 1864, in Ramseur, *Bravest of the Brave*, 299; Ann A. Crenshaw to E. L. Harris, October 18, 1864; and F. Lay to Harris, October 11, 1864, both in E. L. Harris Papers, DUKE; scrapbook, Daniel Papers, SHC.

31. M. D. D. to Rosa Delony, November 6, 1863; Maria Delony to Rosa Delony, August 11, 1864; and Martha D. Duncan to Rosa Delony, November 25, 1863, all in Deloney Papers, UGA; scrapbook, Daniel Papers, SHC.

32. Similarly, Robert McCauley, who died of dysentery in prison, would write in multiple letters, "If we never meet on earth again try to meet me in heaven"; Palmer-McCauley Family Papers, SHSM. Also see Barr, *Let Us Meet*. Ladd to wife, October 29, 1864, Ladd Papers, TSLA.

33. Ramseur, *Bravest of the Brave*, 294; Torrey, *Ideal of Womanhood*, 130, 129.

34. Torrey, *Ideal of Womanhood*, 130–32; Martha D. D. to Rosa Delony, October 13, 1863, Deloney Papers, UGA; Maria Delony to Rosa Delony, August 11, 1864, Deloney Papers, UGA; Sam Adams to Amanda Moore, September 27, 1863, Moore Family Papers, ADAH; Mary E. Flemming to Octavia Stephens, Stephens-Bryant Family Papers, UF; scrapbook, Daniel Papers, SHC.

35. During the war, remaining loyal to the Confederacy was important not just for widows but for most Southerners. While some scholarship suggests that Confederate morale might have plummeted as the war dragged on, historian George Rable believes that "commitment to the Confederacy remained remarkably resilient," as commitment filled with wishful thinking "helped citizens hang onto hope even in the absence of any tangible reasons to do so." Likewise, Jason Phillips's *Diehard Rebels* describes soldiers who not only "knew they were not conquered, but even more, they thought they were unconquerable." "Confederate Loan," July 25, 1861, *Arkansas True Democrat*; *Arkansas True Democrat*, August 29, 1861; "Reading the List," September 3, 1862, *Washington Telegraph*.

36. For further discussion of antebellum mourning poetry reprinted in the *Southern Literary Messenger* during the war, see Schantz, *Awaiting the Heavenly Country*, 97–125. A. B. Meek, "War Song," *Southern Literary Messenger*, 1863, 627.

37. Moore, *Civil War in Song*, 76.

38. Evans, *Macaria*, xvii, 390, 382, 411.

39. Morgan, *Sarah Morgan*, 448.

40. Stiles, *Four Years*, 41–43, 322–23.

41. Wright, *Southern Girl in '61*, 215–16.

42. Wiley, *Civil War Diary*, 79.

43. Guerrant, *Bluegrass Confederate*, 331.

44. W. N. Halderman to Helm, September 25, 1863; Bruce to Helm, September 30, 1863; E. Halderman to Helm, September 25, 1863; undated newspaper clipping; and E. Pickett to Helm, December 31, 1863, all in Helm Papers, KHS.

45. This telegram has not survived, so we have to take Emilie's word about Lincoln's response. Helm, *True Story of Mary*, 221.

46. Helm, 221; *Washington Sunday Herald*, December 5, 1886.

47. Helm, *True Story of Mary*, 224, 229, 230, 231, 233; John L. Helm to Emilie Todd Helm, January 20, 1864, Helm Papers, KHS.

48. Rosa Delony to William Delony, December 13, 1861, Deloney Papers, UGA.

CHAPTER 4

1. Georgia Page King Smith to Henry Lord Page King, October 30, 1862; William Duncan Smith to Georgia Page King, April 10, 1861; Georgia Page King to Henry Lord Page King, July 1, 1861; and Georgia Page King to John Floyd King, July 8, 1861, all in King-Wilder Papers, GHS.

2. "Death of Brig. General Wm. Duncan Smith," newspaper clipping; and Georgia Page King Smith to Henry Lord Page King, October 30, 1862, both in King-Wilder Papers, GHS.

3. Georgia Page King Smith to Henry Lord Page King, October 30, 1862, King-Wilder Papers, GHS.

4. Vaughan to Louisa Clark Boddie, February 22, 1863, Boddie Family Papers, MDAH.

5. Emma Holmes, *Diary*, 179; Swepston Stephens to Octavia Stephens, October 20, 1866, Stephens-Bryant Family Papers, UF.

6. Willie Bryant to Rebecca Bryant, March 8, 1864; and Stephens diary, March 15, 1864, both in Stephens-Bryant Family Papers, UF.

7. Augustina Stephens to Octavia Stephens, March 21, 1864; Mary Branning to Octavia Stephens, May 4, 1864; Catherine Park to Octavia Stephens, June 6, 1864; and Willie Bryant to Octavia Stephens, April 19, 1864, all in Stephens-Bryant Family Papers, UF.

8. Loulie to Octavia Stephens, March 13, 1864; aunt to Octavia Stephens, March 16, 1864; and Augustina Stephens to Octavia Stephens, March 21, 1864, all in Stephens-Bryant Family Papers, UF.

9. For another example of family support, see Foote Family Papers, FHS. Stephens diary, April 22, May 2, 1864, Stephens-Bryant Family Papers, UF.

10. Willie Bryant to Davis Bryant, March 21, 1864; Stephens diary, March 27, 1864; Willie Bryant to Stephens, March 31, April 17, 18, 1864; and Julia Fisher to Davis Bryant, April 4, May 3, 1864, all in Stephens-Bryant Papers, UF.

11. Stephens to Davis Bryant, April 4, 1864; Stephens diary, March 13, 1866, May 25, 1864; Willie Bryant to Stephens, May 4, 1864; and Stephens to Davis Bryant, June 11, 1864, all in Stephens-Bryant Papers, UF.

12. Marshall to Sallie Fair, November 3, 1864, Rutherford Papers, South Caroliniana Library, University of South Carolina, Columbia.

13. Scrapbook, Daniel Papers, SHC.

14. Scrapbook.

15. Nannie Bierne Parkman (1841–94) married Samuel Breck Parkman. The wedding described is that of Bettie Bierne to William Porcher Miles. Nannie would remarry, to Baron Ahlefeldt, a man whom her father (a wealthy Louisiana planter) disliked for his extravagances and habit of sleeping in. De Leon, *Belles, Beaux and Brains*, 158–59; Chesnut, *Mary Chesnut's Civil War*, 448.

16. McGuire, *Diary*, 250; Faust, *This Republic of Suffering*, 150; Etta Kosnegary to mother and sisters, November 1862, Kosnegary Letter, LSU.

17. For more on this flourishing advertising campaign, see Kreiser, *Marketing*. A. A. Crenshaw to Mrs. Harris, October 25, 1864, David Bullock Harris Papers, DUKE; Faust, *This Republic of Suffering*, 151, 91, 94.

18. De Leon, *Belles, Beaux and Brains*, 158; Sidney Harding diary, October 11, 1863, Harding Diaries, LSU; Sarah Kennedy diary, March 19, 1864, Kennedy Papers, TSLA; Hodes, "Wartime Dialogues," 235.

19. For more on the whirl of sociability that happened in the war, see Jabour, *Scarlett's Sisters*, 270–73. Brooks diary, February 8, 1865, as quoted in Rable, "Despair, Hope, and Delusion," 138; Stone, *Brokenburn*, 293, 292, 277; McGuire, *Diary*, 328; Morgan, *Sarah Morgan*, 300.

20. Sherwood, *Manners and Social Usages*, 193; Kennedy diary, March 19, 1864, Kennedy Papers, TLSA.

21. Bell to her husband, September 1, 1863, Bell Papers, TSLA; Coleman to his parents, December 7, 1863, Coleman Papers, TSLA.

22. The prevalence of sexual assault in the war is unknown. A survey of less than 5 percent of the federal court-martial records yielded more than thirty cases of reported rape. Records of the Judge Advocate General's Office (Army), March 15, 1864, entry 101, National Archives Record Group 153, as quoted in Lowry, *Story*, 123, 125.

23. James Madison Bowler to Elizabeth Caleff Bowler, October 23, 1863, in Bowler and Madison, *Go If You Think*, 162; Sarah Kennedy diary, March 19, 1864, Kennedy Papers, TSLA; Ayers journal, May 6, 1864, in Commager, *Blue and the Gray*, 82.

24. Chesnut, *Mary Chesnut's Civil War*, 489, 472.

25. Charles F. Johnson to Mary Johnson, June 19, 1864, in Charles Johnson, *Civil War Letters*, 256; Babcock, *Selections from the Letters*, 94; White diary, May 2–4, 1865, in Wellman, *County of Warren*, 153.

26. Georgia Page King Smith to Henry Lord Page King, October 30, 1862, King-Wilder Papers, GHS.

27. Smith to King.

28. Caperton to Georgia Page King Smith, November 3, 1862; and Smith to Henry Lord Page King, October 30, 1862, both in King-Wilder Papers, GHS.

29. Mary to Fannie Franklin Hargrave Carson, July 17, 1864; and Lou E. Hightower to Carson, July 13, 1864, both in Hargrave Family Papers, UWG.

CHAPTER 5

1. Jane may not be the most reliable of narrators. While she did have a brother, George McCausland, who fought as a captain in the Confederacy, he did not die until September 17, 1861, months after the first battle in Manassas. When confronted by the soldiers, Jane also claimed her husband did not die in the service of the Confederacy. The soldier nonetheless believed he died in the "Rebel Army" and treated her as a widow of the Confederacy. She survived the war and passed away in 1918, at age ninety. Chinn Civil War Reminiscence, LSU.

2. Just as I argue that household reconstruction began at the end of a life, not the end of the war, historian Eric Foner argues that emancipation began the process of reconstruction before the war was over; Foner, *Reconstruction.* James J. Broomall's work on the lingering trauma of the Civil War is also a useful framework for this discussion; Broomall, *Private Confederacies.*

3. William Pender to Fanny Pender, September 22, 1861, in Pender and Pender, *General to His Lady,* 65.

4. Mary Ann Cobb to Howell Cobb, October 14, 1863; and Delony to Mary Ann Cobb, December 7, 1863, both in Coleman, *Athens,* 70, 75.

5. It is possible that Sarah and Lucy were not actually widows but simply women using Confederate widowhood as justification for their turning to this particular occupation. *Daily Dispatch,* May 18, 1862; Records of the Judge Advocate General's Office (Army), Court Martial Case File, file no. MM2388, National Archives Records Group 153, as quoted in Lowry, *Story,* 71.

6. Leeson to Seddon, July 22, 1863, in Escott, *After Secession,* 108; McCurry, *Confederate Reckoning,* 140.

7. Historians Victoria Bynum's and Stephanie McCurry's analyses of government papers have been a significant contribution toward understanding the political activities of women during times of war. Bynum, *Unruly Women*; McCurry, *Confederate Reckoning,* 142–45, 148.

8. "A Case for Sympathy," *Southern Confederacy,* May 18, 1862.

9. Helm to Abraham Lincoln, October 30, 1864, as shared in Berry, *House of Abraham,* 173.

10. Helm to Lincoln.

11. McGuire, *Diary,* 254–55.

12. "Editorial Items," *Yorkville Enquirer,* June 10, 1863.

13. Elizabeth Mildred Powell diary, January 14, 1862, Hereford Papers, SHSM; Civil War Relief Meeting Notice, SHSM; Ella Harper to George W. F. Harper, May 4, August 11, 1863 as described in McGee, "Home and Friends," 377.

14. For more, see West Virginia Civil War Soldiers Database, George Tyler Moore Center for the Study of the Civil War, Shepherdstown, West Virginia. For another strong collection related to the experience of border-state occupation, see Moxley-Offutt Family Papers, FHS. *Staunton Spectator,* January 22, 1861, as quoted in Ayers, *In the Presence,* 100, 154; Sheehan-Dean, *Why Confederates Fought,* 198.

15. Mary Bedinger Mitchell, "Woman's Recollections of Antietam," 686.

16. Lee to Hunter, July 20, 1864, as printed in Bushong, *History of Jefferson County,* 174–76.

17. For a longer piece on the relationship between mothers-in-law and widows, see Elder, "Dead Husband, Dead Son," 248–67. John B. Gordon, *Reminiscences,* 118.

18. Sam, whose sister wrote to him about their mother, was imprisoned near Gettysburg. For a look at relationships between Union soldiers and their mothers, see Reid Mitchell, *Vacant Chair*. For a tragic example of a family who lost both sons to the war, see Foster Family Correspondence, LSU. Marion Dewoody Nelson to Sam Dewoody, December 4, 1864, Dewoody Family Papers, ASA; Dawson to Elodie Todd, June 6, 1861, Dawson Papers, SHC.

19. In the antebellum period, mothers grieved children, too. But most often, children died before the age of five, not as young adults. See Censer, *North Carolina Planters*, esp. chap. 2. Patrick diary, May 22, 1862, ASA; Lucinda Helm to Emilie Todd Helm, October 21, 1863, Helm Papers, KHS.

20. Eunice Richardson Stone Connolly to Lois Davis, March 8, 1863, as quoted in Hodes, *Sea Captain's Wife*, 145; Faust, *Mothers of Invention*, 33; Semmes as quoted in Faust, *Mothers of Invention*, 37; Emma Crutcher to Will Crutcher, March 1, 1862, as quoted in Faust, *Mothers of Invention*, 36–37.

21. In some ways, this is what Charles Frazier's *Cold Mountain* gets right—that women fought their own wars at home, against one another, with one another, condensing new households that would endure after the man that brought them together was gone. McDonald, *Woman's Civil War*, 211; Lucinda Helm to Emilie Todd Helm, October 21, 1863, Helm Papers, KHS; letter to Emma S. Garnett, May 20, 1863, Garnett Family Letters, Library of Virginia, Richmond; Kosnegary to family, November 12, 1862, Kosnegary Letter, LSU.

22. May Louise Comfort to Charlotte Comfort, December 22, 1873; and David Comfort III to Charlotte Comfort, October 3, 1874, both in Comfort Family Papers, VHS; Janett Harrison to Alice Harrison, January 27, 1862, Harrison Family Papers, VHS.

23. Maria Delony to Rosa Delony, April 11, 1864, Deloney Papers, UGA.

24. Lucinda Helm to Emilie Todd Helm, October 21, 1863, Helm Papers, KHS.

25. For an interesting detour, see the Gaillard Civil War Letters, SHC, which feature a widowed husband, fighting with the Second South Carolina, whose children reside with his sister-in-law. McDonald, *Woman's Civil War*, 217–18.

26. Beckie Spears Warren to Sallie Gray Spears, November 23, 1860, October 14, 1862, December 6 [year unknown, but after Sallie's husband's death and before the war ended], Spears and Hicks Family Papers, SHC.

27. Edmund Ruffin Jr. to Charlotte Ruffin, May 24, 1864, Ruffin and Meade Family Papers, SHC.

28. Turner to "My Dear Mother," September 29, October 17, December 12, 1864, Turner Collection, RU.

29. E. Pickett to Emilie Todd Helm, December 31, 1863, Helm Papers, KHS. Edwin "Eddie" J. Lee was aide-de-camp to Stonewall Jackson, and William F. Lee was a young cousin of Robert E. Lee. Edwin J. Lee to aunt, November 18, 1861, Lee Papers, SHSM.

30. Martha D. Duncan to Delony, November 25, 1863; and W. H. Channing to Delony, November 28, 1863, both in Deloney Papers, UGA.

31. "Lt. Col. Delony," *Southern Watchman*, September 26, 1866.

32. Davis Bryant to Stephens, April 10, 1864; and Stephens diary, October 21, November 4, December 25, 1864, December 25, 1866, March 1, 1867, March 1, 1973, November 1, 1904, all in Stephens-Bryant Family Papers, UF.

33. Augustina Stephens to Octavia Stephens, January 8, 1865; Winston Stephens, "The Little Boston Rebel, both in Stephens-Bryant Family Papers, UF; Octavia Stephens

to Mary Hall, January 27, 1883, as quoted in Blakey, Lainhart, and Bryant, *Rose Cottage Chronicles*, 371; Octavia Stephens diary, February 24, 1883; Augustina Stephens to Octavia Stephens, March 21, 1864, both in Stephens-Bryant Family Papers, UF.

34. Sallie Gray Spears to grandson, May 17, 1911, Spears and Hicks Family Papers, SHC.

35. That said, while single white women of the Civil War era feared their chances for marriage would lessen, it turned out to be a false fear; "the vast majority (approximately ninety-two percent) of southern white women who came of marriage age during the war married at some point in their lives," according to Kenzer. Chesnut, *Mary Chesnut's Civil War*, 489–90; Faust, *Mothers of Invention*, 150; Kenzer, "Uncertainty of Life," 125.

36. Emma Holmes, *Diary*, 224–25.

37. Another example of this is in the Ramsay Papers, SHC: After becoming a widow in 1864, within three months, Maggie began courting her late husband's cousin. They would also disguise their handwriting on their envelopes and address their letters "My Dearest" followed by a long dash. Ultimately, they married within a year of her widowhood. Eli Alexander Warlick to Cornelia L. Warlick, April 12, 1866, June 6, 1867; and Samuel P. Tate to Cornelia L. Warlick, August 3, 1867, both in McGimsey Papers, SHC.

38. A biography of the Hargrave family is included in the family papers, the author's name not recorded. Likely it was compiled by Julia Graves Ivey, the donor of the collection. Hargrave biography, Hargrave Family Papers, UWG.

39. Mollie Brannan to Jimmie [James Carson], June 8, 1864; Fannie Franklin Hargrave Carson to James Carson, May 25, June 4, 1864; and Long to James Carson, June 8, 1864, all in Hargrave Family Papers, UWG.

40. Benjamin F. Bigelow to Fannie Hargrave Carson, July 3, 1864; Carson to Lou E. Hightower, July 6, 1864; Hightower to Carson, July 13, 1864; and Fannie Darden to Carson, February 21, 1866, all in Hargrave Family Papers, UWG.

41. Sister to Fannie Hargrave Carson Brannan, November 4, 1865, Hargrave Family Papers, UWG.

42. Fannie Franklin Hargrave Carson Brannan to Bessie H. Long and friends, November 1865; Sister to Brannan, November 4, 1865; Mollie to Brannan, n.d.; Bessie Lowe to Brannan, n.d.; and Meta to Brannan, February 9, 1866, all in Hargrave Family Papers, UWG.

43. Sister to Fannie Hargrave Carson Brannan, November 4, 1865, Hargrave Family Papers, UWG.

44. Fannie Darden to Fannie Hargrave Carson, February 21, 1866, Hargrave Family Papers, UWG.

CHAPTER 6

1. "Relief for the Widows of Confederates," *Louisiana Democrat*, January 30, 1867. The chapter's epigraph is taken from "Orphan Brigade Have Great Time at Xalapa," *Bourbon News*, October 5, 1920.

2. Susan Buck Cooper Thomas diary, January 1, 1864, Corder-Thomas Family Papers, SHSM. For another example, see "An Appeal for the Widows and Orphans from the Confederates in Heaven," Hero Papers, LSU. "The Orphans of the South," *Daily Intelligencer*, September 7, 1866.

3. "Thirty Women Are Starving," *Georgia Weekly Opinion*, September 17, 1867.

4. "The Confederate Widow and Orphan," *Daily Dispatch*, April 25, 1867.

5. *Weekly Democratic Statesman*, February 17, 1876; "Wanted," *Daily Dispatch*, January 26, 1869.

6. *New Orleans Crescent*, March 7, 1869; *Memphis Daily Appeal*, May 12, 1867.

7. *Memphis Daily Appeal*, April 21, 1867; "Boarding," *Alexandria Gazette*, October 5, 1868.

8. "A New Way to Raise Money," *Wheeling Daily Intelligencer*, June 11, 1866; "A Female Swindler," *Charleston Daily News*, January 18, 1869.

9. "Two Little Girls Offered for Adoption," *Daily Intelligencer*, October 14, 1868.

10. "Orphans' Home of the North Georgia Conference of the Methodist Episcopal Church South," *Weekly Constitution*, February 20, 1872.

11. "A Sad Accident," *Weekly Gwinnett Herald*, August 7, 1872.

12. "Clippings," *Carolina Watchman*, July 20, 1867; "Home for the Mothers, Widows, and Daughters of Confederate Soldiers," *Daily Phoenix*, June 14, 1868. For another example of a home, see Savannah Widows' Society, GHS.

13. "Remember the Living," *Daily Phoenix*, June 8, 1866.

14. "The Women of the Late War," *Sunny South*, July 19, 1884.

15. "Widows and Orphans," *Alexandria Gazette*, January 17, 1867; "Relief for the Widows of Confederates," *Louisiana Democrat*, January 30, 1867.

16. "Ex-President Davis—Great Torchlight Procession in His Honor at Macon," *Weekly Star*, November 5, 1887.

17. "The 'Reconstruction Committee' So-Called Make a Report," *New Oregon Plain Dealer*, February 23, 1866.

18. Jackson, *Life and Letters*, dedication, preface.

19. There are other women who made careers out of their Confederate widowhood, such as Varina Howell Davis and LaSalle Corbell Pickett, but they did not lose their husbands during the war like the other widows in this study, so I will not say more about them here. For an introduction to Mary Anna Jackson, see Gardner, "'Sweet Solace,'" 49–68. Jackson, *Memoirs of Stonewall Jackson*, 89, 447, 458, 459, 465.

20. Walker, "Other Days," 94–95, ADAH.

21. Walker, 94–95.

22. For more about Flora Cooke Stuart, see Wert, *Cavalryman*. *Richmond Whig*, May 17, 1864, as quoted in Wert, 362.

23. Ed C. Cook to Eliza Maney, June 6, 1864; and committee invitation, n.d., both in Murfree Family Papers, SHC.

24. Karen Cox picks up this thread, exploring the United Daughters of the Confederacy, a popular Lost Cause organization that developed after the LMAs, in Cox, *Dixie's Daughters*. Janney, *Burying the Dead*, 40, 41, 79, 70, 3.

25. Within the topic of Confederate veterans, historian Brian Craig Miller likewise finds that those who lost the most in the war did not participate in the memorialization of the war. Veterans with amputations often did not have the financial capital or mobility required to attend reunions. Likewise, many Confederate widows appeared to be more interested in garnering pensions for themselves from state legislators than bickering about a "Yankee textbook" or decorating the grave for anyone other than their dead husbands, brothers, or fathers. For more on veterans with amputations, see Brian Craig Miller, *Empty Sleeves*. Janney, *Burying the Dead*, 57, 68, 56, 110–11.

26. For more on Emilie and Mary, see Elder, "Emilie Todd Helm." Elizabeth Dixon,

quoted in Clinton, *Mrs. Lincoln*, 245; Emilie Todd, undated Civil War reminiscence, Helm Collection, KHS.

27. The reader may notice that in some quotations Emilie's name was spelled differently and should note that I refer to her as Emilie for consistency. "The Inauguration," *Frankfort Roundabout*, September 8, 1883; Filson Club membership certificate for Emilie Todd Helm, October 6, 1890, Helm Papers, KHS; "Pertinent Personalities," *Pittsburg Dispatch*, January 14, 1891; "Candidates for State Librarian," *Semi-Weekly Interior Journal*, July 23, 1895.

28. Breckinridge to Helm, October 31, 1863; Quarles to Helm, May 8, 1880; Lyon to Helm, August 30, 1888; Thompson to Helm, February 25, 1868; and "Helm Guards," undated newspaper clipping, all in Helm Papers, KHS.

29. Rodger Hanson's widow was the first "Mother" of the Orphan Brigade, Emilie the second, filling the role after Mrs. Hanson's death. W. O. Bullock to Helm, August 30, 1883; John H. Weller to Helm, September 9, 1884; J. D. Pickett to Helm, September 14, 1884; "Mrs. Helm Made Mother of the Orphan Brigade," *Courier-Journal*; unidentified newspaper clipping; and *Bourbon News*, October 5, 1920, all in Helm Papers, KHS.

30. While Emilie wrote extensively about the purpose of the organization, her personal papers do not indicate whether her main function was as a figurehead invited to speak for publicity or as a more substantial worker within the organization. The most complete history of the UDC is Cox, *Dixie's Daughters*. Emilie Todd Helm, ["Ladies and Daughters of the Confederacy"], undated writing, Helm Papers, KHS.

31. Emilie Todd Helm, ["A third of a century"], undated writing; Emilie Todd Helm, ["God bless the Confederate women"], undated writing; Emilie Todd Helm, ["The duty of a Historian"], undated writing; Emilie Todd Helm, ["Ladies and Daughters of the Confederacy"], undated writing; and *Courier-Journal*, November 22, 1901, all in Helm Papers, KHS.

32. J. Y. Gilmore to Emilie Todd Helm, January 11, 1898; and R. Cobb to Helm, November 26, 1904, both in Helm Papers, KHS.

33. The concept of the Lost Cause has a long and varied history. Books that discuss women's roles in crafting this ideology include Wilson, *Baptized in Blood*; and Foster, *Ghosts of the Confederacy*. Emilie Todd Helm, "The Spirit of 1860," Helm Papers, KHS.

34. Emilie Todd Helm, "Wanting an Occupation," Helm Papers, KHS.

35. "Chivalry Illustrated," *Weekly Clarion*, September 23, 1869.

36. Newspapers throughout the country, including papers in Pennsylvania and New York, reported on Emilie's activities, which speaks to her popularity, fame, and influence. In many ways Emilie's postwar actions are similar to those of George Pickett's widow, LaSalle Corbell. Like Emilie, LaSalle shaped the way her husband would be remembered in history, ignoring and denying facts that did not match the image she desired to create. See the excellent essay by Lesley J. Gordon, "Cupid," 69–86. "A Strange Man," *St. Paul Daily Globe*, September 4, 1898.

37. Nina Silber argues that a sentimental rubric took hold of the reunion process and that "southern women became the domestic and morally refined exemplars of true womanhood." Silber, *Romance of Reunion*, 23; "Kentuckians Pay Tribute to the Memory of Abraham Lincoln at the Unveiling of Statue at Hodgenville," *Courier-Journal*, June 1, 1909; Helm to Lincoln, October 30, 1864, as quoted in Berry, *House of Abraham*, 174; Emilie Todd Helm, ["Ladies and Daughters of the Confederacy"], undated writing, Helm Papers, KHS.

38. Helm to Albert Edwards, August 15, 1899, Ninian W. Edwards Papers, Abraham Lincoln Presidential Library, Springfield, Illinois.

CONCLUSION

1. Margaret Mitchell, *Gone with the Wind*, 121 (incl. epigraph), 95, 94, 120.

2. After dozens of articles flooded the internet with news of this "last" Confederate widow's death, other stories surfaced of older widows still alive, such as Maudie Celia Acklin, who at age nineteen married eighty-seven-year-old William M. Cantrell in 1934. Horwitz, *Confederates in the Attic*, 340; Alberta Martin, "Civil War Widows," interview by Joe Richman, *Radio Diaries*, July 1, 1998, http://www.radiodiaries.org/transcripts/OtherDocs/civilwar.html; "Alberta Martin, 97, Confederate Widow, Dies," *New York Times*, June 1, 2004, http://www.nytimes.com/2004/06/01/us/alberta-martin-97-confederate-widow-dies.html; Horwitz, *Confederates in the Attic*, 341, 342.

3. With regard to historiography, this chapter is in closest dialogue with Gallagher's *Causes Won, Lost, and Forgotten*. Wilson's *Baptized in Blood* is also useful for conceptualizing memory right after the Civil War. For more on ruins as a concept, see Nelson, *Ruin Nation*.

4. The book remains popular, consistently landing on "top 100" lists of all varieties. For a detailed analysis of the making of the book and movie, see Brown and Wiley, *Margaret Mitchell's*. Mitchell as quoted in Brown and Wiley, *Margaret Mitchell's*, 5, 6, 28, 87; "Atlanta History Center Midtown," Atlanta History Center (website), accessed on August 11, 2021, https://www.atlantahistorycenter.com/buildings-and-grounds/atlanta-history-center-midtown/; Edwin Granberry, as quoted in Vertrees, *Selznick's Vision*, 23.

5. Margaret Mitchell, *Gone with the Wind*, 121, 94, 95.

6. Mitchell, 127, 137, 139, 142.

7. Pyron, *Southern Daughter*, 38; Mitchell as quoted in Vertrees, *Selznick's Vision*, 25.

8. Mitchell as quoted in Brown and Wiley, *Margaret Mitchell's*, 76; Vertrees, *Selznick's Vision*, 23; "Cinema: G with the W," *Time*, December 25, 1939, http://content.time.com/time/magazine/article/0,9171,762137,00.html.

9. When earnings are adjusted for inflation, *Gone with the Wind* remains the highest-grossing domestic movie in American history. "Cinema: G with the W"; "Gone with the Wind (1939): Awards," IMDb, http://www.imdb.com/title/tt0031381/awards; Haley and Malcolm X, *Autobiography of Malcolm X*, 36.

10. "High Spots in 'Gone with the Wind,'" *Life*, December 25, 1939, 12; Fleming, *Gone with the Wind*.

Bibliography

ARCHIVES

Alabama

Alabama Department of Archives and History, Montgomery
    Ebenezer B. Coggin Papers, 1862–1889
    Eliza Jane Kendrick Walker, "Other Days: Reminiscences"
    Harris Hardin Averett Papers, 1854–1863
    John F. Davenport Civil War Letters, 1862–1864
    Nancy Gilliam Papers, 1850–1904
    Sarah Randle Perry Diary, 1867–1868
    Sydenham Moore Family Papers, 1833–1873

Arkansas

Arkansas State Archives, Little Rock
    David O. Dodd Papers, 1859–1874
    Dewoody Family Papers, 1858–1944
    Hardin Family Letters, 1861–1878
    Isaac N. Brownlow Letters, 1864–1865
    Mary S. Patrick Diary, 1862–1864

Florida

George A. Smathers Libraries, Special and Area Studies Collections,
        University of Florida, Gainesville
    Dallas Wood Papers, 1863
    James J. Nixon Letters, 1861–1863
    Stephens-Bryant Family Papers, 1664–1989

Georgia

Georgia Historical Society, Savannah
    C. Ann Butler Letter, 1865
    John McCorkle Correspondence, 1863–1864
    King-Wilder Papers, 1817–1946

Savannah Widows' Society, 1822–2001
Hargrett Rare Book and Manuscript Library, University of Georgia, Athens
William Gaston Deloney Papers, 1829–1915
Ingram Library, Annie Belle Weaver Special Collections,
University of West Georgia, Carrollton
Hargrave Family Papers, 1858–1949

Illinois
Abraham Lincoln Presidential Library, Springfield
Ninian W. Edwards Papers, 1791–1908

Kentucky
Filson Historical Society, Louisville
Foote Family Papers, 1759–1897
George W. Vanvalkenburgh Papers, 1861–1907
Grigsby Family Papers, 1818–1884
Moxley-Offutt Family Papers, 1818–1978
Kentucky Historical Society, Frankfort
Emilie Todd Helm Papers, 1855–1943

Louisiana
Hill Memorial Library, Special Collections, Louisiana State University, Baton Rouge
Andrew Jr. and George Hero Papers, 1829–1905
Edmond Vige Letters, 1862
Etta Kosnegary Letter, 1862
James Foster Family Correspondence, 1861–1866
Jane McCausland Chinn Civil War Reminiscence, 1863
John A. Harris Letters, 1854–1864
John N. and Eugenia B. Shealy Letters, 1859–1862
Sidney Harding Diaries, 1863–1865
Thomas Gibbes Morgan Jr. Letters, 1837–1864

Mississippi
Mississippi Department of Archives and History, Jackson
Boddie Family Papers, 1841–1915
Norman S. Fields Papers, 1862–1863
T. J. Koger Collection, 1862–1956

Missouri
State Historical Society of Missouri, Columbia
Civil War Relief Meeting Notice, 1864
Corder-Thomas Family Papers, 1867–1961
Elizabeth Mildred Powell Hereford Papers, 1817–1880
Palmer-McCauley Family Papers, 1858–1915
Thomas Mee Papers, 1863–1864
William Fitzhugh Lee Papers, 1861–1863

North Carolina
David M. Rubenstein Rare Book and Manuscript Library, Duke University, Durham
David Bullock Harris Papers, 1789–1894
E. L. Harris Papers, 1873–1894

Ella Gertrude Clanton Thomas Papers, 1848–1906
William Boone Douglass Papers, 1809–1948
Wilson Library, Southern Historical Collection,
       University of North Carolina at Chapel Hill
C. D. Epps Papers, 1862–1915
Ellen Long Daniel Papers, 1848–1918
Franklin Gaillard Civil War Letters, 1861–1864
John A. Ramsay Papers, 1852–1900
Laura Cornelia McGimsey Papers, 1856–1868
Murfree Family Papers, 1779–1935
Nathaniel Henry Rhodes Dawson Papers, 1851–1917
Polk Family Papers, 1864–1938
Ruffin and Meade Family Papers, 1796–1906
Spears and Hicks Family Papers, 1852–1917

South Carolina

South Caroliniana Library, University of South Carolina, Columbia
Peter Manigault Collection, 1745–1950
William Drayton Rutherford Papers, 1840–1897
Spartanburg County Public Library, Spartanburg
Oliver E. Edwards Diary, 1861–1863

Tennessee

Tennessee State Library and Archives, Nashville
Asa V. Ladd Papers, 1864
Civil War Microfilm Collection
Ben W. Coleman Papers
Joseph R. Mothershead Journal
Mary W. M. Bell Papers
Rains Family Papers
Sarah Kennedy Papers

Texas

Rice University, Houston
Anne Marie Stewart Turner Collection, 1857–1913
Papers of Jefferson Davis, 1828–1879

Virginia

Library of Virginia, Richmond
Garnett Family Letters, 1847–1863
The Home for Needy Confederate Women, 1862–1997
Robert H. King Papers, 1861–1910
Virginia Historical Society, Richmond
Comfort Family Papers, 1848–1900
Harrison Family Papers, 1756–1893
Hunter Family Papers, 1766–1918

West Virginia

George Tyler Moore Center for the Study of the Civil War, Shepherdstown
West Virginia Civil War Soldiers Database

NEWSPAPERS AND PERIODICALS

Alexandria (Va.) Gazette
Arkansas True Democrat (Little Rock)
Bourbon News (Paris, Ky.)
Carolina Watchman (Salisbury, N.C.)
Charleston (S.C.) Daily News
Courier-Journal (Louisville, Ky.)
Daily Dispatch (Richmond, Va.)
Daily Intelligencer (Atlanta)
Daily Phoenix (Columbia, S.C.)
Frankfort (Ky.) Roundabout
Georgia Weekly Opinion (Atlanta)
Life
Louisiana Democrat (Alexandria)
Macon (Ga.) Daily Telegraph
Memphis Daily Appeal
New Oregon (Iowa) Plain Dealer
New Orleans Crescent
New York Times
Pittsburg (Pa.) Dispatch
Recorder (Hillsborough, N.C.)
Savannah Republican

Semi-Weekly Interior Journal
   (Stanford, Ky.)
Semi-Weekly Standard (Raleigh, N.C.)
Southern Confederacy (Atlanta)
Southern Literary Messenger
Southern Watchman (Athens, Ga.)
St. Paul Daily Globe
Sunny South (Atlanta)
Time
Washington (D.C.) Sunday Herald
Washington Telegraph
   (Hempstead County, Ark.)
Weekly Clarion (Jackson, Miss.)
Weekly Constitution (Atlanta)
Weekly Democratic Statesman (Austin)
Weekly Gwinnett Herald
   (Lawrenceville, Ga.)
Weekly Star (Wilmington, N.C.)
Wheeling (W.Va.) Daily Intelligencer
Yorkville (S.C.) Enquirer

PRINT AND DIGITAL PRIMARY SOURCES

Adams, Henry. *The Education of Henry Adams: An Autobiography*. Boston: Houghton Mifflin, 1918.

Akin, Warren. *Letters of Warren Akin, Confederate Congressman*. Edited by Bell I. Wiley. Athens: University of Georgia Press, 1959.

Alexander, Edward Porter. *Fighting for the Confederacy: The Personal Recollections of Edward Porter Alexander*. Edited by Gary W. Gallagher. Chapel Hill: University of North Carolina Press, 1989.

———. *Military Memoirs of a Confederate: A Critical Narrative*. New York: Charles Scribner's Sons, 1907.

Andrew, James O. *The Cross of Christ; Being a Sermon Preached by the Late H. B. Bascom, D.D., LL.D., before the General Conference of the Methodist Episcopal Church, South, in St. Louis, Missouri, May 13th, 1850; To Which Is Added a Brief Sketch of His Illness and Death*. Louisville: Morton and Griswold, 1951.

———. *Family Government: A Treatise on Conjugal, Parental, and Familial Duties*. Charleston, S.C.: Jenkins, 1847.

The Art of Good Behavior; And Letter Writer on Love, Courtship, and Marriage: A Complete Guide for Ladies and Gentlemen, Particularly Those Who Have Not Enjoyed the Advantages of Fashionable Life. New York: C. P. Huestis, 1846.

Babcock, Willoughby. *Selections from the Letters and Diaries of Brevet-Brigadier General Willoughby Babcock of the Seventy-Fifth New York Volunteers*. New York: University of the State of New York, 1922.

Barr, James Michael. *Let Us Meet in Heaven: The Civil War Letters of James Michael Barr, 5th South Carolina Cavalry*. Edited by Thomas D. Mays. Abilene, Tex.: McWhiney Foundation Press, 2001.

Beauchamp, Jereboam O. "The Confession of Jereboam O. Beauchamp." In *The Beauchamp Tragedy in Kentucky*, 7–93. New York: Dinsmore, 1858.

Beecher, Catharine E. *A Treatise on Domestic Economy, for the Use of Young Ladies at Home and at School*. Boston: T. H. Webb, 1842.

Behn, Aphra. *The Widow Ranter, or The History of Bacon in Virginia: A Tragi-Comedy*. In *Women's Writing of the Early Modern Period, 1588–1688: An Anthology*, edited by Stephanie Hodgson-Wright, 369–432. New York: Columbia University Press, 2002.

Berry, Stephen, and Angela Esco Elder, eds. *Practical Strangers: The Courtship Correspondence of Nathaniel Dawson and Elodie Todd, Sister of Mary Todd Lincoln*. Athens: University of Georgia Press, 2017.

Blakey, Arch Frederic, Ann Smith Lainhart, and Winston Bryant, eds. *Rose Cottage Chronicles: Civil War Letters of the Bryant-Stephens Families of North Florida*. Gainesville: University Press of Florida, 1998.

The Book of Common Prayer, and the Administration of the Sacraments; And Other Rites and Ceremonies of the Church, according to the Use of the Protestant Episcopal Church, in the United States of America: Together with the Psalter, or Psalms of David. New York: Dana, 1856.

Bowler, James, and Elizabeth Caleff. *Go If You Think It Your Duty: A Minnesota Couple's Civil War Letters*. Edited by Andrea R. Foroughi. St. Paul: Minnesota Historical Society Press, 2008.

Breckinridge, Lucy. *Lucy Breckinridge of Grove Hill: The Journal of a Virginia Girl, 1862–1864*. Edited by Mary D. Robertson. Columbia: University of South Carolina Press, 1994.

Brevard, Keziah. *A Plantation Mistress on the Eve of the Civil War: The Diary of Keziah Hopkins Brevard, 1860–1861*. Edited by John Hammond Moore. Columbia: University of South Carolina Press, 1993.

Burge, Dolly Lunt. *The Diary of Dolly Lunt Burge, 1848–1879*. Edited by Christine Jacobson Carter. Athens: University of Georgia Press, 1997.

Chesnut, Mary Boykin Miller. *Mary Chesnut's Civil War*. Edited by C. Vann Woodward. New Haven, Conn.: Yale University Press, 1981.

Child, Lydia Maria. *The American Frugal Housewife*. 12th ed. Boston: Carter, Hendee, 1833.

Coleman, Kenneth, ed. *Athens, 1861–1865: As Seen through Letters in the University of Georgia Libraries*. Athens: University of Georgia Press, 1969.

Collis, Septima Maria Levy. *A Woman's War Record, 1861–1865*. New York: Knickerbocker, 1889.

Commager, Henry Steele, ed. *The Blue and the Gray: The Story of the Civil War as Told by Participants*. Vol. 1, *The Nomination of Lincoln to the Eve of Gettysburg*. New York: Bobbs-Merrill, 1973.

Cotton, John, and Mariah Cotton. *Yours Till Death: The Civil War Letters of John W. Cotton*. Edited by Lucille Griffith. Birmingham: University of Alabama, 1951.

Davis, Jefferson. *The Rise and Fall of the Confederate Government*. New York: D. Appleton, 1881.

Douglas, Henry Kyd. *I Rode with Stonewall: The War Experiences of the Youngest Member of Jackson's Staff*. Chapel Hill: University of North Carolina Press, 1940.

Evans, Augusta Jane. *Macaria; or, Altars of Sacrifice*. Edited by Drew Gilpin Faust. Baton Rouge: Louisiana State University Press, 1992.

Fay, Edwin. *This Infernal War: The Confederate Letters of Edwin H. Fay*. Edited by Bell Irvin Wiley with the assistance of Lucy E. Fay. Austin: University of Texas Press, 1958.

Fitzhugh, George. *Sociology for the South; or, The Failure of Free Society*. Richmond, Va.: A. Morris, 1854.

Goodbar, K. D. "Mrs. Richard Ledbetter." In *Confederate Women of Arkansas 1861-'65: Memorial Reminiscences*, 36. Little Rock: United Confederate Veterans of Arkansas, 1907.

Gordon, John B. *Reminiscences of the Civil War*. New York: Charles Scribner's Sons, 1903.

Guerrant, Edward O. *Bluegrass Confederate: The Headquarters Diary of Edward O. Guerrant*. Edited by William C. Davis and Meredith L. Swentor. Baton Rouge: Louisiana State University Press, 1999.

Haley, Alex, and Malcolm X. *The Autobiography of Malcolm X: As Told to Alex Haley*. New York: Ballantine, 1964.

Harrison, Burton. *Recollections Grave and Gay*. New York: Charles Scribner's Sons, 1911.

Holmes, Emma. *The Diary of Miss Emma Holmes 1861–1866*. Edited by John F. Marszalek. Baton Rouge: Louisiana State University Press, 1979.

Holstein, Anna Morris Ellis. *Three Years in Field Hospitals of the Army of the Potomac*. Philadelphia: J. B. Lippincott, 1867.

How to Behave: A Pocket Manual of Republican Etiquette, and Guide to Correct Personal Habits. New York: Fowler and Wells, 1856.

Isham, Edward. *The Confessions of Edward Isham: A Poor White Life in the Old South*. Edited by Charles C. Bolton and Scott P. Culclasure. Athens: University of Georgia Press, 1998.

Jackson, Mary Anna. *Life and Letters of General Thomas J. Jackson*. New York: Harper and Brothers, 1892.

———. *Memoirs of Stonewall Jackson, by His Widow*. Louisville: Prentice, 1895.

Jacobs, Harriet. *Incidents in the Life of a Slave Girl*. New York: Dover, 1861.

Johnson, Charles. *The Civil War Letters of Colonel Charles F. Johnson, Invalid Corps*. Edited by Fred Pelka. Amherst: University of Massachusetts Press, 2004.

King, Anna Matilda Page. *Anna: The Letters of a St. Simons Island Plantation Mistress, 1817–1859*. Edited by Melanie Pavish-Lindsay. Athens: University of Georgia Press, 2002.

Lane, Mills, ed. *Dear Mother: Don't Grieve about Me. If I Get Killed, I'll Only Be Dead: Letters from Georgia Soldiers in the Civil War*. Savannah, Ga.: Beehive, 1990.

Lincoln, Abraham. *Abraham Lincoln: Great Speeches*. Edited by John Grafton. New York: Dover, 1991.

Longstreet, James. *From Manassas to Appomattox: Memoirs of the Civil War in America*. Philadelphia: J. B. Lippincott, 1896.

McClatchey, Minerva Leah Rowles. "A Georgia Woman's Civil War Diary: The Journal of Minerva Leah Rowles McClatchey." Edited by T. Conn Bryan. *Georgia Historical Quarterly* 51 (June 1967): 197–216.

McDonald, Cornelia Peake. *A Woman's Civil War: A Diary with Reminiscences of the War, from March 1862*. Edited by Minrose C. Gwin. Madison: University of Wisconsin Press, 1992.

McGuire, Judith White Brockenbrough. *Diary of a Southern Refugee during the War by a Lady of Virginia*. Lincoln: University of Nebraska Press, 1995.

Mitchell, Mary Bedinger. "A Woman's Recollections of Antietam." In *Battles and Leaders of the Civil War*, edited by Robert Underwood Johnson and Clarence Clough Buel, 2:686–94. Edison, N.Y.: Castle, 1985.

Moore, Frank. *The Civil War in Song and Story 1860–1865*. New York: P. F. Collier, 1892.

Morgan, Sarah. *Sarah Morgan: The Civil War Diary of a Southern Woman*. Edited by Charles East. New York: Simon and Schuster, 1991.

Neal, Alice B. "The Constant; or, The Anniversary Present." *Godey's Lady's Book*, January 1851.

Nutt, Laetitia LaFon Ashmore. *Courageous Journey: The Civil War Journal of Laetitia LaFon Ashmore Nutt*. Edited by Florence Ashmore Cowles Hamlett Martin. Miami, Fla.: Seemann, 1975.

Pender, William, and Fanny Pender. *The General to His Lady: The Civil War Letters of William Dorsey to Fanny Pender*. Edited by William W. Hassler. Chapel Hill: University of North Carolina Press, 1962.

Perry, Theophilus, and Harriet Perry. *Widows by the Thousand: The Civil War Letters of Theophilus and Harriet Perry*. Edited by M. Jane Johansson. Fayetteville: University of Arkansas Press, 2000.

Petty, Elijah P. *Journey to Pleasant Hill: The Civil War Letters of Captain Elijah P. Petty, Walker's Texas Division, CSA*. Austin: University of Texas, 1982.

Ramseur, Stephen Dodson. *The Bravest of the Brave: The Correspondence of Stephen Dodson Ramseur*. Edited by George G. Kundahl. Chapel Hill: University of North Carolina Press, 2010.

Rogers, E. O. "Woman's Proper Sphere." In *The Christian Union, and Religious Memorial*, edited by Robert Baird, 2:676–77. New York: Samuel Hueston, 1849.

Schaller, Frank. *Soldiering for Glory: The Civil War Letters of Colonel Frank Schaller, Twenty-Second Mississippi Infantry*. Edited by Mary W. Schaller and Martin N. Schaller. Columbia: University of South Carolina Press, 2007.

Sherwood, Mrs. John. *Manners and Social Usages*. New York: Harper and Brothers, 1899.

Simms, William Gilmore. *The Sword and the Distaff, or "Fair, Fat, and Forty": A Story of the South at the Close of the Revolution*. Philadelphia: Lippincott, Grambo, 1852.

Solomon, Clara. *The Civil War Diary of Clara Solomon: Growing Up in New Orleans, 1861–1862*. Edited by Elliott Ashkenazi. Baton Rouge: Louisiana State University Press, 1995.

Stephens, Alexander. "Slavery the Cornerstone of the Confederacy." In *Great Debates in American History*, edited by Marion Mills Miller, 5:269–72. New York: Current Literature, 1913.

Stiles, Robert. *Four Years under Marse Robert*. New York: Neale, 1904.

Stone, Kate. *Brokenburn: The Journal of Kate Stone, 1861–1868*. Edited by John Q. Anderson. Baton Rouge: Louisiana State University Press, 1955.

Thompson, Edwin Porter. *History of the First Kentucky Brigade*. Cincinnati, Ohio: Caxton, 1868.

Thornwell, Emily. *The Lady's Guide to Perfect Gentility*. New York: Derby and Jackson, 1856.

Torrey, Lizzie. *The Ideal of Womanhood, or, Words to the Women of America*. Boston: Wentworth, Hewes, 1859.

U.S. Bureau of the Census. United States Federal Census Population Schedules. 1850–1920. Accessed via ancestry.com.

———. United States Federal Census Slave Schedules. 1860. Accessed via ancestry.com.

Vermilion, William. *Love amid the Turmoil: The Civil War Letters of William and Mary Vermilion.* Edited by Donald C. Elder III. Iowa City: University of Iowa Press, 2005.

Wiley, William. *The Civil War Diary of a Common Soldier: William Wiley of the 77th Illinois Infantry.* Edited by Terrence J. Winschel. Baton Rouge: Louisiana State University Press, 2001.

Wright, Louise Wigfall. *A Southern Girl in '61: The War-Time Memories of a Confederate Senator's Daughter.* New York: Doubleday, Page, 1905.

SECONDARY SOURCES

Ash, Stephen V. *Rebel Richmond: Life and Death in the Confederate Capital.* Chapel Hill: University of North Carolina Press, 2019.

Ayers, Edward L. *In the Presence of Mine Enemies: The Civil War in the Heart of America, 1859–1863.* New York: W. W. Norton, 2003.

Berry, Stephen. *All That Makes a Man: Love and Ambition in the Civil War South.* Oxford: Oxford University Press, 2003.

———. *House of Abraham: Lincoln and the Todds, a Family Divided by War.* New York: Houghton Mifflin Harcourt, 2007.

———. "More Alluring at a Distance: Absentee Patriarchy and the Thomas Butler King Family." *Georgia Historical Quarterly* 81, no. 4 (Winter 1997): 863–96.

Blair, William A. *Cities of the Dead: Contesting the Memory of the Civil War in the South, 1865–1914.* Chapel Hill: University of North Carolina Press, 2004.

Brimmer, Brandi Clay. *Claiming Union Widowhood: Race, Respectability, and Poverty in the Post-Emancipation South.* Durham, N.C.: Duke University Press, 2020.

Broomall, James J. *Private Confederacies: The Emotional Worlds of Southern Men as Citizens and Soldiers.* Chapel Hill: University of North Carolina Press, 2019.

Brown, Ellen F., and John Wiley Jr. *Margaret Mitchell's Gone with the Wind: A Bestseller's Odyssey from Atlanta to Hollywood.* Lanham, Md.: Taylor, 2011.

Buckley, Thomas E. *The Great Catastrophe of My Life: Divorce in the Old Dominion.* Chapel Hill: University of North Carolina Press, 2002.

Bushong, Millard Kessler. *A History of Jefferson County, West Virginia, 1719–1940.* Westminster, Md.: Heritage Books, 1941.

Bynum, Victoria. "Mothers, Lovers, and Wives: Images of Poor White Women in Edward Isham's Autobiography." In Isham, *Confessions of Edward Isham,* 83–100.

———. *Unruly Women: The Politics of Social and Sexual Control in the Old South.* Chapel Hill: University of North Carolina Press, 1992.

Carmichael, Peter S. *Lee's Young Artillerist: William R. J. Pegram.* Charlottesville: University Press of Virginia, 1995.

———. *The War for the Common Soldier: How Men Thought, Fought, and Survived in Civil War Armies.* Chapel Hill: University of North Carolina Press, 2018.

Carter, Christine Jacobson. *Southern Single Blessedness: Unmarried Women in the Urban South, 1800–1865.* Chicago: University of Illinois Press, 2006.

Censer, Jane Turner. *North Carolina Planters and Their Children, 1800–1860.* Baton Rouge: Louisiana State University Press, 1984.

Clinton, Catherine. *Mrs. Lincoln: A Life.* New York: HarperCollins, 2009.

———. *The Plantation Mistress: Woman's World in the Old South.* New York: Pantheon Books, 1982.

————. *Tara Revisited: Women, War, and the Plantation Legend.* New York: Abbeville, 1995.

Cloyd, Benjamin G. *Haunted by Atrocity: Civil War Prisons in American Memory.* Baton Rouge: Louisiana State University Press, 2010.

Coffin, Margaret. *Death in Early America: The History and Folklore of Customs and Superstitions of Early Medicine, Funerals, Burials, and Mourning.* Nashville: Thomas Nelson, 1976.

Conger, Vivian Bruce. *The Widows' Might: Widowhood and Gender in Early British America.* New York: New York University Press, 2009.

Coopersmith, Andrew S. *Fighting Words: An Illustrated History of Newspaper Accounts in the Civil War.* New York: New Press, 2004.

Cox, Karen. *Dixie's Daughters: The United Daughters of the Confederacy and the Preservation of Confederate Culture.* Gainesville: University Press of Florida, 2003.

Crawford, Lindsay. "Martha Rutledge Kinloch Singleton: A Slaveholding Widow in Late Antebellum South Carolina." In *Proceedings of the South Carolina Historical Association,* 15–26. Columbia: South Carolina State Library, 2009.

De Leon, Thomas C. *Belles, Beaux and Brains of the 60's.* 1909. Reprint, New York: Arno, 1974.

Delfino, Susanna. "Susan P. Grigsby and the Psychological Dimension of Disease and Death in Antebellum and Civil War Kentucky." In *The Scourges of the South? Essays on "The Sickly South" in History, Literature, and Popular Culture,* edited by Thomas Ærvold Bjerre and Beata Zawadka, 111–32. Newcastle, UK: Cambridge Scholars, 2014.

Edwards, Laura. *The People and Their Peace: Legal Culture and the Transformation of Inequality in the Post-Revolutionary South.* Chapel Hill: University of North Carolina Press, 2009.

————. *Scarlett Doesn't Live Here Anymore: Southern Women in the Civil War Era.* Urbana: University of Illinois Press, 2000.

Elder, Angela Esco. "Dead Husband, Dead Son: Widows, Mothers-in-Law, and Mourning in the Confederacy." In Frank and Whites, *Household War,* 248–67.

————. "Emilie Todd Helm and Mary Todd Lincoln: We Weep over Our Dead Together." In *Kentucky Women: Their Lives and Times,* edited by Melissa A. McEuen and Thomas H. Appleton Jr., 81–98. Athens: University of Georgia Press, 2015.

Escott, Paul D. *After Secession: Jefferson Davis and the Failure of Confederate Nationalism.* Baton Rouge: Louisiana State University Press, 1978.

Eustace, Nicole. *Passion Is the Gale: Emotion, Power, and the Coming of the American Revolution.* Chapel Hill: University of North Carolina Press, 2008.

Faust, Drew Gilpin. *Mothers of Invention: Women of the Slaveholding South in the American Civil War.* Chapel Hill: University of North Carolina Press, 1996.

————. *This Republic of Suffering: Death and the American Civil War.* New York: Random House, 2008.

Fleming, Victor, dir. *Gone with the Wind.* Los Angeles: Warner Bros., 1939. DVD.

Foner, Eric. *Reconstruction: America's Unfinished Revolution, 1863–1877.* New York: HarperCollins, 1989.

Foster, Gaines M. *Ghosts of the Confederacy: Defeat, the Lost Cause, and the Emergence of the New South, 1865–1913.* New York: Oxford University Press, 1987.

Fox-Genovese, Elizabeth. *Within the Plantation Household: Black and White Women of the Old South.* Chapel Hill: University of North Carolina Press, 1988.

Frank, Lisa Tendrich, and LeeAnn Whites, eds. *Household War: How Americans Lived and Fought the Civil War*. Athens: University of Georgia Press, 2020.

Fredette, Allison Dorothy. *Marriage on the Border: Love, Mutuality, and Divorce in the Upper South during the Civil War*. Lexington: University Press of Kentucky, 2020.

Freemon, Frank R. *Gangrene and Glory: Medical Care during the American Civil War*. Cranbury, N.J.: Associated University Presses, 1998.

Friend, Craig Thompson, and Lorri Glover. *Death and the American South*. New York: Cambridge University Press, 2014.

Gallagher, Gary. *Causes Won, Lost, and Forgotten: How Hollywood and Popular Art Shape What We Know about the Civil War*. Chapel Hill: University of North Carolina Press, 2008.

Gardner, Sarah E. "'A Sweet Solace to My Lonely Heart': 'Stonewall' and Mary Anna Jackson and the Civil War." In *Intimate Strategies of the Civil War: Military Commanders and Their Wives*, edited by Carol K. Bleser and Lesley J. Gordon, 49–68. New York: Oxford University Press, 2001.

Garrison, Elise P. "Attitudes toward Suicide in Ancient Greece." *Transactions of the American Philological Association* 121 (1991): 1–34.

Giesberg, Judith. "The Work That Remains." *Civil War Monitor Magazine* 1, no. 1 (Fall 2011): 39–45.

Glymph, Thavolia. *The Women's Fight: The Civil War's Battles for Home, Freedom, and Nation*. Chapel Hill: University of North Carolina Press, 2020.

Gordon, Lesley J. "Cupid Does Not Readily Give Way to Mars: The Marriage of LaSalle Corbell and George E. Pickett." In *Intimate Strategies of the Civil War: Military Commanders and Their Wives*, edited by Carol K. Bleser and Lesley J. Gordon, 69–86. New York: Oxford University Press, 2001.

Green, Carol C. *Chimborazo: The Confederacy's Largest Hospital*. Knoxville: University of Tennessee Press, 2004.

Griggs, Walter S., Jr. *General John Pegram, C.S.A.* Lynchburg, Va.: H. E. Howard, 1993.

Gross, Daniel M. *The Secret History of Emotion: From Aristotle's Rhetoric to Modern Brain Science*. Chicago: University of Chicago Press, 2006.

Gross, Jennifer Lynn. "'And for the Widow and Orphan': Confederate Widows, Poverty, and Public Assistance." In *Inside the Confederate Nation: Essays in Honor of Emory M. Thomas*, edited by Lesley J. Gordon and John C. Inscoe, 209–29. Baton Rouge: Louisiana State University Press, 2005.

———. "'Good Angels': Confederate Widowhood in Virginia." In *Southern Families at War: Loyalty and Conflict in the Civil War South*, edited by Catherine Clinton, 133–54. New York: Oxford University Press, 2000.

———. "The United Daughters of the Confederacy, Confederate Widows, and the Lost Cause: 'We Must Not Forget or Neglect the Widows.'" In *Women on Their Own: Interdisciplinary Perspectives on Being Single*, edited by Rudolph M. Bell and Virginia Yans, 180–200. New Brunswick, N.J.: Rutgers University Press, 2008.

———. "'You All Must Do the Best You Can': The Civil War Widows of Brunswick County, Virginia, 1860–1920." MA thesis, University of Richmond, 1995.

Hacker, J. David. "A Census-Based Count of the Civil War Dead." *Civil War History* 57, no. 4 (2011): 307–48.

Hacker, J. David, Libra Hilde, and James Holland Jones. "The Effect of the Civil War on Southern Marriage Patterns." *Journal of Southern History* 76, no. 1. (February 2010): 39–70.

Helm, Katherine. *The True Story of Mary, Wife of Lincoln*. New York: Harper and Brothers, 1928.

Hodes, Martha. *Mourning Lincoln*. New Haven, Conn.: Yale University Press, 2015.

———. *The Sea Captain's Wife: A True Story of Love, Race, and War in the Nineteenth Century*. New York: W. W. Norton, 2006.

———. "Wartime Dialogues on Illicit Sex: White Women and Black Men." In *Divided Houses: Gender and the Civil War*, edited by Catherine Clinton and Nina Silber, 230–46. New York: Oxford University Press, 1992.

———. *White Women, Black Men: Illicit Sex in the Nineteenth-Century South*. New Haven, Conn.: Yale University Press, 1997.

Holmes, Amy E. "'Such Is the Price We Pay': American Widows and the Civil War Pension System." In *Toward a Social History of the American Civil War: Exploratory Essays*, edited by Maris A. Vinovskis, 171–96. New York: Cambridge University Press, 1990.

Horwitz, Tony. *Confederates in the Attic: Dispatches from the Unfinished Civil War*. New York: Random House, 1998.

Jabour, Anya. "Days of Lightly-Won and Lightly-Held Hearts: Courtship and Coquetry in the Southern Confederacy." In *Weirding the War: Stories from the Civil War's Ragged Edges*, edited by Stephen Berry, 95–121. Athens: University of Georgia, 2011.

———. "'It Will Never Do for Me to Be Married': The Life of Laura Wirt Randall, 1803–1833." *Journal of the Early Republic* 17, no. 2 (Summer 1997): 193–236.

———. *Scarlett's Sisters: Young Women in the Old South*. Chapel Hill: University of North Carolina Press, 2007.

Jalland, Pat. *Death in the Victorian Family*. Oxford: Oxford University Press, 1996.

Janney, Caroline. *Burying the Dead but Not the Past: Ladies' Memorial Associations and the Lost Cause*. Chapel Hill: University of North Carolina Press, 2008.

Johnson, Walter. *Soul by Soul: Life Inside the Antebellum Slave Market*. Cambridge, Mass.: Harvard University Press, 1999.

Jones-Rogers, Stephanie E. *They Were Her Property: White Women as Slave Owners in the American South*. New Haven, Conn.: Yale University Press, 2019.

Kasson, John F. *Rudeness and Civility: Manners in Nineteenth-Century Urban America*. New York: Hill and Wang, 1990.

Kenzer, Robert. "The Uncertainty of Life: A Profile of Virginia's Civil War Widows." In *The War Was You and Me: Civilians in the American Civil War*, edited by Joan E. Cashin, 112–35. Princeton, N.J.: Princeton University Press, 2002.

Kete, Mary Louise. *Sentimental Collaborations: Mourning and Middle-Class Identity in Nineteenth-Century America*. Durham, N.C.: Duke University Press, 2000.

King, Grace Elizabeth. *Creole Families of New Orleans*. New York: Macmillan, 1921.

Kreiser, Lawrence A., Jr. *Marketing the Blue and Gray: Newspaper Advertising and the American Civil War*. Baton Rouge: Louisiana State University Press, 2019.

Laderman, Gary. *The Sacred Remains: American Attitudes towards Death, 1799–1883*. New Haven, Conn.: Yale University Press, 1996.

Leavitt, Sarah A. *From Catharine Beecher to Martha Stewart: A Cultural History of Domestic Advice*. Chapel Hill: University of North Carolina Press, 2002.

Lebsock, Suzanne. *Free Women of Petersburg: Status and Culture in a Southern Town, 1784–1860*. New York: W. W. Norton, 1984.

Lowry, Thomas P. *The Story the Soldiers Wouldn't Tell: Sex in the Civil War*. Mechanicsburg, Pa.: Stackpole Books, 1994.

Lystra, Karen. *Searching the Heart: Women, Men, and Romantic Love in Nineteenth-Century America*. New York: Oxford University Press, 1989.

Matt, Susan J. *Homesickness: An American History*. New York: Oxford University Press, 2011.

Mays, Ashley. "'If Heart Speaks Not to Heart': Condolence Letters and Confederate Widows' Grief." *Journal of the Civil War Era* 7 (2017): 377–400.

McClintock, Megan J. "Civil War Pensions and the Reconstruction of Union Families." *Journal of American History* 83 (September 1996): 456–80.

McCurry, Stephanie. *Confederate Reckoning: Power and Politics in the Civil War South*. Cambridge, Mass.: Harvard University Press, 2010.

McDonough, James Lee. *Stones River: Bloody Winter Tennessee*. Knoxville: University of Tennessee Press, 1980.

McGee, David H. "Home and Friends: Kinship, Community, and Elite Women in Caldwell County, North Carolina, during the War." *North Carolina Historical Review* 74, no. 4 (October 1997): 363–88.

McMillen, Sally G. *Motherhood in the Old South: Pregnancy, Childbirth, and Infant Rearing*. Baton Rouge: Louisiana State University Press, 1990.

McPherson, James M. *For Cause and Comrades: Why Men Fought in the Civil War*. New York: Oxford University Press, 1997.

McPherson, Tara. *Reconstructing Dixie: Race, Gender, and Nostalgia in the Imagined South*. Durham, N.C.: Duke University Press, 2003.

Miller, Brian Craig. *Empty Sleeves: Amputation in the Civil War South*. Athens: University of Georgia Press, 2015.

Miller, Richard F. "For His Wife, His Widow, and His Orphan: Massachusetts and Family Aid during the Civil War." *Massachusetts Historical Review* 6 (2004): 70–106.

Mitchell, Margaret. *Gone with the Wind*. New York: Macmillan, 1936.

Mitchell, Reid. *The Vacant Chair: The Northern Soldier Leaves Home*. New York: Oxford University Press, 1993.

Mohr, Clarence L. *On the Threshold of Freedom: Masters and Slaves in Civil War Georgia*. Baton Rouge: Louisiana State University Press, 2001.

Muhlenfeld, Elisabeth. *Mary Boykin Chesnut: A Biography*. Baton Rouge: Louisiana State University Press, 1981.

Nelson, Megan Kate. *Ruin Nation: Destruction and the American Civil War*. Athens: University of Georgia Press, 2012.

Ott, Victoria E. *Confederate Daughters: Coming to Age during the Civil War*. Carbondale: Southern Illinois University Press, 2008.

Phillips, Jason. *Diehard Rebels: The Confederate Culture of Invincibility*. Athens: University of Georgia Press, 2007.

Prinz, Jesse J. *Gut Reactions: A Perceptual Theory of Emotion*. New York: Oxford University Press, 2004.

Pyron, Darden Asbury. *Southern Daughter: The Life of Margaret Mitchell*. New York: Oxford University Press, 1991.

Rable, George C. "Despair, Hope, and Delusion: The Collapse of Confederate Morale Reexamined." In *The Collapse of the Confederacy*, edited by Mark Grimsley and Brooks D. Simpson, 129–67. Lincoln: University of Nebraska Press, 2001.

Reddy, William. *The Navigation of Feeling: A Framework for the History of Emotions*. Cambridge: Cambridge University Press, 2001.

Rutkow, Ira M. *Bleeding Blue and Gray: Civil War Surgery and the Evolution of American Medicine*. New York: Random House, 2005.

Salmon, Marylynn. "Equality or Submersion? Feme Covert Status in Early Pennsylvania." In *Women of America: A History*, edited by Carol Ruth Berkin and Mary Beth Norton, 92–111. Boston: Houghton Mifflin, 1979.

Schantz, Mark S. *Awaiting the Heavenly Country: The Civil War and America's Culture of Death*. Ithaca, N.Y.: Cornell University Press, 2008.

Schlesinger, Arthur M. *Learning How to Behave: A Historical Study of American Etiquette Books*. New York: Macmillan, 1946.

Schoenbachler, Matthew G. *Murder and Madness: The Myth of the Kentucky Tragedy*. Lexington: University Press of Kentucky, 2009.

Sheehan-Dean, Aaron. *Why Confederates Fought: Family and Nation in Civil War Virginia*. Chapel Hill: University of North Carolina Press, 2007.

Silber, Nina. *The Romance of Reunion: Northerners and the South, 1865–1900*. Chapel Hill: University of North Carolina Press, 1993.

Silkenat, David. *Moments of Despair: Suicide, Divorce, and Debt in Civil War Era North Carolina*. Chapel Hill: University of North Carolina Press, 2011.

Simkins, Francis Butler, and James Welch Patton. *The Women of the Confederacy*. Richmond, Va.: Garrett and Massie, 1936.

Smith-Rosenberg, Carroll. "The Female World of Love and Ritual: Relations between Women in Nineteenth-Century America." *Signs* 1, no.1 (Autumn 1975): 1–29.

Sommerville, Diane Miller. *Aberration of the Mind: Suicide and Suffering in the Civil War Era South*. Chapel Hill: University of North Carolina Press, 2018.

———. "A Burden Too Heavy to Bear: War Trauma, Suicide, and Confederate Soldiers." *Civil War History* 59, no. 4 (December 2013): 453–91.

———. "Will They Ever Be Able to Forget? Confederate Soldiers and Mental Illness in the Defeated South." In *Weirding the War: Stories from the Civil War's Ragged Edges*, edited by Stephen Berry, 321–39. Athens: University of Georgia Press, 2011.

Speer, Lonnie R. *War of Vengeance: Acts of Retaliation against Civil War POWs*. Mechanicsburg, Pa.: Stackpole Books, 2002.

Stanley, Amy Dru. *From Bondage to Contract: Wage Labor, Marriage, and the Market in the Age of Slave Emancipation*. New York: Cambridge University Press, 1998.

Stearns, Peter N. *American Cool: Constructing a Twentieth-Century Emotional Style*. New York: New York University Press, 1994.

Stearns, Peter N., and Jan Lewis, eds. *An Emotional History of the United States*. New York: New York University Press, 1988.

Stegeman, John F. *These Men She Gave: Civil War Diary of Athens, Georgia*. Athens: University of Georgia Press, 1964.

Stephan, Scott. *Redeeming the Southern Family: Evangelical Women and Domestic Devotion in the Antebellum South*. Athens: University of Georgia Press, 2008.

Sutherland, Daniel E. *Seasons of War: The Ordeal of a Confederate Community, 1861–1865*. New York: Free Press, 1995.

Tracy, Susan J. *In the Master's Eye: Representations of Women, Blacks, and Poor Whites in Antebellum Southern Literature*. Amherst: University of Massachusetts Press, 1995.

Ulrich, Laurel Thatcher. *Good Wives: Image and Reality in the Lives of Women in Northern New England, 1650–1750*. New York: Vintage Books, 1980.

Varon, Elizabeth R. "Southern Women and Politics in the Civil War Era." In *Women and the American Civil War: North-South Counterpoints*, edited by Judith Giesberg and Randall M. Miller, 3–19. Kent, Ohio: Kent State University Press, 2018.

Vertrees, Alan David. *Selznick's Vision: Gone with the Wind and Hollywood Filmmaking*. Austin: University of Texas Press, 1997.

Vinovskis, Maris A. "Have Social Historians Lost the Civil War? Some Preliminary Demographic Speculations." In *Toward a Social History of the American Civil War: Exploratory Essays*, edited by Maris A. Vinovskis, 1–30. New York: Cambridge University Press, 1990.

Wellman, Manly Wade. *The County of Warren, North Carolina, 1586–1917*. Chapel Hill: University of North Carolina Press, 1959.

Wert, Jeffry D. *Cavalryman of the Lost Cause: A Biography of J. E. B. Stuart*. New York: Simon and Schuster Paperbacks, 2008.

Wills, Garry. *Lincoln at Gettysburg: The Words That Remade America*. New York: Simon and Schuster, 1992.

Wilson, Charles Reagan. *Baptized in Blood: The Religion of the Lost Cause, 1865–1920*. Athens: University of Georgia Press, 2009.

Wood, Kirsten E. *Masterful Women: Slaveholding Widows from the American Revolution through the Civil War*. Chapel Hill: University of North Carolina Press, 2004.

Woods, Michael E. *Emotional and Sectional Conflict in the Antebellum United States*. New York: Cambridge University Press, 2014.

Index

Bourne, Dorothea, 30
Brannan, Hiram King, 129
breakdown, emotional, 10, 95–102
Breckinridge, John C., 145
Breckinridge, Lucy, 83
Brevard, Keziah, 39, 40
Brooks, Abbie, 103
Brown, Ardella, 42
Brown, Mary, 25–26
Brownlow, Isaac, 74
Bruce, H. M., 90
Bryant, Davis, 98
Bryant, Octavia "Tivie." See Stephens,
    Octavia "Tivie" Bryant
Bryant, Willie, 96, 97, 98
Bumpass, Frances, 39
burials, 76–78, 143; directions for, 174n18;
    reinterment, 122–24, 130, 142, 143, 146,
    147; status and, 124. See also graves
Burson, Jennie, 17
Bush, George W., 3
Butler, William, 173n4

Calhoun, John C., 31
Callaway, Morgan, 55
callousness, 62–63
Campbell, Frances, 6
Caperton, Lizzie, 107
Carolina Watchman, 136
Carson, James N., 128, 130
Cary, Hetty, 42
cemeteries, 76–77. See also burials; graves
Chancey, Kenneth, 152
Channing, W. H., 76
charity, 115. See also support for widows
Charlotte Temple (Rowson), 24
Chesnut, Mary Boykin, 9, 30, 93; on
    behavior of widows, 126; on flirtation,
    105; opinion of African Americans, 56;
    on Parkman, 102; on Singleton, 38
Child, Lydia Maria, 20–21; The American
    Frugal Housewife, 20–21
childbirth, 26, 57. See also motherhood
children: death of, 95, 124, 136, 179n19;
    finances and, 135; inability to find
    peace from, 95; mothers-in-law and,
    120–21; names of, 125; as orphans, 8, 120,

135–36, 138; support for, 135–36, 137, 138;
    transition to widowhood and, 84–85, 96.
    See also motherhood
Church, William, 78
civic engagement, 141, 143. See also
    memorialization; political engagement
Civil War, beginning of, 40–41
Clanton, Gertrude, 72
class, economic: expectations of women
    and, 24–26; memorialization and, 132,
    138–50; mourning clothes and, 102;
    remarriage and, 126. See also women,
    poor/working-class
closure, 79
clothing. See mourning clothes
Cobb, Mary Ann, 111
Coggin, Ann, 49–50, 69–70, 71
Coggin, Ebenezer B., 49–50, 62, 69–70
communication, 47. See also letters
community, 28, 95, 97, 106
condolence letters, 83–86, 90–91, 96–97,
    98–99
Confederacy: importance of widows
    to, 68–69, 86, 107–8; inability to find
    peace from, 95; legitimacy of, 2, 3–4, 5,
    9, 139; loyalty to, 175n35; mourning for,
    143; in popular culture, 151–57; positive
    memories of, 134; requests for support
    from, 111–13; widows' devotion to, 89–92,
    138; widows' lack of devotion to, 105, 106.
    See also country; Lost Cause ideology;
    South (region)
Confederate Insurance Company, 62
Confederate Medical Department, 72
conflict: in wartime marriages, 56–60;
    between women, 7–8, 117–22
Conger, Vivian, 35
control: clothing and, 102; decision to
    marry and, 47
Cook, Ed C., 142
Cook, Eliza Maney, 142
Cooke, Anna, 24
Cooley, Elizabeth Ann, 17
Cooper, Susan, 132
Corbell, LaSalle, 182n36
correspondence. See letters
cotton, 113, 114

Cotton, John W., 54–55, 64
Cotton, Mariah, 61
country: wife equated with, 51–52.
    See also Confederacy; patriotism
courtship, 15, 17–20, 43–47
Crutcher, Emma, 53, 61, 119
Culpeper, Thomas, 30
cultural capital, 2

Daily Dispatch (Richmond), 111
Daily Intelligencer (Atlanta), 132
Daily South Carolinian, 102
Dale, Mary, 26
dancing, 21, 104, 154, 156
Daniel, Ellen Long, 99
Daniel, Junius, 99
Davenport, John F., 64
Davidson, James, 30
Davis, David, 91
Davis, Jefferson, 1–2, 4–5, 9, 81–82;
    *The Rise and Fall of the Confederate
    Government*, 1–2
Dawson, Nathaniel, 50–51
Dawson, Thomas, 104
death: acceptance of, 62–63, 79–80, 97,
    107; causes of, 68, 69–74, 75, 94, 151, 154;
    desire to know details of, 76; fear of,
    61–62; Good Death, 31, 75, 76, 103; initial
    reactions of widow, 78–81; of in-laws,
    121–22; notifications of, 130, 141, 144;
    proof of, 79–80; soldiers' reflections on,
    41; surrounded by strangers, 31, 173n4;
    wives told to prepare for, 64
debts, 34, 38–39. *See also* finances
defeats, military, 90
Delony, Rosa, 10, 61, 76, 78, 111, 123–24
Delony, William Gaston, 49, 62, 71, 76, 78,
    124, 130
diaries, 65, 96
Dictionary of Love, 18
direction: for burial, 174n18; from
    husbands, 53–55; to prepare for husband's
    death, 64; transition to widowhood and,
    85. *See also* responsibility
disease, 71, 72, 74, 75, 94, 151, 154
disorientation, 78
distractions, 103–4

diversity, 132, 149, 157
divorce, 9, 29, 30, 37, 38
Douglass, Frances, 34
dower thirds, 110
Dreux, Charley, 70
duty, 45, 52–53, 131–44
dysentery, 94

Early, Jubal A., 143
economic stability: single women and,
    36–37; wartime marriage and, 43.
    See also finances
economy of mourning, 102–3
education, 15
Edwards, Laura, 3
Edwards, Rebecca Jane Cary, 173n3
Elizabethtown Volunteers, 146
embalming, 103
emotion: definitions of, 164–65n16; history
    and, 9–10, 165n16
emotional currency, 130. *See also* support
    for widows
emotional expression: analyzing, 5, 6–8;
    authenticity of, 47–50; consistency in, 11;
    through language, 10; potential political
    consequences of, 8–11. *See also* anger;
    grief; love
emotional freedom, widowhood as
    opportunity for, 75
emotional regime, 3–4
employment, 133–34
emptiness, 8, 79
engagements, in antebellum South, 20; in
    wartime South, 42–47
enlistment, 52–53. *See also* soldiers,
    Confederate; soldiers, Union
enslaved people: happy slave narrative,
    148; management of, 55–56, 171n30;
    portrayal of, 156; resistance by, 56; sexual
    relationships with, 30, 37–38, 103. *See also*
    African Americans
Epps, C. D., 55, 62, 69
etiquette: challenges to, 68, 156; initial
    reactions of widows and, 68; O'Hara's
    challenge to, 156; perpetual widowhood
    ideal in, 85; remarriage and, 127, 129. *See
    also* behavior; expectations; mourning

Emilie Todd; Stephens, Octavia "Tivie" Bryant); politics and, 8–11, 59; postwar, 132; power and, 4; public, 83, 140; reality of, 94–95, 98 (*see also* reality of wartime widowhood); remarriage and, 127, 129; of sweetheart vs. widow, 45; as woman's work, 6. *See also* behavior; etiquette; expectations

mourning clothes, 32–33; in *Gone with the Wind*, 151–52; ideal of widows' behavior and, 83; inability to purchase, 102; as standard of public widowhood, 83; status and, 114

mythology, classical, 8

Nashville, 113
nationalism, 9
Neblett, Lizzie, 56
newspapers: ideals of Confederate widowhood in, 86–87. *See also individual newspapers*
Nixon, James J., 54, 55–56, 62, 71
Norcom, James, 30
Norman, James, 37
notifications of death, 130, 141, 144
Nutt, Laetitia Lafon Ashmore, 47

obedience, 23, 57
O'Hara, Scarlett, 5, 11, 151–57
O'Hear, Annie, 80–81
opportunity, widowhood as, 74–75
Orphan Brigade, 131, 144, 145, 146, 147, 182n29. *See also* Helm, Emilie Todd
orphans, 8, 120, 135–36, 138
Ott, Victoria, 3
Owens, Carryn, 3

Parkman, Nannie Bierne, 93, 100–102, 177n15
patriarchy, 4, 14, 53–54
Patrick, Mary, 118
patriotism, 52, 61. *See also* Confederacy; country; duty
Patterson, Mary Adaline, 26
Pegram, John, 42
Pender, William Dorsey, 48, 54, 56–59, 61–62

pensions, 165n19, 181n25
Peres, James Bodie, 174n16
Perry, Harriet Eliza, 171n25
Perry, Theophilus, 53, 171n25
personal, political as, 5
Pettus, John J., 109
Petty, E. P., 55
physical reminders, 100–102
Pittsburg Dispatch, 145
plantation management. *See* management
poetry, vi–vii, 50, 87, 99–100
political, as personal, 5
political culture, 11
political engagement, 3, 111–14. *See also* civic engagement
politics, widows and, 3, 8–11
popular culture, 5, 11, 35, 110, 151–57
Porter, Madam, 89–90
poverty, 28. *See also* finances
power: of Confederate women, 3; gender roles and, 53–54; of men, 16–17, 22, 37; mourning and, 4; transition to widowhood and, 107; of wealthy widows, 38; in wives' letters, 41
pregnancy: in antebellum South, 26; dangers of, 59; transition to widowhood and, 84. *See also* children; motherhood
Preslar, Alvin, 29
Price, Lucy Harris, 37
Price, R. M., 26
prisoners, 73–74, 173–74n13
property, destruction of, 116–17
prostitution, 111
protection, male, 104
Pyron, Darden Asbury, 155

Quarles, George W., 146

racial hierarchy, desire to maintain, 56, 148
racial tensions, 147–48
Rains, James Edward, 54, 60
Ramseur, Ellen "Nellie" Richmond, 42
Ramseur, Stephen Dodson, 49, 52, 85
reactions of widows, initial, 68–69, 74, 78–81
reality of wartime widowhood, 95; attractiveness of widows, 104–6, 127,

129–30; condolence letters and, 83–86, 90–91, 96–97, 98–99; flirtation by widows, 105; inability to purchase mourning clothes, 102; King's, 106–8; mourning and, 94–95, 98; physical reminders, 100–102; sexual behavior and, 103, 106; social functions and, 103–4; Stephens's, 95–98

rebellion, politics of, 47

Reconstruction, 132. *See also* memorialization

reconstruction of widows' lives: beginning of, 110, 157, 178n2; in border states, 115–17; children and, 120–21; conflict in, 122; diversity in, 157; on foundation of grief, 124–25; in-laws and, 117–22; requests for support, 111–13; status of widows and, 114; support for Confederacy and, 114. *See also* finances; remarriage; support for widows

Reddy, William, 3, 4, 10

Reeves, Timothy, 73

Reid, Ann, 15

reinterment, 122–24, 130, 142, 143, 146, 147

relatives, male, 38, 120

religion: acceptance of death and, 107; advice to widows and, 120; comfort from, 96; condolence letters and, 83–84, 96, 97; ideals and, 22–23; lack of comfort from, 95; marriage and, 22; reunions in Heaven and, 96, 125, 175n32; widows' behavior and, 34–35

remarriage, 110, 127–30, 180n37; age and, 126, 169n52; in antebellum South, 34, 36–38; avoidance of, 38–39; class and, 126; etiquette and, 127, 129; opportunity for, 126; as unpatriotic, 103. *See also* reconstruction of widows' lives

resistance: by enslaved people, 55; female, 47

responsibility, 53–54. *See also* direction; management

retaliation, acts of, 73, 173n12

Retreat. *See* King, Anna Page

reunification, national, 149–50

reunion, in Heaven, 96, 125, 175n32

reunions, veterans', 142, 146, 147, 182n37

Richardson, Martha, 16

Richmond, Virginia, 11

Richmond Enquirer, 23

Richmond Whig, 141

Rise and Fall of the Confederate Government, The (Davis), 1–2

Rivers, Eurith D., 155

Roane, Newman, 29

Rogers, E. P., 22

Rosser, Thomas "Tex" L., 137

Rowson, Susanna, 24

Rutherford, Sallie Fair, 98–99

Rutherford, William Drayton, 98

sacrifice, weariness of, 61

sadness, descriptions of, 11, 100–102

Savannah Republican, 6

Saville, Victor, 155

Schaller, Frank, 40, 43

Schantz, Mark, 11

scrapbooks, 99–100, 140

Second Virginia Infantry, 116

Seddon, James, 111

Selznick, David O., 155, 156

Semi-Weekly Standard (Raleigh), 60

Semmes, Jorantha, 119

separation, emotions and, 53

sexual assault, 104, 177n22

sexual attractiveness of widows, 104–6, 127, 129–30

sexual behavior: of antebellum widows, 35; infidelity, 30, 37–38, 57–59, 174n16; promiscuous widows, 103, 106; prostitution, 111; sexual relationships with enslaved people, 30, 37–38, 103. *See also* flirtation

Shealy, John N., 17

Sheehan, Cindy, 3

Sherman, William Tecumseh, 128

shortages, 102, 103–4, 111

Singleton, Martha Rutledge Kinloch, 38

slave management, 55–56, 171n30

slaves. *See* enslaved people

Smith, Georgia Page King, 41, 43, 45–47, 50, 93–94, 106–8, 153

Smith, William Duncan, 43, 45–47, 50, 93–94, 106

social capital, 9, 12, 108, 110, 149
social functions, 103–4. *See also* behavior
soldiers, Confederate: enlistment viewed as duty, 52–53; image of, 140, 147; mothers of, 117–22; number of deaths, 173n3; positive memories of, 134; reunions of, 142, 146, 147, 182n37; widows' devotion to, 88–89. *See also* memorialization; veterans, Confederate
soldiers, Union, 105–6
solidarity, assumption of, 7
Solomon, Solomon P., 70
Sommerville, Diane Miller, 6, 10
South (region): conditions in, 132; power dynamics in, 41. *See also* Confederacy
South, antebellum: courtship in, 17–20; emotional expression in, 14; expectations of marriage in, 20–26; Good Death in, 31; motherhood in, 26–27; mourning in, 31–35; poor white women in, 24–26; schoolgirl relationships in, 15; single women in, 166n6; widows in, 31, 38–39
Southern Express, 102
Southern Literary Messenger, 23, 87
Southern Poems of the War, The (Mason), vii
Southern Watchman, 124
Speer, William, 73
Stanley, Amy Dru, 3
starvation. *See* hunger; support for widows
Stearns, Peter N., 9
Stephens, Alexander, 56
Stephens, Octavia "Tivie" Bryant, 18–19, 26, 48, 61, 78, 106, 130; grief of, 95–98, 107, 124–25
Stephens, Winston, 13–15, 18–19, 48, 95–96
Stickney, Sarah, 35
Stiles, Robert, 88–89
Stilwell, Mary, 113
Stone, Kate, 103–4
St. Paul Daily Globe, 148
Stuart, Alexander H. H., 115
Stuart, Flora Cooke, 141
Stuart, J. E. B., 141
suffering, 6, 114, 136
suicide, 8, 10, 24, 122
support for widows, 4–5, 165n19; calls for, 109–10, 131–34; as duty, 136–38; Helm

and, 113–14; lack of, 113; pensions, 181n25; requests for, 111–13. *See also* finances
sweetheart, vs. widow, 45
Sword and the Distaff, The, 36
sympathy, 98, 133–34. *See also* letters, condolence

Telfair, Mary, 15, 17
Thompson, Edwin Porter, 146
Thornwell, Emily, 33; *Lady's Guide to Perfect Gentility*, 33
Todd, Elodie Breck, 50–51
Todd, Emilie. *See* Helm, Emilie Todd
Todd family: image of, 148–49. *See also* Helm, Emilie Todd; Lincoln, Mary Todd
Torrey, Lizzie, 33; *The Ideal of Womanhood*, 33
transition to widowhood, 68–92; cause of husband's death and, 69–74; children/pregnancy and, 84–85, 96; details of husband's death and, 76; initial reactions of widows, 68–69, 74, 78–81; instructions left by husbands and, 85; memory of husband and, 85–86; phases of, 68; power and, 107. *See also* behavior; etiquette; letters, condolence; mourning
Treatise on Domestic Economy (Beecher), 21
Trice, Martha, 37
Trump, Donald, 3
Turner, Ann Marie Stewart, 122
Turner, Rebecca, 27

UDC (United Daughters of the Confederacy), 142, 143, 146–47
uncertainty, 43, 65
Uncle Tom's Cabin (Stowe), 9, 21
United Confederate Veterans, 147
United Daughters of the Confederacy (UDC), 142, 143, 146–47

Van Dorn, Earl, 174n16
Varon, Elizabeth R., 5
Vaughan, Mary, 95
Verstille, Charlotte, 31
Veteran Cavalry Association of the Army of Northern Virginia, 142

veterans, Confederate, 142, 146, 147, 181n25, 182n37. *See also* memorialization

Victoria, Queen, 8

victories, military, 90

violence against women, 29, 37

Virginia, 11, 116

visual imagery, ideal female mourner in, 34

Wainwright, Charles, 62

Walker, Eliza Jane Kendrick Lewis, 140–41

Walters, Elizabeth, 30

Watchman of the South, 23

Waud, A. R., 80

weariness, 60–61, 132–33

Webb, Laura, 134

weddings, wartime, 43, 46–47. *See also* marriages, wartime

Weekly Democratic Statesman (Texas), 133

West, Frances, 104

West Virginia, 116

Wheeling Daily Intelligencer, 134

White, Mary J., 105

widowers, remarriage of, 169n52

widowhood, 4; in classical mythology, 8; in *Gone with the Wind*, 151–57; image of, 2; as lived experience, 11; as opportunity, 74–75; perpetual, 85, 141, 142, 143–50 (*see also* Helm, Emilie Todd; Jackson, Mary Anna; Stephens, Octavia "Tivie" Bryant); preference for, 36–37. *See also* reality of wartime widowhood; support for widows; transition to widowhood

Widow Ranter, The (Behn), 35

widows: age of, 38–39, 84, 103, 151; in antebellum South, 31, 38–39; cultural standing of, 3; defiant, 11; deviant, 5, 11, 151–57; disappearance of from academic narrative, 5; elite, 38, 138–50; image of, 2; legend of, 153; number of, 2, 11, 66, 164n3; oldest Confederate, 152, 157; political meaning of, 2; returning to narrative of Civil War, 11; selfless, 11; vs. sweethearts, 45. *See also* reality of wartime widowhood; support for widows; transition to widowhood; women

wife, true, 85

Wiley, William, 89–90

Williams, Beard, 127

Wise, Henry A., 131

woman, covered, 16–17

women, 1; conflict between, 7–8; diversity among, 149, 157; essentialization of, 7; ideals of Confederate widowhood and, 89; scholarship on, 2–3

women, poor/working-class, 11, 24–26, 65, 102

women, single, 166n6, 169n4. *See also* widowhood; widows

Wood, Dallas, 83

worry, 61–64

Wright, Louise, 89

X, Malcolm, 156

Yeatman, Ida, 60

Yorkville Enquirer, 115